THE NEW
WORSHIP

The New Worship moves us beyond a selfish "meism," which champions only one style of worship, to a creative integration employing a blend of the best in traditional and contemporary styles.

Dr. Gary L. McIntosh, Talbot School of Theology,
author of *The Issachar Factor* and *Three Generations*

The style is very readable and the charts are exceptionally helpful. *The New Worship* deserves a wide reading and wide implementation.

Dr. J. Daniel Bauman,
author of *An Introduction to Contemporary Preaching*

It is tragic that many churches are being divided over the subjects of worship and music. It should not be so. This excellent volume by Barry Liesch will enable local churches to develop meaningful worship experiences which will bring glory to God and unity to his Body!

Paul A. Cedar, president,
Evangelical Free Church of America

This is the kind of book I've been waiting for. It gets to the heart of issues and is still full of practical ideas.

Edna Grenz, director of music and worship,
First Baptist Church, Vancouver, B.C.

Dr. Barry Liesch has done his "homework"—the result is a fine, comprehensive treatise.

Kurt Kaiser, composer

A very useful resource for music directors.

Laurey Berteig, director of music and worship,
Broadway Church, Vancouver, B.C.

All churches expanding the role of contemporary music in worship will benefit from this practical, down-to-earth book, written much like a set of workshops for pastors and musicians. Seminaries will also find his descriptive analyses and guidelines most helpful for preparing a new generation of worship leaders.

Emily Brink, Calvin College,
music and liturgy editor of the Christian Reformed Church

There is a wealth of thought-provoking material here! *The New Worship* offers insightful guidance through the current maze of worship issues. Liesch calls us to a vigourous reconsideration of the biblical and theological foundations for the ministry of music in Christian worship. In his examination of Christ-led worship, as modeled in Hebrews, he effectively reminds us that our song can be nothing more (nor less) than response—the initiative is always God's.

Dianne Bowker, BRE, MCM, ThM,
worship planner/coordinator, Abbotsford, B. C.

EXPANDED EDITION

THE NEW WORSHIP

Straight Talk on Music and the Church

BARRY LIESCH

FOREWORD BY DONALD P. HUSTAD

Baker Books

A Division of Baker Book House Co
Grand Rapids, Michigan 49516

Published by Baker Books
a division of Baker Book House Company
P.O. Box 6287, Grand Rapids, MI 49516-6287

Second printing, February 2002

Printed in the United States of America

Library of Congress Cataloging-in-Publication Data

Liesch, Barry Wayne, 1943–
    The new worship : straight talk on music and the church / Barry Liesch ; foreword by Donald P. Hustad.—Expanded ed.
        p.   cm.
    Includes bibliographical references and index.
    ISBN 0-8010-6356-6
    1. Music—Religious aspects—Christianity. 2. Public worship. 3. Church music. 4. Evangelicalism. I. Title
    BV290.L54   2001
    264'.2—dc21
                                              00-066810

This book is dedicated
to my brother, businessman and musician,
Donald Brian Liesch (b. 1946),
his wife Diane,
and their talented children,
Chelan, Koby, and Shelby—
keep practicing!

When your dad and I were boys,
I'd play the piano softly and our dog Sparky
would rest his chin on my foot and fall asleep.
Then Don would come in and honk at him with his clarinet.
Sparky would jump up, growl, and show his teeth!
Then Don would play,
first in the warm, low range,
then the middle range,
and finally in the high range,
letting go thrilling, high tones.
Sparky, transfixed and inspired, would rise,
lift his nose high, and howl in harmony—
ahroooo, ahrooooo!
Your dad was a great player!

CONTENTS

FOREWORD

Why would an author like Barry Liesch prepare a second edition of a book he has written? Does he need to correct errors in the first edition? Has he learned more about the subject that he wants to share with readers? The answer to both questions is "possibly, yes," and the same would be true for almost any author of any book. But, more likely, the original publication is out of date simply because "things are different now."

Many leaders believe that the tide has turned in the worship revolution, which has occupied the church's attention for more than forty years. Perhaps the most radical warriors assume that they have won the battle, because most churches have altered their services to a greater or lesser degree. At any rate, they have almost ceased conducting their conferences and workshops promoting "contemporary worship."

The attention today has shifted to serious study sessions sponsored by local church groups, where historic, biblical concepts are shared and demonstrated. In many places, the idea of "contemporary" has given way to "blended." Nowadays, certain leaders criticize the "chorus" tradition for its weaknesses and urge its patrons to "sift the tiny hymns carefully and use only the best." Certain churches have judged that the skits they once planned to prepare for the sermon were really little more than titillating interludes and have decided rather to use dramatic techniques in the sermon or the Scripture reading. Finally, we hear that the baptized New Community members of the trendsetting Willow Creek Church near Chicago are insisting that they need symbolism in their worship room, which up to now has displayed neither a cross nor a Bible in deference to the "seekers" for whom the building was planned.

All of this is evident in this revised edition. Barry Liesch is excited about the new worship, and he describes and analyzes many of the forms that are familiar to evangelical Christians. However, he wants all evangelical worship to be founded on sound biblical and theological foundations. He also wants it to reflect and promote the unity of God's people, not a fractured and divided church. For these reasons, his Bible-based arguments are thorough and in some cases more scholarly than some readers would prefer. Liesch calls for "stronger choruses" and for "traditional hymns with contemporary language": I am convinced that both are already available, but not everyone has the know-how and the patience necessary to find them. He also acknowledges the value of the church organ along with the typical guitar and drums that are preferred by younger generations.

This newer-and-better edition is also extremely "user-friendly." In the introduction Liesch tells how to read the book, suggesting that "picking and choosing" chapters is perfectly acceptable, and in almost any order. I prefer to start with Part Two, because I need a convincing and complete theology-philosophy of worship to precede its practical application. In addition, Liesch credits certain friends for the graphics that grace the volume. Logos, concept icons, variety in typeface, graphs, and sketches abound to make the pages more eye-catching and more understandable.

Above all, I recommend the book because it allows readers to share the heart and mind of a gifted, thoughtful musician and teacher. Barry Liesch has a passion for worship and its music that is exemplary, and he expresses it convincingly. He even gives some insight into a musical technique I consider to be almost unteachable by traditional methods—the art of improvisation. In that art, as well as in the ones required to produce this fine book, Barry Liesch is well endowed.

Thanks be to God!

Donald P. Hustad
Senior Professor of Church Music and Worship
Southern Baptist Theological Seminary
Louisville, Kentucky

ACKNOWLEDGMENTS

Rising on the shoulders of many authors, the expanded edition of *The New Worship* has benefited greatly from the following writers: Harold Best, Judson Cornwall, David Detwiler, Gordon Fee, John Frame, Andrew E. Hill, Donald Hustad, David Pass, David Peterson, and James B. Torrance.

Friends, professors, and worship leaders also graciously critiqued the text and contributed ideas: Marva Dawn, Edna Grenz, Leo Holt, Mike Kent, James Melton, Gail Neal, Ron Rogalski, Philip Rust, Ron Sprunger, and especially Dianne Bowker (you were incredible!). My sincere thanks to each one of you!

Faculty from Biola University read chapters and offered improvements: Clint Arnold, Tom Finley, Bob Krauss, Bill Lock, Victor Rhee, Jack Schwarz, Gregg TenElshof, and Rod Vliet. Students in my Introduction to Music classes contributed their perspective and drew attention to areas that needed clarification.

To Dave Russell (director of Instructional Resources at Biola University), my special thanks for the "concept icons" and figures that have added "dimension" to this book.

To my editor, Mary L. Suggs, who improved the wording, transitions, the flow and sequencing of paragraphs, and scoured the footnotes, I admire your skill and appreciate so much your warm, friendly manner. Thank you for your insightful questions, and for the care you lavished on every page. To the staff at Baker Book House, thanks for going the extra mile on the design and layout.

I must acknowledge two individuals who have profoundly impacted my life. To Richard Johnson, elder and faithful friend who has nurtured me as a loving father for over fifteen years, I thank God for you! To

Rowlie Hill, my grade-school piano teacher, who taught me to place a high value on ministry, picking me up Sunday nights and involving me in his youth choir, thank you for the exciting environment, the YFC piano competitions, and for guys like Tom Keene and Franklyn Lacey. You got me going in those crucial, formative years.

To everyone, my deepest gratitude.

INTRODUCTION

Nothing short of a revolution in worship styles is sweeping across North America. Pastors, worship leaders, and congregations face new and powerful forces of change—forces that bring renewal to some churches and fear to others. No group or denomination can sidestep the hot debate over the benefits of hymns versus choruses, seeker services versus worship services, choirs versus worship teams, traditional versus contemporary styles, and flowing praise versus singing one song at a time.

The New Worship is a resource for everyone embroiled in the planning and leading of worship. If you need practical material you can use every Sunday, this book is for you. Pastors, ministers of worship, worship leaders, and worship teams have used it widely as a study and discussion guide, and seminaries and schools of music have adopted it as a required text.

The New Worship will aid you not only with the entire scope and direction of your worship program but also with your philosophy of worship. Though I particularly focus on worship that employs a blend of traditional and nontraditional music in the free-flowing praise format, I don't limit my attention to that. The free-flowing style is not without its flaws—in fact, I think the concept needs some refining. So I'll be tackling head-on some tough questions and controversial issues that don't always get answered, offering both practical application and analysis. This book aims to accomplish the following:

- provide biblical and theological perspective
- discuss contemporary trends and technology
- teach concepts and illustrate techniques
- help churches in a worship transition
- build up the pastor/musician relationship

What's New in the Expanded Edition?

Each chapter of the expanded edition has been enhanced. Chapters 1, 2, 6, 10, and 11 have undergone major revision. Chapter 1 now includes the perspectives of college students on worship. Chapter 2 makes a strong case for the teaching role of music in worship. Chapter 6 discusses the use of computer images and offers fresh applications for drama. Chapter 10 shares insights on "Jesus Christ as our Worship Leader" from the book of Hebrews. Chapter 11 combines chapters 10 and 11 of the old version.

In addition a wealth of supplemental materials is now available at worshipinfo.com—including sixteen free PowerPoint presentations, one for each chapter. These presentations have been used in church retreats, seminars, classes taught by college and seminary teachers, as well as introduction to music courses. The result? The expanded edition of *The New Worship* is both deeper and more practical.

How to Read This Book

You may enjoy reading this book in different ways than simply straight through. Here are a few options:

- Read any chapter in any order
- Read any pair of chapters
- Begin with part 2

Many chapters are arranged in pairs. If you select a pair of chapters, let your area of interest guide your choice:

The argument for hymns, choruses, diversity (1, 2)
Understanding free-flowing praise (3, 4)
Service design (5, 6)
The issue of performance (8, 9)
Theology of worship (10, 11)
Reducing divisiveness over music style (12, 13)
Staff issues (14, 15)

If you want the complete rationale before the application, then begin with part 2: Read chapters 8 through 16 first and return later to chapters 1 through 7. This book unfolds in the reverse of most books: Solutions are sometimes presented before the problem is discussed in detail. Why?—because musicians are application hungry! I'm attempting to keep musicians engaged throughout, so I dive into application in the first seven chapters.

Chapters That Are "Must Reading"

I regard chapters 2 and 10 as the major contribution of the expanded version. Each of the sixteen chapters is intended to appeal to a wide variety of readers, but pastors will find chapters 2, 5, 7, 10, 11, 14, and 15 particularly helpful. Musicians will be especially drawn to chapters 1, 3, 4, and 7. Introduction to music classes will find chapters 1, 2, 10, 12, and 13 useful.

The New Worship is not a rehashing of my previous book, *People in the Presence of God,* but it does develop ideas alluded to there. And, although it is fairly comprehensive, it does not address everything. For example, I was not able to deal with the Lord's Table or the subject of prayer (neglected in much contemporary worship) as I would have liked.

Field-tested in seminars, church retreats, and undergraduate and graduate college classrooms, this book has been greatly shaped by the concerns of many individuals. I hope the Questions for Reflection and Discussion at the end of each chapter will spark lively and constructive discussion between pastors and musicians, students and teachers. Additional questions for classroom written assignments are available at worshipinfo.com.

 This logo is your signal that free, downloadable material dealing with keyboard modulation and improvisation, *The New Worship Musician Software,* is available at worshipinfo.com.

The charts convey a lot of information and are offered free of copyright restriction. You are at liberty to print or project them for your sermons, Sunday school classes, college teaching, seminars, or any other noncommercial activity.

Finally, I want to declare myself as being passionately *for* the church! For over four years I have been crafting, refining, eating, and sleeping this book. I believe it has the potential to do some good, and so with great joy I present it to you.

PART 1

CONTEMPORARY
WORSHIP SERVICES

CULTURE, CHORUSES, AND HYMNS

Culture is the software of the mind.
George Hunter

They function like the "top forty," a kind of musical fireworks. Each new one shoots into the air, bursting into a kaleidoscope of color, only to fall all too quickly, burned out through overuse like songs on the hit parade.

"Worship choruses! Are they here to stay?" pastors ask. Definitely! "Should their use be supported?" Absolutely! Their spectacular rise to a near dominant position in our worship has been breathtaking. The new choruses communicate a freshness to our faith and relate Christianity to contemporary culture. They are understandable to the visiting nonbeliever and help new Christians become spiritually grounded. They are effective in educating children and they inspire enthusiasm in young people for experiencing worship. Some are literal expressions of the Word of God—verses of Scripture set to song. Their contribution is enormous, and I love and play them continually.

For many churches, praise and worship songs form the heart of their service. Walk into these churches and you may not hear one chorus that is familiar! Each church has its unique repertoire. Their congregations are always learning new songs, and singles, young families, and even senior citizens find these churches attractive.

19

Why Choruses Are Meaningful to Gen-Xers

I teach a 101 Introduction to Music course at a fine, interdenominational Christian university. I asked my students, "Why are worship choruses meaningful to you?" Most are first-year, non-music majors who have grown up in conservative, evangelical churches in the western United States. Their comments express how choruses are uniquely *their* cultural form:

They are up-to-date with where we are, therefore making the worship real with life. I also like that new pieces are continually being written.

Choruses are their means of intimate worship expression:

They help me feel closer to God in a one-on-one relationship. They really show the intensity of the relationship between God and myself.

With choruses I can be transparent with him and just offer him my soul.

Choruses are a means of prayer:

I like worship choruses that focus on one attribute of God or on my relationship with him. They can function as a casual prayer for me.

The repetition in choruses facilitates understanding, retention, and spiritual formation:

They usually repeat, and this helps me focus. . . . Sometimes repetition is the best way to really know what you're singing.

They're catchy and get stuck in my head and stay with me pleasantly through the day.

The repetition of choruses helps to really stick it not only into my mind, but my soul.

Choruses are integral to their spiritual journey—plus they're fun:

Songs like "Seek Ye First" and "You Are My All in All" remind me of the moment I chose to follow Christ and of the awesome journey that was ahead of me.

I have fun singing choruses. I think it can be a very good thing to have fun during worship as long as your center of focus is still on God. So whatever works for you, I say, keep rolling with it.

I find these statements revealing and significant—not shallow. The postmodern generation greatly values direct experience. Would an older saint be inclined to think of worship as a time to be "transparent" before the Lord, a time to "just offer him my soul"? That wording seems unlikely.

Older people and young people today tend to have different expectations in worship. Older saints see worship usually *as a response* in which they honor and praise God. Young people see worship often *as a personal, experiential encounter* in which they come, vulnerably, into his presence.[1] Biblical support exists for both views. Notice also that some of the things older adults "dislike" about choruses (i.e., repetition) are viewed by college students as spiritually beneficial.

Seeking Balance

In our culture, choruses are flourishing and hymns are dying. Here is my point. Despite the many benefits of worship choruses, we must acknowledge that they tend to reflect values of popular culture that should not be "bought into" without question—values that include "instant gratification, intellectual impatience, ahistorical immediacy, and incessant novelty."[2]

Used exclusively, choruses have real limitations. Choruses excel at expressing celebration and intimacy but, in general, lack intellectual rigor and fail to offer a mature exposition of the broad range of biblical doctrines. Often choruses shortchange the full reality of sin and human weakness and fail to capture adequately the agony and suffering of Christ on the cross. They emphasize sin defeated and gloss over persistent sin in our lives. There's very little emphasis on corporate confession or repentance. And the cost of discipleship and need for perseverance in the Christian life get scant attention.[3] The lyrics of choruses are often so short that thoughts about God cannot be developed or expanded. In fairness, we must acknowledge that some of the new choruses are addressing these deficiencies.

How should we look at different forms of music and worship in our culture? The issues of form and content will rise to the forefront throughout this book and command our attention.

21

Form—Confused with Spirituality

We often confuse form with spirituality. Worshiping a certain way or in a certain style doesn't make us spiritually superior. True, the content in forms can encourage us to pursue maturity in Christ, but the forms themselves don't make us spiritual. To be spiritual is to be conformed to the image of Christ through the power of the Holy Spirit. *Behavior and holy living reflect spirituality.*

The form of a liturgical service is not more spiritual than that of a thematic or free-flowing praise service. The form of Baptist worship is not more spiritual than Presbyterian; nor is the form of Methodist worship less spiritual than that of Calvary Chapel or the Assemblies of God Church. *Forms are cultural phenomena.* Free-flowing praise, for example, does not have a monopoly on the Holy Spirit.

It is unfair (and dangerous!) to equate spirituality with any form. I mention this even though I'm an avid supporter of flowing praise and contemporary expression. In fact, in chapters 3 and 4 I attempt to enrich free-flowing praise, make it more viable, and elevate it to a new level of sophistication conceptually. Ultimately the Spirit of God must animate *any* form with his presence and power if we are to experience authentic worship. We are dependent on God not forms: "righteousness . . . is the product of the Spirit's empowering."[4]

Is something of value being neglected, though, in some nontraditional worship? I think so, and this is what I want to convey to worship leaders: "I love your band and wholeheartedly support your use of choruses. But couldn't you include at least *one* hymn—or any chorus with a longer lyric—that has a solid teaching function?" Why not perform hymns or longer choruses to the very best of your ability *within your style?* This has the weight of biblical precedence, as I will try to show in the next chapter. The length of the lyric is important, for it takes a number of lines of text to build and shape thoughts. The contemporary song "As the Deer" meets this standard because its three stanzas develop a train of thought.

I've observed a disturbing trend among our university students. Increasingly our incoming students—whom I take to be representative of the evangelical population—are ignorant of even the most well-known, historic hymns. My informal survey suggests that college students who have grown up in the church in California are familiar, on the average, with about fifteen to twenty-five hymns today—that's after having been in the church for eighteen years.[5] That's not many! Only a couple of decades ago, students would have been familiar with one or two hundred hymns. A stunning change has taken place before our very eyes in so short a time! Local churches have let down our young people.

A significant number of my students are concerned that their generation is not being exposed to hymns:

I personally have never been really introduced to singing hymns at my church and I do feel as if I'm losing out on a great tradition of praising God.

Back home my Calvary Chapel is very worship-strong, and the worship is very contemporary. About once every two months they will have a song that will require the congregation to blow the dust off the hymnals. As I think about that, it upsets me, because those songs are the classics. They deserve to be played just as much as choruses do.

Some students are very concerned about the future:

If we stop singing hymns, I think our theology and knowledge of God will diminish quite rapidly.

I think that in this stage of our history, the church is going to be made or broken by what we do with choruses and hymns.

What will be the "worship tradition" of Gen-Xers in another twenty-five years? Will the choruses of praise and worship become *the tradition?* Jeremy Begbie rightly challenges us: "Roots down! Walls down!" Once we know our tradition, then we can expand. Everyone needs a center.[6] If we step back and look at "tradition" in the more remote sense—our Protestant roots since 1517—it's clear that hymns have played a crucial role in defining our Protestant identity. In practical terms, we have been a people of two books, the Bible and the hymnbook.

Given this backdrop, I want to explore two basic questions:

1. What different yet valuable functions can both choruses and hymns perform?
2. What can we do to create contemporary hymns and energize old ones?

For purposes of clarity, first let's define the differences between hymns, gospel songs, and worship choruses. A hymn, ancient or modern, is a metrical poem with multiple stanzas, often without a refrain (chorus). A gospel song usually has multiple stanzas plus a memorable refrain. A chorus is a mini-poem consisting of a refrain, but usually without stanzas or with only one stanza.

Hymns often tell us about God and his works and are usually sung in the first person plural ("we"). The following contemporary songs have several stanzas and a refrain and thus could conceivably fall into either the hymn or gospel song category: "Amazing Love" and "Shine, Jesus, Shine" by Graham Kendrick, and "There Is a Redeemer" by Melody Green. Choruses are often sung directly to God and have a very personal tone ("I"). The *hymn* definition by the Hymn Society of America, however, contains several characteristics that could conceivably overlap with choruses:

> A Christian hymn is a lyric poem, reverently conceived, designed to be sung, which expresses the worshiper's attitude to God or God's purposes in human life. It should be simple and metrical in form, genuinely emotional, poetic and literary in style, and its ideas so direct and so immediately apparent as to unify a congregation while singing it.

Both worship choruses and hymns tend to be direct, simple, reverent, and emotional, and they have the capacity to unify congregations. Now let's address our questions.

Stars or Fireworks?

Hymns may not explode or dazzle like fireworks, but they shine like stars. Stars, ablaze so many millions of miles away, pierce our atmosphere and reach us with their light. Similarly hymns bring deep theological truth within our reach in portions we can grasp and with melodies we can remember.

One could argue that hymns are ultimately more rewarding than choruses. Hymns have stood the test of time. They communicate the profundities of faith and offer a thoughtful exposition of church doctrines. For example, this weighty stanza of "It Is Well with My Soul" expresses the doctrine of the atonement:

> My sin—O the bliss of this glorious thought—
> My sin, not in part, but the whole,
> Is nailed to the cross, and I bear it no more:
> Praise the Lord, praise the Lord, O my soul!

Hymns provide texts for a wider variety of subjects and themes than most worship choruses. There are hymns for virtually any sermon topic or occasion, any doctrine, any emotion. Hymns such as "How Firm a Foundation" paraphrase whole Scripture passages.

"How Firm a Foundation" Paraphrases Isaiah[7]

Scripture	Hymn Paraphrase
Fear thou not; for I am with thee:	Fear not, I am with thee;
be not dismayed;	O be not dismayed;
for I am thy God:	for I am thy God,
I will strengthen thee;	and will still give thee aid;
yea, I will help thee;	I'll strengthen thee, help thee,
yea, I will uphold thee	and cause thee to
with the right hand of my	stand, upheld by my
righteousness (Isa. 41:10 KJV).	righteous, omnipotent hand.
When thou passest through	When through the deep waters
the waters, I will be with thee;	I call thee to go, the rivers
and through the rivers,	of woe shall not thee overflow;
they shall not overflow thee	for I will be with thee,
(Isa. 43:2 KJV).	thy troubles to bless,
	and sanctify to thee
	thy deepest distress.

During the Reformation, Protestant leaders educated worshipers through singing. Calling his people "theological barbarians," Martin Luther taught them basic theology by devoting Thursday evenings to congregational hymn singing.[8] Two centuries later, the Lutheran composer J. S. Bach recounts his congregation singing up to forty stanzas of one hymn! An unrelenting *perseverance* pervaded their culture. Some services lasted four hours. The Hebrew people in the Old Testament too, under the leadership of Ezra, read the Scriptures for three hours and praised God for another three hours (Neh. 9:1–6). Think about that!

Is our "sound bite culture" serving our long-term interests?[9] By majoring so heavily on short choruses, are we watering down the teaching capacity of congregational song? Are we singing up to our theology?

Incredible Stories behind Incredible Texts

Hymns have been written under incredible circumstances. The hymn "It Is Well with My Soul" was composed by Horatio Spafford, a lawyer born in 1828 who had a close relationship with evangelist D. L. Moody. Profound tragedy struck Spafford. His only son died, and the Chicago fire of 1871 wiped out his real estate holdings. Desiring a vacation for his wife and four daughters, he sent them by ship to Great Britain to join D. L. Moody. Last-minute business delayed Spafford's departure, and as he was making preparations to join his family, he received a cable from his wife that read, "Saved alone." On November 22, 1873, the English vessel his wife and daughters were on, the *Lochearn*, was struck and sank in twelve minutes.

Anguished and heartbroken, Spafford immediately left by ship to join his wife. It is believed that as his ship passed near the place where his four daughters drowned, he penned the words so familiar to us and yet so graphic in their disclosure of overwhelming grief: *"When sorrows like sea billows roll."* Prevailing faith was granted Spafford, however, for he was able to write: "Whatever my lot, Thou hast taught me to say, *'It is well, it is well with my soul.'* "[10]

We must share these stories! They are our heritage. Knowing the circumstances behind hymns helps us love and appreciate them all the more. Encourage young people to take a second look. If we unthinkingly allow our youth to be severed from their magnificent past—their cloud of witnesses—are we serving them well? "Therefore, since we are surrounded by such a great cloud of witnesses, . . . let us run with perseverance the race marked out for us" (Heb. 12:1).

Why not seek for your services a *blend* of hymns and choruses that reflects the composition of your church? Or look at it another way: What will our sons and daughters have after thirty years of *exclusive* chorus singing? A few choruses of enduring quality and the memory of hundreds of worn-out ones?

Overcoming Polarization

Besides visiting contemporary churches, I also visit older, traditional churches. My heart goes out to churches that are aging: The youngest person may be fifty years old. They have not adjusted to today's cultural patterns. Some members would like to draw in younger blood, but to achieve this they must be willing to undergo change. This is an extremely difficult proposition, especially for the "older saints," who are usually established in their ways. Yet many desire change because they know the future lies with the youth.

Congregations often experience tension between the young who want choruses performed in contemporary styles, and the old who want hymns rendered in traditional ways. Polarization is not uncommon. Both sides often insist on their own rights and experience untold hurt and rejection.

Is there an answer? Some churches have separate traditional and contemporary services on the same Sunday morning. Or they have a traditional service Sunday morning but a contemporary service Saturday or Sunday evening. In the contemporary services, the pastor and the people don't wear ties. They meet in the church gym, where they can set up their guitars, synthesizers, and percussion instruments, whereas the traditional service meets in the sanctuary with a choir and the organ, and the dress is more formal.

When churches establish a second service in a different style, they are creating, in essence, another church. Pastors must be willing to devote much extra time in order to see the project through. They must not "bail out" if the going gets tough.[11] Often a different team of musicians is needed for each service, for most musicians do not possess the skill to cross over between musical styles.

Pastors report that different-style services appeal to the divergent cultures represented in their congregations and reach out to a wider variety of nonchurched individuals. Some have discovered that services originally designed for Gen-Xers are attracting entire families, even older singles. Similarly, the traditional services are attracting young people who prefer traditional structure. In other words, attendance has not divided so strictly along age lines as might have been expected. This is a healthy sign! We should encourage as broad a range of age groups as possible in each style of service. Maintaining intergenerational interaction in all services is crucial. Young people—whatever the style—need the presence and mentoring of older, more seasoned believers.

Another solution to the need for different styles of worship, and the one I prefer, is to seek a *blend* of the old and the new. More than one type of blended service can occur where multiple-style services exist at a single church location. *Blend* does not necessarily mean a 50/50 balance. *Blend* could mean a 25/75 or 60/40 weighting of hymns and choruses, for example, depending on the composition of the congregation(s).

It's interesting that the great majority of students in my college classes report that they do not want to see hymns eliminated. Some desire more diversity:

> I love the idea of a more musically diverse church. I go to a church that has a separate service for contemporary and traditional tastes. I wonder if there's a way they could blend the two.

This student is not alone—many others are thinking the same thought! A recent survey of 200 evangelical churches in British Columbia indicated two primary needs: (1) training for worship leaders on how to lead and play for church services, and (2) how to address the whole blended worship issue.[12] How can this blend be achieved? One way is to link hymns and choruses having common themes together. James Melton, director of choral activities at Vanguard University of Southern California, suggests having young people read hymn stories to the congregation: "This involves them personally and is 'another voice' from the congregation. Even better, have them 'act out' the hymn story. There is a huge resource of dramas, even monologues, available for meaningful production."[13]

Another way is to have a "what this hymn/chorus means to me" time. When older people share how a hymn has impacted their faith in times of crisis, it helps young people understand where they are coming from. Sometimes a college student can be inspired just by hearing older people sing with conviction:

Sometimes the hymns we sing in our worship service are unfamiliar to me, but I love it when the older adults around me sing out and engulf my, sometimes ignorant, ears. When this happens, I have the opportunity to learn and be taught by the words in the hymnal (and on the screen), and by the elders who surround me with their brilliant knowledge of such rich hymns.

This comment underscores the crucial importance of good singing by the adult community.

Moreover, if a young person sings a hymn as a solo, and expressions of appreciation and affirmation follow, improved relations between the young and old are given a real chance to develop. A student told me a related story:

In our college and youth group, we have a band and we love it. We sang last week to our elderly people, and they didn't really like it, but they said they gladly welcomed it—which should be our same attitude to hymns.

This demonstrates refreshing honesty.

Again, it's important that leaders on either side not undertake this task with a begrudging attitude that smacks of tokenism. The effort must be a real and costly one—it should summon your very best. This kind of give-and-take pleases God because it promotes and advances spiritual maturity and is a powerful demonstration of Christian respect for one another on the congregational level:

> Make my joy complete by being of the same mind, maintaining the same love, united in spirit, intent on one purpose. Do nothing from selfishness or empty conceit, but with humility of mind let each of you regard one another as more important than himself; do not merely look out for your own personal interests, but also for the interests of others.
>
> Philippians 2:2–4 NASB

Dianne Bowker, a scholar who is interested in how worship, theology, and the arts interface, cautions against falling into the trap of musical chauvinism, and her concern intersects with the spirit of these verses. "Musical chauvinism," she maintains, "consists of thinking of one's preferred style more highly than we ought to" (see Rom. 12:3).[14]

Are You Saying Hymns Are Better?

Since I've spent so much time talking about hymns in this chapter, you may think I'm saying that hymns are better.[15] Not really. I'm arguing for diversity, musically and textually. Hymns do some things better, and choruses do some things better, as the chart below suggests.

Hymns and Choruses Edify Differently

Hymns	Choruses
enduring "stars"	momentary "fireworks"
historic, classic	contemporary, popular
lengthy, developed	short, repetitious
numerous thoughts	one general thought
transcendent	intimate
more cognitive	more emotional
full of content	minimal content
appealing to mature believers	appealing to mature believers, children, and the unchurched
require attention to text	free attention to God
lyrics sometimes dated	lyrics contemporary
vocally demanding	vocally easy
rhythmically regular	rhythmically varied
extensive theology	basic theology

In Acts 2 the Holy Spirit descended with tongues of fire and the gospel was preached in a stunning array of languages. Pentecost, as parable, demonstrates that the gospel is comfortable in any thought style and culture. Our God is not western or eastern. Harold Best urges us to "live pentecostally" and actively seek out and welcome a variety of music styles:

> Pentecost tells that each of us must live pentecostally—in the spirit of Pentecost—among the musics of the world. Living pentecostally does not imply a change of denomination or worship style; it means that we strive to seek out and welcome a variety of music to our own lives, even as Jesus welcomes them into his kingdom.[16]

Harold Best insists that, as much as possible, we should "revel in the whole world of musical creativity—transculturally, transstylistically, and transhistorically," for no one culture can "say it all." Choruses help us do this too.

Contemporary choruses can have a broadening effect culturally. Worship choruses put us in touch with ethnic groups and styles—Hispanic (ska, reggae, bossa nova, Cajun, Latin jazz), African American (straight ahead/smooth jazz, gospel, blues, funk, hip-hop), Hebrew (Messianic Jewish), as well as Taizé, country, Celtic, and the various rock styles and fusions.

This is no mean thing, for the gospel must be contextualized for each generation. For example, in the music of Franz Schubert (1797–1828), we hear the galloping of horses, but in Bob James, our contemporary, we experience the feeling of powering along the freeway.[17] That's a crucial difference, reflecting today's culture.

What about popular music? We should not condemn the *entire* popular music scene, nor make light of our impressive European classical music heritage. Gifted people are working in both areas.[18] We should be discerning and seek quality *wherever* it may be found. Some students, however, are critical of choruses:

> We focus way too much on emotions when worshiping. So often we sing the same five words over and over, something like "Jesus, I need You," and it becomes more of a mantra than an act of glorification. I almost want to say, ENOUGH, GET ON WITH IT!

> Most of our praise choruses today are about us and how much we've done wrong, and how he should come and touch our hearts. That's all well and good, but how can we call them "praise choruses" if they're about us?

30

I dislike choruses. They are lyrically, musically, and spiritually inferior to hymns. They are a crutch for today's casual Christian, oversimplified and mass-produced.

Nevertheless, some choruses like "We Give Thanks" (Henry Smith), though brief, draw on deep scriptural concepts, and seasoned Christians can appreciate the better ones. But many choruses are inadequate for encouraging Christian maturity.

The Main Problem

In general, my university students tell me that the music of hymns is more of a problem to them than the lyrics. That's a critical observation! For a small minority of students, hymns are either at their musical center or very distant from their home base of preference. But for the vast majority, hymns are adjacent—off to the side of their musical center. I find this encouraging—it tells me the task of energizing hymns is not impossible.

College students are more attracted to the content of hymn lyrics than the music. The overwhelming majority do not dismiss hymns as culturally irrelevant. Most believe a blend of hymns and choruses is the best solution. Yet it is clear that if hymns are to survive with the younger generation, they must undergo musical transformation. Here are some comments from an e-mail discussion:

From visiting my grandma's church, I've been exposed to some hymns. When I visit her church, I enjoy singing the "boring" old hymns. They are usually close to one's heart and can be sung with real desire.

I would love for musicians in our church to play a contemporary version of an old hymn like "A Mighty Fortress" and just go crazy with it.

I DO think, though, that it would be impossible to sing ALL hymns in a contemporary church full of a young crowd.

College students appreciate hymn lyrics more than hymn music:

Maybe we should brighten up the beat a bit on some of them [hymns], but man, keep the words, for they are very impacting.

I'll admit I like singing choruses more, but when we sing hymns in church, a new type of spirituality stirs within me.

31

Not to say that I don't love the lyrics. But when it comes to the rhythm and music aspect of hymns, THEY ARE DRY.

I usually do not get much out of hymns for a number of reasons. First of all, I don't understand most hymns as I'm singing them. They take a lot more thought process to understand the meaning of the words.

I believe we need to take the young man's comment—that some hymns are difficult to understand—much more seriously than we have. Accessibility and relevancy are important issues (see chapters 2 and 7 for ideas addressing these concerns). But for now, here's my question. *Must all texts be immediately accessible?* Shouldn't Scripture set our standards for the issue of accessibility?

Is all Scripture uniformly easy to understand? Doesn't Peter say that some of Paul's writings are difficult to understand (2 Peter 3:16)? Doesn't Scripture speak about growing in maturity and encourage the progression from "milk" to "meat" (Heb. 5:12)? Isn't it healthy to have some lyrics that are dense in meaning—that keep yielding new insights to us each time we sing them?

I say this though I too didn't care much for the great historic hymns when I was a teenager. I was interested in the hot chords and rhythms— the lyrics went straight over my head, even though I was learning them unconsciously. My experience was like this university student in one of my classes:

I was well educated in a Christian high school in which we were required to learn hymns to graduate. I hated this at first, but I learned to respect hymns more. I now have a greater respect for their value in the long run.

Options for Impacting Our Time

In these days of breathtaking change and cultural pluralism, I believe we must take calculated risks to bridge communication barriers. To do so, *we need to see tradition as an ongoing, ever-renewing process.* Here are six suggestions for energizing hymnody, which I take to be one of our thorniest problems.

First, *sound a call for a new genre of hymn texts.* Especially encourage pastors to write contemporary lyrics that contain good theology and flesh out their pastoral concerns. Most of our nineteenth-century English hymns were written by pastors.

We also need lyrics by gifted poets. Martin Luther, for example, actively sought out those endowed with the art of words. Here's an excerpt from his letter of 1524 to Spalatin:

> Our plan is to follow the example of the prophets and the ancient fathers of the Church, and to compose psalms for the people in the vernacular, that is, spiritual songs, so the Word of God may be among the people in the form of music. Therefore we are searching everywhere for poets. Since you are endowed with a wealth of knowledge and elegance in handling the German language, and since you have polished your German with much use, I ask you to work with us on this project.[19]

Second, *continue to paraphrase Old and New Testament Scripture,* both closely and freely, in songs. This course of action has a long and venerable history.

Third, *conceive longer worship choruses that develop and expand on thoughts.* This will require more skill and crafting. Some could address particular theological truths; others could be seasonal in nature—for Christmas, Easter, and so on.

 Fourth, *create contemporary band charts and choral and instrumental arrangements of historic hymns for congregational singing.* Public domain hymns (those not under copyright) may be altered, arranged, displayed, reproduced, and distributed by any means without fear of copyright infringement.[20] For example, "Blessed Assurance," "Come Ye Disconsolate," and "My Tribute" (refrain) can be sung in a black gospel swing style (see endnote).[21]

Fifth, *create refrains, bridges, even new tunes and rhythms, for classic hymns.* Arrangements may not be enough. Bridges like Tommy Walker's addition to "A Mighty Fortress" may be required.[22]

Moreover, the idea of creating original refrains for hymns has enormous potential. Many hymns consist of only verses; contemporary, captivating refrains could be created for them. What a combination that would be! In a similar vein, Bob James has transformed classical pieces into contemporary styles.[23]

Also, compose new tunes and rhythms to old texts. Missiologist Alan R. Tippett related a revealing story from the Fiji Islands along these lines. In the 1840s missionaries who had real insight into the Fiji language paraphrased Wesley's lyrics into Fijian and invited the native people to chant them in their own scales and idioms. The project was a spectacular success. Forty years later, a new group of missionaries arrived and insisted that the old tunes be sung exactly as notated in their English hymnbooks. This new constriction, he told me, was never well received; the tunes and rhythms felt strange to the people. This story has significance for us today.

In fact, did you know that many classic hymns we use today have undergone revision—melodically, rhythmically, and textually—over the centuries? We do not sing "A Mighty Fortress Is Our God" the way it was sung in Martin Luther's time. Current settings have a sturdy, military feeling to them, whereas the original setting around 1550 conveyed a lighter, dancing, Renaissance feeling.

Sixth, *contemporize old hymn lyrics (when feasible)*. A friend sent me a photocopy of the original lyric of Charles Wesley's "O for a Thousand Tongues to Sing" obtained from a library in England. The original contained about sixteen stanzas, some breathing hellfire and brimstone. One stanza included something like this:

That stanza has been omitted from our hymnbooks![24] The wording of other stanzas has also been "toned down" by editors so as not to offend the sensitivities of today's worshipers. Understand, I'm not suggesting we change *all* hymn lyrics, rather that adjustments have been and *must* continue to be made.

Really, to be truly successful, we need hundreds and hundreds of individuals working from many different angles in all of these areas. In the academic world, for instance, a host of authors in the music area are continually writing on music theory, history, conducting, sight-singing, technology, and instrumental and vocal pedagogy. Authors borrow and rework ideas from one another. Eventually the cream rises to the top, and from the massive effort put forth, ultimately real quality emerges.

We need the same kind of concerted, sustained effort in *all areas* of Christian worship, including the visual and dramatic arts. We need the theoretical, the practical, the pedagogical—all of it! We need a great, continuous, costly offering of materials pouring forth from local churches, parachurch organizations, and the music and arts departments of Christian colleges and universities everywhere.

With the advent of the Internet, it is possible to target even a very small niche market and self-publish our own material. Let's publish those theological works, training manuals, service designs, arrangements, and compositions. Do it!—whether you are a professional or an amateur. Make a difference in your time! I pledge myself to be a part of this effort (see www.worshipinfo.com).

The Power of Song

When I was eighteen, my home church graciously paid my tuition to go to our denominational Bible college for a year. In those days the dorm life was authoritarian—really strict! Everyone was expected to have devotions at 10:15 p.m., and the lights had to be out by 10:30—no exceptions.

One night my roommate came up with a brilliant plan. "Why don't we quote hymns for our devotions tonight?" We shut off the lights, lay back comfortably in our beds, and started quoting hymns to each other. An hour went by—two hours went by. At the third hour we decided to include choruses, Sunday school songs, even tunes learned at vacation Bible school. Everything!

Around the fourth hour, one of us would be on the verge of dozing off when the other would say, "Do you know this one?" This went on and on. Amazingly, the two of us, working together, could often perfectly piece together three or four stanzas of almost any hymn. I'd get one phrase; he'd get the other. Somehow the rhyme, rhythm, or tune would help us draw out the text stored away deep in our long-term memory traces. I can't tell you exactly when we finished, but it must have been at least three or four o'clock in the morning when we finally fell asleep. The next day we were in awe of the marathon of the night before—really stoked! We were amazed at what we had been able to remember.

Some months later, I began to ask myself, Could I have quoted Scripture verses for three or four hours without a break? What makes hymns and choruses so special? How did all of those songs get into my brain so easily and stay there in such perfect condition? The more I mulled this over, the more I got to thinking, This has profound theological and educational implications! I began to note how much I enjoyed humming hymns and choruses throughout the day. It indeed had become an established, unconscious habit of mine. These songs were—as one of the students I've quoted said—"pleasantly" dwelling with me.

The next chapter explores the relationship of worship songs to spiritual formation—how songs can teach and develop us.

For an amazing student response on the value of hymns, see chapter 1 of The New Worship Supplement *at worshipinfo.com.*

How I did weep, in Your Hymns and Canticles, touched to the quick by the voices of Your sweet-attuned Church! The voices flowed into mine ears, and the truth distilled into my heart, whence the affections of devotion overflowed and tears ran down, and happy was I therein.

Augustine

Questions for Reflection and Discussion

1. Which student responses caught your attention?
2. Was the "stars/fireworks" imagery useful? In what way?
3. What blend (percentage) of hymns and choruses would be appropriate for your church? Why?
4. How can intergenerational polarization be overcome?
5. If the singing of hymns were to cease, what (if anything) would be lost?

TEACHING, THE SPIRIT,
AND OUR CONGREGATIONAL SONGS

A congregation is just as responsible to sing the gospel as the preachers are to preach it. Those two acts (singing and preaching) jointly taken to their fullest, then reduce themselves to one common act.

Harold Best, *Music Through the Eyes of Faith*

Sometimes we come across an incredible verse in the Bible that both informs and tantalizes. Our understanding is enlarged, yet nagging uncertainties remain. Until recently that is how I felt about Colossians 3:16 and Ephesians 5:18–21, that is, until I acquired more clarity as a result of the research of David Detwiler.[1] Detwiler has conducted a thorough exegetical inquiry into these verses, and I am eager to share some of his results with you. He writes, "The importance of Colossians 3:16 in clarifying the role of music in worship can hardly be overstated."[2] I agree. In fact I would like to *shout* the message of this chapter—and keep shouting it—to church leaders everywhere. The issues need to be discussed and debated widely.

A cursory reading of Colossians 3:16 and Ephesians 5:18–21 shows that these verses overlap considerably. Each has been used to clarify the meaning of the other; scholars consider them to be parallel passages:

Let the word of Christ richly dwell within you, with all wisdom *teaching and admonishing one another with psalms and hymns and spiritual songs, singing with thankfulness in your hearts to God.*

Colossians 3:16 NASB

And do not be drunk with wine, in which is dissipation; but be filled with the Spirit, *speaking to one another in psalms and hymns and spiritual songs, singing and making melody in your heart to the Lord,* giving thanks always for all things to God the Father in the name of our Lord Jesus Christ, submitting to one another in the fear of God.

Ephesians 5:18–21 NKJV

Paul's restatement of part of the verse a second time underscores its importance to us. Several questions arise. Is there a connection between how the word of Christ dwells in us and singing? Is there a connection between being filled continually with the Spirit and worship? To whom do we sing? Is there a scriptural basis for urging a rich blend of materials? What should motivate our response? These are the questions we will address.

Structural Overview

Let's begin with an overview of Colossians 3:16, which may contain the most explicit statement for the use of music in the New Testament. Paul's words are directed to the Christian community as a whole—not the individual believer—as the people gather to worship.[3] Paul confirms that the early church was a singing church.

Paul addresses the entire community with a basic command: Let the word of Christ dwell in your midst richly, abundantly, lavishly! The opening clause—*let the word of Christ richly dwell within you*—has the central verb "let dwell."[4] The balanced symmetry of the remainder of the verse is directly dependent on it.

> *Let the word of Christ richly dwell within you,*
>> with all wisdom
>>> teaching and admonishing **one another**
>>> with psalms and hymns and spiritual songs,
>> singing with thankfulness
>>> in your hearts **to God.**

Sing to God . . . and to One Another

The phrases *to God* and *one another* reveal the presence of not one but two audiences in our worship, (1) God and (2) our fellow worshipers. The words "singing . . . to God" point to the object of our song, God himself, our primary audience. The preposition "to" may appear

38

trivial, yet it carries the full weight and force of Old Testament precedence and practice. "Sing to the Lord" occurs more than 100 times in the Psalms, and it is found elsewhere, without variation, repeatedly. If you check a concordance, you will find the repetition most striking.

If singing "to God" or "to the Lord" could become our true focus, our passionate center—not the leadership style, the production and staging, or the music performance of our worship—what a difference it would make in our churches! Instead, our people often find themselves observing rather than participating, evaluating rather than releasing praise, analyzing the musical performance rather than contributing a rich, heartfelt response to our Lord. Encourage your people to be different! Teach your people to be proactive, aggressive, and intentional in their worship. Singing "to the Lord" is central and foundational for authentic worship.

Notice also the verse says teaching and admonishing *"one another with psalms,"* indicating the presence of a secondary audience, our fellow worshipers. It's often overlooked today that we have a responsibility to one another in worship. Paul envisions the entire worshiping community interacting as a synergistic body. From this verse I would argue that our worship should not be the privatized experience of many Gen-Xers today.

Increasingly in our highly individualized society, I hear my students saying, "Worship is a private affair. It's just between you and God. It's about how it makes me feel." Most assuredly there is nothing wrong with raising your hands and closing your eyes, "getting lost in worship," and "pouring out your heart" to God in a personal way. In fact we need to encourage that. I'm not attacking intensity in worship. But we must also, as God's people, embrace our *teaching and admonishing role* to one another. Our singing, though directed to God, is also meant to build up our brothers and sisters in Christ.

Worship is not just an inside, personal experience. As we sing with conviction, our fellow worshipers become awakened to truth and aroused to respond. Our worship becomes a witness that impacts believers and nonbelievers who may be present (1 Cor. 14:24–25). This emphasis on proclamation and mutual edification is huge in the New Testament and it's an integral part of worship. Edification in the New Testament sense has less to do with individual growth and advancement (or what is *personally* helpful) and more to do with what contributes to the life and development of the *whole* Christian community.[5] Paul has a corporate focus in mind here and employs the concept of edification to "oppose individualism."[6] Therefore, we must insist on the importance of singing not only to the Lord but to one another. Worship is not only vertical but horizontal. Our songs should strengthen our people: "What shall we say then, brothers? When you come together, everyone has a hymn, or a word of instruction, a tongue or an interpretation. All of this must be done for the strengthening of the church" (1 Cor. 14:26).

"Psalms and Hymns and Spiritual Songs"

What is the meaning of "psalms and hymns and spiritual songs" in Colossians 3:16? The terms have been translated variously. Clearly they indicate the presence of a variety of forms, but is it possible to differentiate these terms into distinct song categories? Textually does the word *psalms* refer to Old Testament psalms, *hymns* to New Testament hymns, and *spiritual songs* to improvised or ecstatic songs?

The vast majority of commentators maintain that such differentiation is not possible.[7] Scholars report that the New Testament, the Septuagint (Greek Old Testament), and the writings of Philo and Josephus do not support differentiated usage. Rather, the terms are often used interchangeably, though the words *psalm* and *hymn* have a more sacred connotation than *song,* which has a more general meaning and is often used in Scripture with a modifier as in "new song," "song of Moses," "song of the Lamb," or "spiritual songs."

Two representative examples show why differentiation has not been possible. When Paul writes, "When you come together, everyone has a hymn" (1 Cor. 14:26), he actually uses the word *psalm* (*psalmon* in the Greek), but modern translators render the term as "hymn." Why?— because the context strongly suggests the music was composed by members of the congregation, not taken from an Old Testament psalm. Similarly, Mark records, concerning Jesus and the disciples after the final Passover meal, "When they had sung a hymn [*hymnoo* in the Greek], they went out. . . ." (Mark 14:26). The word *hymn* here, however, almost certainly refers to the Jewish practice of singing an Old Testament psalm from the Hallel.[8]

So far we have talked about the words *psalms, hymns,* and *songs,* but what about the combination, *spiritual songs?* Four translations have been advanced. First, since the word *pneumatikai* (spiritual) agrees in gender with the nearest noun, *odes* (songs), the translation "spiritual songs" is often rendered.

Second, since *pneumatikai* is ordinarily translated in the Bible as "spirit," the translation "spirit songs" is possible. Fee prefers this view,

40

and thinks it likely indicates "a kind of 'charismatic hymnody' in which Spirit-inspired, and therefore probably spontaneous, songs were offered in the context of congregational worship" (see 1 Cor. 14:15–16, 26).[9]

Third, *pneumatikai* can also be translated "songs on the breath,"[10] and thus perhaps means some form of ecstatic expression, or singing in the spirit. However, Fee is doubtful that "singing in tongues" is in view, as some hold, "since one neither teaches nor admonishes with unintelligible words."[11] If the songs are for teaching and admonishing, then they can't be sung in tongues.

Fourth, *pneumatikai* could be applied to all three nouns. In this view, "spiritual psalms, hymns, and songs," or "spirit psalms, hymns, and songs" results. Fee concludes, however, that the word *spiritual* or *spirit* is probably most appropriately used to qualify the word *song*, for without qualification, the word "song" could refer to any nonreligious song.[12]

The Argument for Variety

Despite the impossibility of exact differentiation, commentators are convinced a diversity of materials is suggested by "psalms and hymns, and spiritual songs." This seems reasonable, for it takes Paul three terms to describe the *full range* of the musical activity occurring. Indeed, Fee writes of the Colossian church: "The riches of the gospel are to be present with them in great 'richness' . . . [and] songs of all kinds are to play a significant role in that richness."[13]

Moreover, the pluralistic culture of Colossae suggests the use of a variety of materials. Historically, the church at Colossae was in all likelihood a blend of Jewish and Gentile believers drawn from a variety of backgrounds:

> The Christians at Colossae lived in an environment of religious pluralism. They coexisted with people who worshiped Anatolian, Persian, Greek, Roman, and Egyptian deities and with Jews who were devoted to the worship of one God. . . . The manner of devotion and religious expressions was quite varied among the different groups.[14]

Their music probably reflected their multicultural environment, an aspect our pluralistic society in North America has in common with the early church.

Clint Arnold asserts that the city of Ephesus (the passage parallel with Colossians 3:16 is Ephesians 5:19) had a much more pluralistic and culturally diverse population than Colossae.[15] Consisting of Asians,

41

Persians, Romans, Greeks, and Egyptians, it was strongly multicultural. Josephus reports that many Jews who lived in Ephesus had emigrated from Babylon, not Jerusalem. Likely they continued to use the music styles from their places of origin, for immigrants cannot easily shed their cultural upbringing.

Another factor attests to the presence of variety. Consider the precedence of Old Testament psalms. The Hebrews, under the inspiration of the Holy Spirit, preserved their old songs, sang contemporary songs, and looked forward to the composition of yet unwritten new songs ("Sing to the Lord a new song," Ps. 98:1). The Book of Psalms spans about a thousand years, from the time of Moses (ca. 1400 B.C.), through to David (ca. 1000 B.C.), and into the postexilic period (ca. 400 B.C.). Still other psalms call for a "new song."

Psalms run the whole stylistic and emotional gamut. Some psalms are short, others long. Some are historical and didactic, others intensely personal. Some provide words of challenge, others the wail of defeat. Some are structurally complex (the acrostic or the symmetrical pattern, for example); others, straightforward and repetitious. There are psalms of adoration, confession, petition, lament, thanksgiving, and proclamation. A commitment to richness of expression is implied in the compilation of the Psalms.

Does your approach to church music embody this kind of breadth? If we took all of the music lyrics you use at your church and made a book out of them, would they have the variety found in the Psalms?

Note that Paul wants the word of Christ to dwell in us *richly,* and links that richness to *a richness of expression.* I believe that because we are forsaking the old hymns, we are losing some richness today. Hymns could add depth to our worship, yet through disuse they are faltering badly. (Isn't it odd that the jazz culture values and continues to perform its "standards" or classic pieces, while we in the church do not?)

An ancient worship principle—*lex orandi, lex credendi,* the law of prayer is the law of faith and belief—states that the way we sing or pray is the expression of what we really believe. Much of our basic theology is assimilated and reinforced by the songs we sing in worship week after week. In fact our texts could be dangerous if they are habitually too simplistic. Dianne Bowker explains, "The danger exists because *music multiplies the potency of the text.* A text set to music is more readily learned and more easily retained."[16] Robert Dale concludes, "The person who chooses the hymns [choruses] for worship is potentially the most important theologian in the congregation."[17] *Think about that!*

Now let's look at the connection between music and teaching in more detail. Stay with me! I will need to launch into some grammatical discussion, but it will lead to a rewarding result.

Spirit-Inspired Songs That Teach and Admonish

If you consult a number of Bible translations, you will discover a wide range of interpretations for Colossians 3:16—a substantial lack of agreement exists. For example, depending on the translator's view of the context, the three participles—"teaching," "admonishing," "singing"—can be rendered with (1) imperative, (2) attendant circumstance, (3) result, or (4) instrumental (modal) force. In abbreviated form, here is the sense of the translations:

1. Imperative view: *Let the word of Christ dwell richly* [**period**]. *Teach and admonish one another with wisdom* [**period**]. *Sing psalms with gratitude* [**period**]. In this view, three separate commands result. Psalms, hymns, and spiritual songs don't have a teaching function and are not a means by which the word of Christ dwells.
2. Attendant circumstance view: *Let the word of Christ dwell richly,* **as** *you teach and admonish one another with wisdom, and as you sing psalms. . . .* In the attendant view, the word of Christ dwells along with or alongside the teaching and admonishing (which is not connected with the singing of psalms) in a somewhat loose relationship.
3. Resultant view: *Let the word of Christ dwell richly,* **then** *you will teach and admonish one another. . . .* In the resultant view, the word of Christ results in songs.
4. Instrumental view: *Let the word of Christ dwell richly,* **by** *teaching and admonishing one another. . . .* In the instrumental view, the word (or message) of Christ dwells by means of teaching and admonishing one another with psalms, hymns, and spiritual songs and by means of singing to God.

As you can see, the four views result in very different meanings—meanings that have the potential to affect greatly one's philosophy of worship! Appendix 1 presents a detailed, persuasive argument for why the instrumental view is preferable, both grammatically and contextually. Take the time to absorb this.

Without getting into the technicalities here, I want to say that the instrumental view is a very powerful yet natural rendering. It makes contextual sense, for in this case the word or message of Christ becomes integrated into hearts by means of song texts that teach about Christ. Moreover, having commanded them to let the word of Christ dwell richly, it is logical to expect Paul to talk about the means by which this could be accomplished.

The Role of Music

What is the significance of the instrumental interpretation? Clearly we have here a very strong case for the teaching or didactic role of music. The word (or message) of Christ is to dwell richly within us, teaching and admonishing (encouraging or warning) us, by means of the texts that we sing. Clint Arnold adds:

> Colossians 3:16 is not a formula, but one of the important ways of enabling people to absorb the teaching about Jesus. This was especially important since there was a high degree of illiteracy in Greco-Roman culture, perhaps especially in a rural context like Colossae.[18]

An implication that follows is that worship leaders ought to evaluate their texts. Do our texts have a strong teaching and warning emphasis? Are texts long enough to teach and develop thoughts? Paul's words should provoke us to question whether the texts of choruses (when used exclusively) are sufficient to meet the scriptural demands of Colossians 3:16. This also leads us to a related question: What were New Testament songs during Paul's time like—did they in fact teach and warn?

If we look at passages that scholars recognize as early church hymnody, we discover they are strongly christological and instructional in function. The following passage has the look, grammatically and structurally, of a New Testament hymn:

> Your attitude should be the same as that of Christ Jesus:
>
> Who, being in very nature God,
> did not consider equality with God something to be grasped,
> but made himself nothing,
> taking the very nature of a servant,
> being made in human likeness.

And being found in appearance as a man,
he humbled himself and became obedient to death—
even death on a cross!

Therefore God exalted him to the highest place
and gave him the name that is above every name,
that at the name of Jesus every knee should bow,
in heaven and on earth and under the earth,
and every tongue confess that Jesus Christ is Lord,
to the glory of God the Father.

Philippians 2:5–11

These verses teach us much about the nature of Christ, his attitude in ministry, his death, and his final exaltation. By way of contrast, compare the popular chorus "God Is So Good."

God is so good,
God is so good,
God is so good,
He's so good to me.

I praise his name,
I praise his name,
I praise his name,
He's so good to me.

Quite a contrast it is! I have no intention of denigrating this chorus. It is certainly one of the simplest of all of the choruses: Not only adults but children can sing it. Its repetitive character is somewhat like Psalm 136:

Give thanks to the LORD, for he is good.
    His love endures forever.
Give thanks to the God of gods.
    His love endures forever.
Give thanks to the Lord of lords:
    His love endures forever.
to him who alone does great wonders,
    His love endures forever.
who by his understanding made the heavens,
    His love endures forever.

45

Yet in terms of its ability to advance believers to maturity in Christ, "God Is So Good" is severely limited. Psalm 136, though repetitious, is much more developmental, as each pair of lines extends the train of thought and eventually tells a story (see the rest of the psalm). Nevertheless, there is a place for both the simple and the complex. Thankfully, there are choruses that have a clear teaching function. The following is an example of such a chorus and, in fact, addresses the text of Philippians 2 quoted above.[19]

> You came to us a man, in very nature God,
> Pierced for our iniquities as you hung on the cross.
> But God exalted you to the highest place
> And gave you the right to bear the Name Above All Names,
> That at the Name of Jesus we should bow,
> And every tongue confess that you are Lord.
> And when you come in glory for the world to see,
> We will sing,
>
> Hail to the King in all his splendor and majesty.
> Hail to the King of Kings, Lord Jesus, Our God.
>
> Larry Hampton
> © 1995 Mercy/Vineyard Publishing

We need to applaud songs like this! Furthermore, I agree with John Frame that teaching is not "merely" an intellectual process—the "emotions, will, imagination, etc., are interdependent, and all of them play a role in learning."[20] I also agree that the example of Scripture itself should set the parameters (limits) for how intellectual our songs should be.[21]

But consider this: Recent scholarship has discovered that the Old Testament psalms are richer, denser, and more sophisticated than previously thought. Thomas H. Troeger writes:

> . . . ancient Hebrew worshipers had the capacity to use in their praise of God a poetry that was not only "denser and richer" than prose, but "denser and richer" than the simple language which is often held up as an ideal for hymn writers. This is not to discredit the value of simplicity, but it is to suggest that a church whose hymnody embodies only simplicity is a diminishment of the tradition whose congregational poetics were much more sophisticated in nuance and form than we have previously realized.[22]

Along this line, an interesting thing happens in Colossians. As we have learned, Paul exhorts the Colossians in chapter 3 to use their songs to teach and admonish one another. But in chapter 1, Paul cites a New Testament hymn that models his emphasis on teaching. Paul practices what he preaches![23] Most scholars consider the passage below to be a New Testament hymn:[24]

> He is the image of the invisible God,
> the firstborn over all creation.
> For by him all things were created:
> things in heaven and on earth,
> visible and invisible,
> whether thrones or powers or rulers or authorities;
> all things were created by him and for him.
> He is before all things,
> and in him all things hold together.
> And he is the head of the body, the church;
> he is the beginning and the firstborn from among the dead,
> so that in everything he might have the supremacy.
>
> Colossians 1:15–18

And what a remarkably compact and instructive text it is! In fact both Scripture hymn texts above are deeply theological—almost creedal in content—and complex in thought. Again I must ask, Do our choruses teach us as much about the nature of Christ as these passages do? Are our songs sufficiently long and well-crafted to elaborate a significant train of thought? I realize that in order to be effective, our songs must communicate at the appropriate level for their intended audience. Complex texts not understood do not serve anyone and do not "teach." Intelligibility is basic to edification (1 Cor. 14:2–5). Nevertheless, I am impressed that Paul chose not to "dumb down" to the young church at Colossae. Both texts represent sublime moments in the New Testament canon.

More questions: How does Paul view his calling as a minister and preacher of the gospel? Do you think he would see his role as different (qualitatively) from that of a worship leader? It is common for people today to think that worship is for celebration and the sermon for teaching. Would Paul agree with that formulation?

It is highly significant that Paul uses the very same phrase that occurs in Colossians 3:16 in relation to music and worship—"with all wisdom teaching and admonishing"—to characterize his own ministry

47

in Colossians 1:28: "We proclaim him, *admonishing and teaching every-one with all wisdom,* so that we may present everyone perfect in Christ." The phrases are the same, the comparison compelling. Worship leaders have a high calling! Like Paul, we proclaim Christ through our texts, teaching and admonishing our people, so that we too "may present everyone perfect in Christ." The comparison breaks down the assumption that truth can only be spoken or read, and frees us to receive the Word through art forms. Harold Best writes, "A congregation is just as responsible to sing the gospel as the preachers are to preach it. These two acts (singing and preaching) jointly taken to their fullest, then reduce themselves to one common act."[25] I think Paul would agree with that.

You may also be wondering, Which well-known translation best expresses the views advanced in this chapter? Unfortunately the popular NIV Bible does not. Rather, the New American Standard Bible (NASB) appears to come closest:

> Let the word of Christ richly dwell within you, with all wisdom **teaching and admonishing** one another with psalms and hymns and spiritual songs, **singing** with thankfulness in your hearts to God.

It falls short in one respect, however: "with thankfulness" may not be the most accurate rendering of the Greek. Gordon Fee says the word *thankfulness* is never rendered as "thankfulness" or "gratitude" in the New Testament, as is common in translations of Colossians 3:16, but rather as "the grace" or "in the grace," which turns out to be an awkward phrase for Colossians 3:16. Therefore, he suggests the phrase "in God's grace" or "by God's grace," adding, "the focus is not so much on our attitude toward God as we sing, but on our awareness of *his* attitude toward us. . . ."[26] That is, we sing with a growing recognition of God's grace on our lives; and it is "our standing in grace that makes such singing come from the heart."[27] A truly great thought! Kenneth Wuest's translation preserves the literal rendering:

> The word of Christ, let it be continually at home in you in abundance; with every wisdom teaching and admonishing each other by means of psalms, hymns, spiritual songs, **with the grace** singing in your hearts to God (emphasis added).[28]

When the New King James version deletes the article *the,* however, a smoother translation results:

> ... teaching and admonishing one another in psalms and hymns and spiritual songs, singing **with grace** in your hearts to the Lord.
>
> Colossians 3:16

Finally, what about the phrase "singing . . . in your hearts to God"? "In your hearts" should not be taken to mean "silent praising of God," says Fee, but rather singing "with your whole heart," for in Paul's culture "both private reading and praying were 'aloud.'"[29]

Be Continually Filled with the Spirit

Now let's turn to Ephesians 5:18–21, which focuses on the issue of the Holy Spirit and worship. Colossians 3:16 does not talk about being filled continually with the Spirit, so the Ephesians passage contains a new emphasis.

Ephesians 5:18–21 begins with a command (an imperative): "Be filled with the Spirit." Fee calls it "the ultimate imperative in the Pauline corpus."[30] The structure is similar to that of Colossians 3:16, but now there are five participles (not three)—"speaking," "singing," "psalming," "giving thanks," and "submitting."

> Do not be drunk with wine, which is excess, but be continually filled with/by the Spirit
> **speaking** to one another
>   with psalms and hymns and spiritual songs
> **singing** and **psalming**
>   in your heart
>   to the Lord
> **giving thanks**
>   always for all things
>   in the name of our Lord
>   to our God and the Father
> **submitting** to one another
>   in the fear of God.[31]

Again the question arises, How are the four dependent clauses beginning with the participles "speaking," "singing and psalming," "giving thanks," and "submitting" to be translated? Which of the four views (imperative, attendant, result, or instrumental) provides the best translation?

49

Detwiler argues (once more) that in terms of the context, which is the most decisive factor, the instrumental view is preferable—that Paul commands us to be continually filled with the Spirit, *by* speaking, *by* singing, *by* psalming, *by* giving thanks, and *by means of* submitting to one another (see appendix 1 for the argument).

The passage is not a formula for being filled with the Spirit, though it may very well suggest ways—but not the only ways to be filled with the Spirit. Paul may be "providing insight on how his readers could be continually filled with the Spirit"—something, Detwiler says, that is "not altogether clear today."[32] In his own worship leading experience, Detwiler has observed that on numerous occasions "the fullness of the Spirit (both in a personal as well as community sense) seemed to follow a rich time of fellowship and worship."[33] Perhaps you have experienced that too.

Passages in Acts and the Old Testament relating worship to the action and presence of the Spirit appear to support Detwiler's observation. In Acts 4:31 the believers "were all filled with the Holy Spirit" *following* a time of raising their voices together in prayer (v. 24). Their prayer, which invoked Psalm 2, could have been sung. In Acts 13:1–3, while the church at Antioch was absorbed in corporate worship, the Holy Spirit gave them direction, saying, "Set apart for me Barnabas and Saul for the work to which I have called them." Both times, the presence of the Spirit followed a time of worship.

In 2 Chronicles, vocal and instrumental worship is offered prior to the power of God being unleashed during the dedication of the temple:

> They [the Levitical musicians] were accompanied by 120 priests sounding trumpets. The trumpeters and singers joined in unison, as with one voice. . . . in praise to the LORD and sang: "He is good; his love endures forever."
>
> Then the temple of the LORD was filled with a cloud, and the priests could not perform their service because of the cloud, for the glory of the LORD filled the temple of God.
>
> 2 Chronicles 5:12–14

In 1 Samuel music is associated with prophesying in the Spirit as King Saul is approached by a procession of prophets:

> you will meet a procession of prophets coming down from the high place with lyres, tambourines, flutes and harps being played before them, and they will be prophesying. The Spirit of the LORD will come

upon you in power, and you will prophesy with them; and you will be changed into a different person.

1 Samuel 10:5–6

In 2 Kings Elisha prophesies while the harpist is playing. Elisha says: "'But now bring me a harpist.' While the harpist was playing, the hand of the LORD came upon Elisha and he said, 'This is what the LORD says'" (2 Kings 3:15).

My sense is that these passages afford additional incentive for us to take seriously the relationship between music and worship and being filled with the Spirit.

The Key Principles

These six principles from Colossians 3:16 and Ephesians 5:18–21 are valid for any worship style:

- Sing to the Lord.
- Sing to one another.
- Teach and admonish one another with songs.
- Value variety.
- Recognize that grace motivates praise.
- See worship as one way to be filled with the Holy Spirit.

Share these principles with your worship team/choir during rehearsals. The principles could also form the outline of a great sermon on worship.

My concern is that we need to take the teaching role of music and song much more seriously. This is true regardless of the music style that is used in worship. Set short- and long-term systematic goals for teaching biblical content through congregational song. Such an emphasis could have a salutary effect on our current practice of contemporary worship.

For the argument behind the instrumental view, see appendix 1. For a musical example demonstrating textual diversity, see chapter 2 of *The New Worship Supplement* at www.worshipinfo.com.

Let me write the hymns [choruses] of a church and I care not who writes the theology.

R. W. Dale

Questions for Reflection and Discussion

1. Is the worship leader the most important theologian in the church? Why or why not?
2. Is worship for celebration and the sermon for teaching?
3. Is worship a means of being filled with the Holy Spirit?
4. Do you have a good balance of singing to the Lord and to one another in your church?

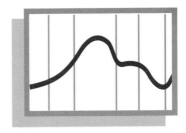

FREE-FLOWING PRAISE

By wisdom a house is built,
and through understanding, it is established;
through knowledge its rooms are filled
with rare and beautiful treasures.
Proverbs 24:3–4

During the past four years I have visited 120 churches, representing some 26 denominations (plus Catholic and Greek Orthodox) in the LA area, in order to gain some perspective of the variety of worship practices in Southern California. Three formats seemed dominant:

- the liturgical service organized around the lectionary and the church year
- the thematic service, where the music and readings serve the sermon
- the free-flowing praise service, where the music and sermon are independent[1]

The last format is a major part of the "new worship" sweeping North America today. Though fast becoming the dominant form on the West Coast, free-flowing praise is still not well understood. So in this chapter and the next, I want to help us get a better grasp of it. For worship musicians who have already adopted this style, I'll offer practical suggestions for refinement.

Alarms continue to be sounded concerning the free-flowing praise format. Some find it too repetitive and aimless. Some contend it results in services too dependent on music. Others maintain free-flowing praise invites abuse—that it manipulates people into emotional highs by engineering induced, psycho-aesthetic worship experiences. All of these are serious concerns that we will attempt to address. It is time to examine the rationale underlying free-flowing praise. We need more perspective and reasoned explanation because it is not likely that free-flowing praise will fade away in the foreseeable future.

This chapter demonstrates how free-flowing praise can be adopted wholly or in part in contemporary and traditional formats. The intent is to educate, not to convey the impression that free-flowing praise is a better form—it is simply *different.*

One of the differences is how the free-flowing praise service is organized. The liturgical and thematic forms of worship are organized according to *discrete events* and the free-flowing praise form is organized in *continuous sections.* Let me explain.

In a service organized as a list of discrete events, a hymn might be followed by a prayer, another hymn, the choir, the offering, a solo, a Scripture reading, and a sermon—the "traditional" format. Each event is a different type of activity and relatively independent and short.

The free-flowing praise arrangement, however, consists of one or more sweeping sections of *one type* of activity—a more romantic form. Sustained singing, for example, could last for ten to forty minutes without breaking the flow.

Both types of worship service can be equally edifying. An interesting development is the multitude of ways churches are innovating variations *within* and mixes *between* the three forms.

The Wimber Five-Phase Model

What is the rationale for the free-flowing style? Eddie Espinosa, formerly of the Vineyard in Anaheim Hills, California, where John Wimber was founding pastor,[2] likens it to a physical workout. Just as sustained periods of exercise are good for the cardiovascular system, so sustained singing for fifteen to forty minutes is good for worshipers' spiritual systems. Long, uninterrupted sections of worship allow people time to offer their whole selves (mind, will, and emotions) to the Lord without distraction. Espinosa also likens free-flowing praise to sitting down to a leisurely meal, lingering and enjoying fellowship with those around the family table.

Sustained sections of public singing also require more planning, *more skill and insight*—not less—in order to execute them smoothly. Because five to ten choruses or hymns may be selected, each must flow into the other, and transitions must be handled deftly so as to produce the effect of a seamless event.

To achieve these smooth transitions, Espinosa and Wimber developed the five-phase pattern. This pattern did not occur to them suddenly; rather, it evolved after years of experience of leading worship—and only later crystallized in their thinking. They found that different types of choruses could be categorized and linked into a five-phase sequence: (1) invitation, (2) engagement, (3) exaltation, (4) adoration, and (5) intimacy (plus a summarizing closeout). The need for the model probably arose because their choruses were short and their worship set was so long that a method for linking choruses smoothly and providing a sense of progression became important.

Espinosa finds support for the five-phase model in Psalm 95.

Invitation	Come, let us sing for joy to the LORD; let us shout aloud to the Rock of our salvation. (v. 1)
Engagement	Let us come before him with thanksgiving and extol him with music and song. (v. 2)
Exaltation	For the LORD is the great God, the great King above all gods. In his hand are the depths of the earth, and the mountain peaks belong to him. The sea is his, for he made it, and his hands formed the dry land. (vv. 3–5)
Adoration	Come, let us bow down in worship, let us kneel before the LORD our Maker; (v. 6)
Intimacy	For he is our God and we are the people of his pasture, the flock under his care. (v. 7)

Five-Phase Worship Curve Respects Psychological Dimension

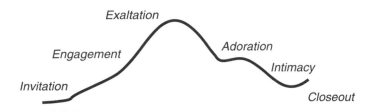

The Invitation Phase

The first phase, the *invitation phase,* is a call to worship. It accepts people where they are and begins to draw them into worship. It can be celebratory and accompanied by hand clapping. The key point is that the lyric is directed mostly to the people—and less directly to God—and it tells them what they are about to do. The lyric does the focusing without your having to resort to verbal scolding ("Can we have quiet!"):

> I will celebrate, sing unto the Lord,
> Sing to the Lord a new song.
> With my heart rejoicing within,
> With my mind focused on Him.
> With my hands raised to the heavens,
> All I am worshiping Him.
>
> Linda Duvall
> ©1982, 1985 by Maranatha! Music and Grace Fellowship

The tempo and feeling can vary. For a moderate tempo, consider "Come, Now Is the Time to Worship" (Doerksen). A slower, more mellow call would occur with "We have Come into His House," or "Come, Worship the Lord." Alternatively, a hymn and a scriptural call to worship could occur before the engagement phase.

Leaders continue in the *invitation phase* until they have made contact with the people and everyone is focused. "The skillful leader woos the congregation into worship like the patient lover draws the beloved."[3] The invitation phase is particularly helpful for churches meeting in schools and hotels not designed for worship where there is an absence of symbols for setting an atmosphere of worship: stained glass windows, banners, open Bible, candles, kneeling benches, or arched ceilings.

The Engagement Phase

In the *engagement phase* the people begin to draw near to God, and the lyric is now addressed to the Lord, not one another (e.g., "How Majestic," "Come Thou Almighty King"):

> Come Thou Almighty King
> Help us Thy praise to sing.

Espinosa likens this phase to the engagement period before marriage, for we are now attentive, serious. Some churches may be able to skip the invitation phase and begin here immediately.

The Exaltation Phase

In the *exaltation phase* the people sing out to the Lord with power, giving meaningful expression to the *words* of transcendence, such as *majestic, worthy, reigns, Lord,* and *mountains.*

> Shout to the Lord all the earth, let us sing,
> Power and majesty, praise to the King.
> Mountains bow down and the seas will roar
> At the sound of your Name.
>> Darlene Zschech
>> ©1993 Darlene Zschech/Hillsong

The pitch spans are greater than in the other phases because high notes help bring out a dynamic response and project a sense of God's greatness. If the people stand throughout the invitation, engagement, and exaltation phases, response will be stronger.

The Adoration Phase

In the *adoration phase* the people can be seated, the dynamics subside, the melodic range may reduce to five or six notes, and the key words may be *you* and *Jesus* (e.g., "We Worship and Adore You"). Transitions and modulations can be longer and more expressive in the adoration phase. Don't rush it!

In the *exaltation* and *adoration phases,* two sides of God's character receive expression: his transcendence (majestic greatness) and his immanence (closeness to us). The expression of both together tends to allay contrived emotion. In the *engagement* and *exaltation phases* praise is *about* God, but in the *adoration phase* we are singing directly *to* God, as in this hymn:

> Jesus, the very thought of Thee,
> With sweetness fills my breast.

The Intimacy Phase

The last phase before the close, the *intimacy phase,* is the quietest and most personal of all. We address God as Abba or Daddy (e.g., "O Lord, You're Beautiful"):

> O Lord, You're beautiful,
> Your face is all I seek;

And when Your eyes
Are on this child,
Your grace abounds to me.

Keith Green
©1980 Birdwing Music

Whereas the lyrics may emphasize the corporate "we" in the exaltation phase, they may now take the personal form of "I" ("Father, I Love You"). "Our" can change to "my" in songs like:

Marvelous grace of *my* loving Lord,
grace that exceeds *my* sin and *my* guilt!

And "him" or "his" can change to "you" or "your" in:

'Tis so sweet to trust *you* Jesus,
Just to take *you* at *your* word.

The acoustic guitar could be used to project intimacy. Brushes or no percussion sounds may be most appropriate.

It all ends when the people stand for a *closeout* chorus or hymn (e.g., "My Tribute" or "Yes, We All Agree") that leads out of *intimacy* and helps everyone adjust to the next event in the service. Musically, big, summarizing pieces are often effective. Textually, songs of dedication, aspiration, exaltation, or songs relating directly to the theme of the pastor's sermon may be appropriate.

A Variety of Music

The following chart illustrates the variety of song possibilities for each phase. The categories are not rigid; a song may serve more than one category. Note: *Older choruses were chosen to communicate to a wide readership. Quotation marks = choruses; italics = hymns.*

Arrange your repertoire list into hymns, fast choruses, and slow choruses. (Quality fast choruses are hard to find!) Engagement and exaltation songs normally fall into the fast category, whereas adoration and intimacy songs are usually slow.

Be guided by these principles:

• Have a goal and direction to your worship.
• Respect the psychological dimension.
• Reflect the character of God (transcendency, intimacy).

Examples of Five-Phase Hymns and Choruses[4]

Invitation	Engagement	Exaltation
"We Bring a Sacrifice of Praise"	"We Declare Your Majesty"	"Shout to the Lord"
"As We Gather"	"He Reigns"	"All Hail King Jesus"
"Come into His Presence"	"Lord, I Lift Your Name on High"	"Our God Reigns"
"From the Sunrise"	"How Majestic"	"Majesty"
Come, Christians, Join to Sing	O Worship the King	Crown Him with Many Crowns
Praise the Savior, Ye Who Know Him	All Creatures of Our God and King	Immortal, Invisible
My Faith Has Found a Resting Place	Guide Me, O Thou Great Jehovah	Rejoice, the Lord Is King!
We Have Come to Join in Worship	Come, Thou Almighty King	How Great Thou Art

Adoration	Intimacy	Closeout
"We Worship and Adore You"	"O Lord, You're Beautiful"	"No Higher Calling"
"Glorify Your Name"	"Jesus, Draw Me Close"	"In My Life, Lord, Be Glorified"
"I Love You, Lord"	"Alleluia, Alleluia"	"Shine, Jesus, Shine"
"Emmanuel"	"In Moments Like These"	"We Declare Your Majesty"
Fairest Lord Jesus	O to Be Like Thee!	My Tribute
My Jesus, I Love Thee	Jesus, the Very Thought of Thee	To God Be the Glory
Be Thou My Vision	Close to Thee	Our Great Savior
Majestic Sweetness Sits Enthroned	Savior, Like a Shepherd	May the Mind

- Sing *about* and later *to* God.
- Mix hymns and choruses for richness and variety.
- Link pieces and phases with smooth transitions.
- Avoid distractions by not jumping around.
- Use common tempos, words, keys.
- Be prepared but still open to the leading of the Spirit.

Notice, this model is mainly psychological, not thematic. It is designed to bring people before God, a great objective in itself. The model is not as conducive to the designing of thematic services, where the content of the pastor's sermon drives the service.

The five-phase model can be complementary to the sermon but usually is not strongly connected to it. Why? Flowing praise has its own shape and structure, and it is hard to find thematic songs that fit back-to-back for the phases. As the service progresses in time, however, leaders may introduce thematic elements that form a bridge to the sermon—songs, prayers, readings, vignettes, and so on.

It should be obvious that free-flowing praise will not be achieved without discipline and spiritual insight. Crafting and testing a set can easily take two hours! I hope this chapter broadens your thinking and offers ways to improve your skill. What is helpful, absorb; disregard the rest.

Musical Considerations

Tempos and Transitions

When planning a free-flowing set, be sure to test the tempo connections. If you desire the *invitation* and *engagement phases* to be brisk, ensure that the tempos are the same and provide enough momentum to lead into the *exaltation phase.* Tap the tempos—faltering tempos will impede momentum. If you tap the tempos for the songs in the chart on page 62, you will find that "We Bring a Sacrifice of Praise" through "Glorify Thy Name" are fairly brisk; the big change to a slower tempo comes with "I Love You, Lord" in the *adoration phase.*

Employ *short* transitions between upbeat praise songs to maintain the momentum. Dead space kills any sense of drive. Use common keys where possible (note the D-majors in the chart), or fashion quick, one- to two-measure modulations. In Assemblies of God churches, song leaders voice short expressions of praise to smooth the transitions. (I prefer purely instrumental transitions, but that is your choice.) Just remember, a number of abrupt tempo changes can be disruptive. Metaphorically speaking, we don't want to stumble or break our stride while running. Overall, think of the tempos the following way: *invitation* and *engagement* (running), *exaltation* (jogging), *adoration* (walking), and *intimacy* (stopping, silent communion, gazing).

Hand Signals

Flowing praise demands a flexible delivery. Hymns and choruses may benefit from an extra repetition, a change in dynamics, or a modulation. The following hand signals for the team can increase communication and help to maintain the flow:

- fingers pointing up for sharp keys, fingers down for flat keys
- curved thumb and forefinger in a C shape for the key of C
- thumbs up for a modulation up a half step
- palm up means louder, palm down, softer
- rotating the wrist and index finger means another repetition
- hand on head means "da capo"—go back to the beginning

Psychological Underpinnings

A basic premise of the five-phase model is that *praise normally precedes adoration.* By "praise," I'm referring to upbeat songs of transcendence in the *engagement* and *exaltation phases;* and by "adoration," reflective songs in the *adoration* and *intimacy phases.* This fundamental principle—that praise normally precedes adoration—is strategic.[5] It's behind much of the best worship leading because it makes sense psychologically. People simply cannot come to church and plunge into adoration without preparation. People need time before they are ready to express true adoration and intimacy. Beginning with praise makes sense too. People need to wake up and be energized—especially in early morning services.

Incorporating Hymns into the Model

Hymns *are* more difficult to incorporate into the model. The wide range of thoughts from stanza to stanza tends to spill over into more than one phase, whereas choruses contain only one major thought and fall into a single phase more easily. When hymns are included, organists can share in the worship. The organ can be particularly effective during a hymn of exaltation or during the closeout. (If your church organ is retrofitted with MIDI,[6] the organist can participate even in contemporary choruses.)

The chart below demonstrates that hymns and choruses can be effectively combined. *The New Worship Musician* software (see appendix 3) notates each of the modulations. *Older, well-established choruses were chosen to communicate to a wide readership.*

A Model Five-Phase Set

Phase	Piece	Key Word	Key
	Stand		
Invitation	"We Bring a Sacrifice of Praise"	praise	D
	"He Has Made Me Glad"	glad	D
Engagement	"Rejoice in the Lord Always"	rejoice	D
Exaltation	"Rejoice, the Lord Is King!"	rejoice	C
	"Crown Him with Many Crowns"	crown	C
	Sit		
Exaltation/ Adoration	"Glorify Your Name"	glorify	B♭/C
Adoration	"I Love You, Lord"	love	F
Intimacy	"As the Deer"	you	C
	Stand		
Closeout	"Fairest Lord Jesus"		D♭/D/E♭

Sensitively craft your set. I've pitched the keys *low,* anticipating an early morning service where voices will need to warm up. Raising the key a half or whole step between repetitions or stanzas can increase intensity (for help on performing modulations, see appendix 3). Try not to overuse this technique, though; determine from the text which stanza(s) will benefit most. For example, raising the last stanza of "Fairest Lord Jesus" a half step up helps immeasurably to express the regality of the text ("Lord of creation"). Key changes up a fourth or down a fifth (as in "Glorify Your Name" and "I Love You, Lord" above)[7] usually require no modulation material at all.

Note: The use of common words between adjacent choruses pre-vents patchiness and builds unity (see "rejoice" in the "Key Word" col-umn above). Charles Wesley also used this device in "O for a Thou-sand Tongues to Sing" to link stanzas. The bold lettering below shows how the word ending a stanza is reused in starting the next stanza. Clever! A good idea for us too.

End of stanza	1. the triumphs of his **grace**
Start	2. My **gracious** Master and my God
End	3. the honors of Thy **name**
Start	4. Jesus, the **name** that calms my fears

Flexibility

The five-phase progression has a balanced, graduated arch. Use it to guide your thinking. You can be flexible about *time:* The same pro-gression can be used in either short or long worship sets. You can also be flexible about *content:* Use all choruses, all hymns, or any mixture or weighting of hymns and choruses. Use any number of hymns or cho-ruses in any phase.

You can be flexible about *place:* Use the whole model before the ser-mon as the dominating activity. Use part of the model during the pre-lude or at the end of your service. Use it in Sunday evening services when you're singing a bunch of favorites.

Cut out some phases or weight them differently. The *exaltation* and *adoration phases* seem to form the core of the model. They mirror the basic character of God: his transcendence and his immanence. They help us project an accurate, faithful image of God to the people—a vital concept. I *always* try to have moments of transcendence and intimacy in every worship service. A good place for a Scripture reading is between these phases, if you need a break in the set (option one). I've also tried moving from exaltation to adoration and back to exaltation (option two).

Flowing Worship Options

Option One	Option Two
Exaltation	Exaltation
Break (Scripture/prayer/solo?)	Adoration
Adoration	Exaltation

You can also give a single phase like *adoration* more weight than the others. I've experimented with short adoration sets (ten minutes long) toward the middle of the morning service. They work especially well when the set emerges out of a time of prayer or the communion service.

Getting Started Safely

If you are introducing free-flowing praise into a traditional service format, begin conservatively. First, start with one chorus; extend that to two, then three continuous hymns or choruses. As your skill increases, and the people become accustomed to the change, gradually lengthen the set.

What about the objection that "hymns and choruses don't go together"? This simply is not true. People who say this often know few hymns and feel threatened by them. However, guitarists do find them awkward to play because hymnbook harmonizations are written for keyboardists. The chords change too quickly. If more hymnbooks would offer slower "harmonic rhythms," and pop symbols in keys with sharps (G, D, A, E), it would help make hymns more accessible to guitarists. Some do.[8] Another solution is to have keyboardists play the hymns and guitarists the choruses.

One more alternative is to place hymns and choruses in different parts of your service. You could open with a chorus section and include two hymns toward the middle of your service. Or you could open with a hymn, continue with choruses, and close your worship set with a hymn. Hymns can even be functional within the center of a set.

One benefit of the model is that it encourages us not to jump around between categories within a set. Jerking about tends to be disorienting, results in a lack of direction, and distracts from the spiritual focus of the service. It's like a home decorated without integrated colors, furniture, and paintings.

Another advantage: Even if worship teams are not given the complete song list, they'll have a mental image of the overall shape and will be able to anticipate how to function dynamically.

Important! *If there is an abrupt change of tempo* in beginning a new song, have the group emerge two or four measures after the leader. That's a safe way to establish a new tempo.

What about technology? Sequenced drum machine parts,[9] MIDI files, and software such as "Band-in-a-Box"[10] may function better at the beginning where steady tempos are normative. The rubato inherent in *adoration* and *intimacy phases* is more difficult to perform with a preset track.

Accumulation, Not Repetition

 Finally, what about the objection that chorus singing is boringly repetitious? That perception, more than anything, reveals a lack of musicianship. When resourceful musicians repeat a chorus, it's not boring and it's not simple repetition. It's *accumulation*. On each repetition the insightful musician will do something subtle—change the rhythm, the chords, or the dynamics in order to add a sense of unfolding newness. In fact there is a real danger that expert leaders may use these techniques to manipulate the people. *Worship leaders have an obligation not to manipulate the people. They must earn and never betray the trust people put in them.*

Let me further expand on the idea of accumulation. If you say to your spouse, "I love you," that means something. But if you declare, "I love you! I love you! I love you!"—it's more than simple repetition! That reiteration communicates intense feeling. In the same way, when praise is offered in the Book of Revelation with the sevenfold repetition—"Worthy is the Lamb, who was slain, to receive power and wealth and wisdom and strength and honor and glory and praise!" (Rev. 5:12)—it is far more than repetition. It has an extolling function. And recall further, the words "holy, holy, holy" are intoned ceaselessly around the throne.

The Danger of Manipulation

Some critics believe contemporary worship is guilty of promoting manipulative, self-indulgent worship experiences. They object to the use of music to induce, urge, cause, or empower a worship experience—to push people's "worship buzzer"—like a conditioned reflex. Some even object to the concept that music can be used to aid, facilitate, or enhance a worship experience.

It is important to hear these critics. Let's be open: Self-examination is beneficial. Dr. Harold Best, former dean of the Music Conservatory at Wheaton College, passionately identifies with each of these concerns. He writes against using music to "aid," "induce," or "enhance" worship: "Depending on music to aid, induce, or enhance worship is idolatry dressed up in psycho-aesthetic finery. It confuses the power of music with the presence of God."[11]

Best believes that contemporary worship is too dependent on music, music styles, and music leaders: ". . . how wrong it is to place the burden of proof so heavily on the music and musicians, on the worship style and leader, instead of the Spirit, whose sovereign purpose, after all, can override or undergird any of our devices."[12]

In chapter 3 of *The New Worship Supplement* at worshipinfo.com, I quote Dr. Best's criticisms at more length and defend the ideas in this chapter. I think you will find my response, as well as his rebuttal, lively and enlightening. Don't miss this!

The five-phase model is valuable for unpacking free-flowing praise technically to worship leaders. But you ask, "Is there more scriptural support for it? And how could I explain the dynamic flow and purpose of the model succinctly to the people?" The next chapter helps us with that. We'll look at a powerful image of worship—"The Journey into the Holy of Holies."

> *. . . art is a means of worship, not an end, the way we formulate, share, and present to the far-off and unfathomed firmament the yearnings of our souls toward higher things.*
>
> Bruce Bawer

Questions for Reflection and Discussion

1. Should praise precede adoration?
2. Do you discern any weaknesses in the five-phase model?
3. How does the five-phase model relate to evangelism, fellowship, and worship services?
4. Are liturgical, thematic, and free-flowing praise formats employed in the churches of your area? What is your experience with each?
5. What distracts you most in worship sets?
6. Are we too dependent on music in our worship?

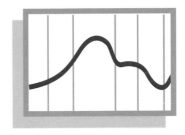

JOURNEY INTO THE HOLY OF HOLIES

Only to sit and think of God,
Oh what a joy it is!
To think the thought, to breathe the Name;
Earth has no higher bliss.

Frederick W. Faber

Students of worship have discovered a powerful pattern for leading congregational praise. This model is called "The Journey into the Holy of Holies," "Worship in the Outer and Inner Courts," or most commonly, "Praise and Worship." The basic movement goes from celebration to adoration, and it follows the Old Testament idea of people making pilgrimages to Jerusalem, beginning by entering the city's gates with praise, and ending in the Holy of Holies.[1]

Imagine Jews traveling in caravans from near and far to the temple:

Along the trails resound the songs of pilgrims wending their way to observe the great festival. One leads a goat, another an ox, a third a sheep to offer to God at the sanctuary. There they will recite prayers and sing hymns and dance in religious procession about the altar. Speaking many dialects they come from many lands, but for all of them Jerusalem is the Holy City. Ascending while singing the Hallel with ever-enlarging throngs, the pilgrims catch first sight of the temple ("that is where the tribes go up, the tribes of the Lord, to praise the name of the Lord"), its gold plates and white marble glistening in the sun. And in the swarming crowds, fathers with their sons and daughters tour the perimeter of the temple examining each gate.[2]

"Enter his gates with thanksgiving and his courts with praise," exclaims Psalm 100:4. As the people march through the gates, there is joyful celebration and loud proclamation of God's greatness. Brass, string, and percussion instruments accompany their singing and clapping, as the people break free from the burdens of life and count their blessings.

Today we can join that journey from the altar and laver to the Holy Place (lampstand, bread, incense) and finally into the Holy of Holies in our congregational song. As we do, exuberant joy turns to mysterious wonderment and solemn adoration. And we can reflect on the temple furniture and wonder at its meaning for us.

The Meaning of the Temple Furniture

As each male Israelite brought an *offering* for sacrifice, so we bring a sacrifice of praise: "Through Jesus, therefore, let us continually offer to God a sacrifice of praise—the fruit of lips that confess his name" (Heb. 13:15). At the *altar* in the inner court, the offering is wholly consumed and goes up in smoke to heaven, illustrating the need for total

Close-up of the Inner Tabernacle

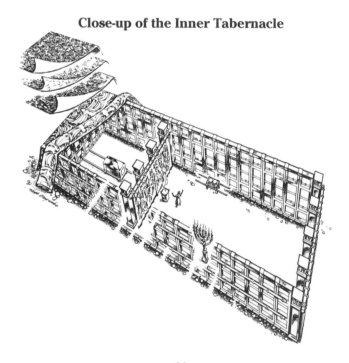

Overview of the Tabernacle

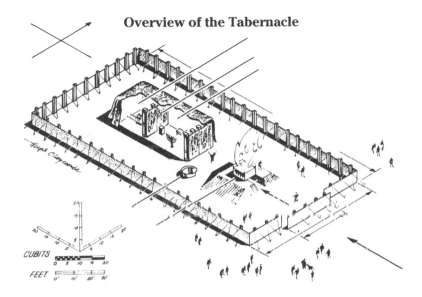

CUBITS

FEET

consecration. The *laver,* the washing basin for the priests, speaks of our need for cleansing before we come into the presence of a holy God. Psalm 24:3 reads: "Who may ascend the hill of the LORD? Who may stand in his holy place? He who has clean hands and a pure heart."

Advancing into the Holy Place, we see the *table of shewbread,* which foreshadows the Lord's Supper and reminds us that we come as members of one body. In the enclosed space, the *seven-branched golden candlesticks* burn continually, replenished by a continuous supply of oil (Zechariah 4). It symbolizes the Holy Spirit, who illuminates the Word of God and enables us to perceive spiritual things (1 Cor. 2:12). In front of the veil, now torn and open wide, stands the *altar of incense,* a symbol of prayer, the gateway into the Holy of Holies. It typifies the risen Christ offering prayers on our behalf before the throne. His prayers, along with ours commingled, rise as sweet perfume before the Lord.

In stillness and awe we enter the Holy of Holies where the *adoring cherubim* guard the ark; the wooden *chest* overlaid with gold inside and out represents the presence of God. On the *mercy seat,* the lid of the chest, we see sprinkled blood, the price paid for our forgiveness by the completed work of Christ. We now cease from any effort to make ourselves acceptable to God. Christ has done it all, and we are clothed in his righteousness.

Inside the ark we see the tablets of stone, the pot of manna, and the budded rod. The *tablets of stone* tell of the demands of the law, now totally satisfied by the death of Christ. The *pot of manna* points to Christ, the self-proclaimed Bread of Life: "I am the bread of life. Your forefathers ate the manna in the desert, yet they died. But here is the bread that comes down from heaven, which a man may eat and not die. I am the living bread" (John 6:48–51).

When Aaron's *budded rod* comes into view, we understand that as this dead stick flowered and bore fruit, so also Christ arose and lives forever. He has obtained "a permanent priesthood" (Heb. 7:24). Because we are "in Christ" and share in the power of his resurrection, we too have become a "royal priesthood" and shall one day become "a kingdom of priests" (Rev. 5:10).

The temple furniture, therefore, foreshadows how we may enter into the Holy of Holies and have a genuine meeting with God: God desires us to be totally consecrated (altar), pure in spirit (laver), unified in fellowship (bread), dependent on the Holy Spirit (candlestick), and in a spirit of prayer (incense). Access to a holy and intimate worship has been made available through the work of our Lord and Savior Jesus Christ:

> Since we have confidence to enter the Most Holy Place by the blood of Jesus, by a new and living way opened for us through the curtain, that is, his body, and since we have a great priest over the house of God, let us draw near to God with a sincere heart in full assurance of faith.
>
> Hebrews 10:19–22

The metaphor of the "Journey into the Holy of Holies" has noteworthy characteristics: (1) It is easy to explain in a few words. Its imagery is visual and connects readily, and leaders wanting to communicate the overall pattern of worship for the day find it valuable. (2) Its imagery is biblical. It has a strong connection with the tabernacle and temple, as well as with the worship in the books of Hebrews and Revelation. Revelation depicts ultimate and final worship as occurring around the throne of God—the Holy of Holies in heaven. The "journey imagery" is also found in the remarkable Hebrews passage quoted above.

Indeed, Scripture implores us, metaphorically, to "draw near to God," to "enter the Most Holy Place," and to go "through the curtain," knowing that Christ, through his body, has opened a way for us into the very Holy of Holies. That's powerful! (See chapter 10 for more on Hebrews.) It's a concept that worship leaders have found immensely practical: Leaders can sense the movement from outer court to inner court worship. *Inner court–outer court imagery* is a major idea for countless worship leaders today. Moreover, it "connects" with the thought processes of musicians in uniquely musical ways that may not be apparent to the average person in the congregation. I'm convinced this imagery will be around a long time! It's become a new paradigm.

Cornwall's Adaptation

Judson Cornwall, a Pentecostal worship writer from the late '70s and '80s, promoted the idea that the worship leader can take the people on a worship journey that mirrors the "Journey into the Holy of Holies" at every point. He cited Psalm 100 as scriptural support.

The leader, he said, must know where the people are, where he wants to take them, and when they have arrived. Cornwall's "worship progression" has five phases.

First: Songs of Personal Testimony in the Camp

The first object is to meet the worshipers where they are, outside the gates in the camp. Here worshipers are concerned with people, places, things, and personal needs, and they have little God consciousness. The worship leader gets their attention through personal testimony hymns, gospel songs, and "I am" and "I have" songs. "Let the congregation enjoy singing songs of testimony until they are sufficiently united," says Cornwall. Sound similar to Wimber's *invitation phase?* One difference, though, is that Cornwall, being from an older generation, makes explicit reference to the use of old gospel songs—songs like "Count Your Many Blessings" and "Bless That Wonderful Name of Jesus."

Second: Through the Gates with Thanksgiving

Cornwall equates the "gates of thanksgiving" with the beginning phase of the service:

> The procession through the eastern gate into the outer court should be a joyful march, for thanks should never be expressed mournfully or negatively. While the people are singing choruses of thanksgiving they will be thinking both of themselves and of their God, but by put-

71

ting the emphasis upon the giving of thanks, the majority of the thought patterns should be on their God. Singing at this level will often invoke a beginning level of **praise,** but it will not produce **worship** [adoration], for the singers are not yet close enough to God's presence to express a worship response.[3]

Psalm 24:7 says, "Lift up your heads, O you gates . . . that the King of glory may come in." These gates are the gates of our hearts. Our King desires to be enthroned in our hearts.

Note above that Cornwall was one of the first writers to make the now popular distinction between "praise" and "worship": "Praise" occurs in the outer court during the beginning of the service, whereas authentic, profound "worship" takes place later in the inner court.

Third: Into His Courts with Praise

Here the emphasis changes from what God has done to who he is, to blessing his name and to thinking less of one's self and more of God. Cornwall candidly admits that "soulish worship" (focused on the self) may occur outside the gates or in the court:

Soulish worship is *feeling* motivated and depends upon external impetus. . . . If a "worship service" requires emotional stories and psychological impetus to stir it into being, it is very likely soulish worship. So much of America's "evangelistic services" and "gospel music" are soulish both in origin and in result.[4]

He would not have the people stop there, however, but push on toward the purer worship occurring in the Holy Place.

Fourth: Solemn Worship inside the Holy Place; and Fifth: In the Holy of Holies

In these phases all attention is now directed solely to God, Jesus Christ, or the Holy Spirit. Cornwall explains: "Nothing in there speaks of man; it is in its every aspect a revelation of God."[5] In Israel's inner sanctuary, an atmosphere of quiet reverence enveloped the space: The flickering flame of the candlesticks, the smell of the incense, and the outstretched wings of adoring cherubim contributed to that. Cornwall's description of a congregation worshiping in the Holy Place reflects that same reverence, and he notes mistakes leaders often make.

> If the leader has been successful in bringing the people step by step into the outer court and on through it into the holy place, there will be a rise in the spiritual response of the people. Instead of mere soulish, emotional responses, there will be responses from the human spirit that have depth and devotion in them. Clapping will likely be replaced with devotional responses of upturned faces, raised hands, tears, and even a subtle change in the timbre of the voices. When there is an awareness that we have come into the presence of God we step out of lightness into sobriety.
>
> It is at this point that too many leaders make a serious mistake by jerking the people back into the outer court with an emotional chorus of thanksgiving. *Worship takes time; don't rush the people.* Let them sing: *let them repeat any chorus or verse of a hymn* that seems to give honest expression to what they are feeling and doing at the moment. The mind can jump from one concept to another far faster than the spirit can. Allow the spirit time to savor the sense of the presence of the Lord.
>
> Just worship. Cleverness is inappropriate. Talk is unnecessary. Directions for response are superfluous. Let the people worship. Silence may be threatening to the leader, but it is golden to the worshiper. A gentle sustained chord on the organ and a song of the Spirit on the lips of the leader should be more than sufficient to carry a worship response of the entire congregation for a protracted period of time.[6]

Note: Cornwall encourages the repetition of songs, so typical of contemporary worship, and warns leaders not to rush the people. Of the worship leader, he says, "If he succeeds, he will be more a leader of worshipers than a leader of songs."[7]

Rounding Off

Two options emerge for concluding this reverential worship. After the Holy of Holies phase is completed and the people have had a quiet time of worship, they may be invited to sit down "in the Lord's presence" or be led back to the outer court with a celebratory hymn in preparation for the preaching of the Word.

73

Comparing the Models

Sound familiar? Yes! Cornwall's model, in form and spirit, bears a lot of resemblance to Wimber's five-phase model, though the terminology is different. How would they look side by side? A comparison in the following chart (see outer columns) reveals a remarkable correspondence.

Liturgical and Free-Flowing Praise Synthesis

Wimber's Five Phases	Webber's Liturgical Model: Isaiah 6	Cornwall's "Journey into Holy of Holies"
1. Invitation	[Call to Worship]	1. Personal Testimony: "Inside the camp"
2. Engagement	[Invocation]	2. Thanksgiving: "Through the gates"
3. Exaltation	1.Transcendent Praise: "I saw the Lord"	3. Praise: "Into his courts with praise"
	2. Confession of Sin: "Woe to me"	
	3. Words of Forgiveness: "Your guilt is taken away"	
4. Adoration		4. Holy Place
5. Intimacy		5. Holy of Holies
Closeout		Rounding Off
Scripture Reading	[Scripture Reading]	Scripture Reading
Preaching	4. Preaching: "Whom shall I send?" Lord's Supper	Preaching
Dismissal	5. Commitment: "Here am I"	Dismissal

The chart reveals another insight: Songs of repentance could be incorporated into flowing praise.[8] Robert Webber's liturgical model (center), emphasizing repentance, could be synthesized into the outer columns. (We look more closely at Webber's model in the next chapter.) Choruses like "Change My Heart, O God" (Espinosa) and "Create in Me a Clean Heart, O God," and hymns like "Kind and Merciful God" (Leech) and

"Whiter than Snow" (Nicholson) could express this emphasis. Prayers of repentance and words of forgiveness could even be *spoken.*

On reflection, it should be evident that the Wimber and Cornwall models

- relate most to a worship-oriented service, less to a fellowship service, and perhaps least of all to an evangelistically oriented service, though not incompatible with any of the above[9]
- are somewhat resistant to a thematically conceived service, though the "closeout" can tie in thematically with the sermon
- may require pastors to delegate to their worship leader the responsibility of choosing pieces that link together

My objective has not been to impart a "formula" to be rigidly followed with the expectation that it can, of itself, deliver a great worship experience. That is the Holy Spirit's work. Yet we all need tools to use, to modify, and to depart from. We don't need to fear structures.[10]

True worship is a matter of the spirit, as Jesus explained to the Samaritan woman:

> The water I give . . . will become . . . a spring of water welling up to eternal life. . . . A time is coming and has now come when the true worshipers will worship the Father in spirit and truth, for they are the kind of worshipers the Father seeks. God is spirit, and his worshipers must worship in spirit and in truth.
>
> John 4:14, 23–24

The five-phase and Holy of Holies models have a logic to them and a sensitivity to the psychological dimension that respects the human person and the character of God. More than a passing fad, they have been found to be demonstrably valuable. If you employ them, eventually you may sense gaps and weaknesses, but you can address those deficiencies. The next chapter widens our focus to consider three major ways of designing the service.

Suggestion: When you are reflecting on this chapter, link it with the first half of chapter 10, where Christ our worship leader leads us into the Holy of Holies.

> *Narrow is the mansion of my soul;*
> *enlarge it, that You may enter it.*
> Saint Augustine

Questions for Reflection and Discussion

1. What are the merits of "The Journey into the Holy of Holies" model?
2. Why has "praise and worship" become so popular?
3. Do you find the distinction between "outer court" and "inner court" helpful? Explain.
4. Do you agree or disagree with this statement: "Silence may be threatening to the leader, but it is golden to the worshiper"? Explain.

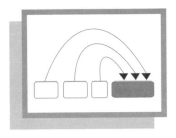

DESIGNING THE SERVICE

Worship is the dramatic celebration of God in his supreme worth in such a manner that his "worthiness" becomes the norm and inspiration of human living.

Ralph Martin, *The Worship of God*

We do not find in Scripture a prescribed order of service for New Testament Christians to follow. Apparently the Holy Spirit wisely left the designing of the service for each culture to determine. While Scripture does not offer explicit guidance, it does indicate that revelation and response are basic to worship. Donald P. Hustad has helped us all with this guiding principle:

Insofar as we are able to conceive and achieve it, there should be a *full revelation* of God [Jesus Christ and the Holy Spirit], his actions and his will for us, and a *full response* by men and women, involving body, emotions, intellect, and will.[1]

In this chapter I'm going to present three forms of worship—liturgical, thematic or free-church, and open/free-flowing praise. I refuse to stand in judgment on which is best. That determination is best made by the people involved. My intention is to promote understanding and to present each form fairly. The three forms are *not mutually exclusive;* they can be *blended.*

The Formats Being Blended Today

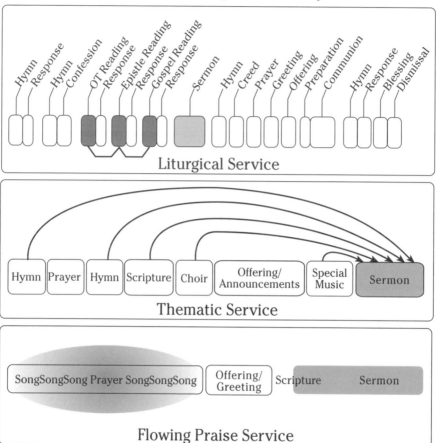

The chart shows three formats that dominate the worship landscape today. The liturgical format has been in continuous use since the Protestant Reformation and can be traced back to Catholic and synagogue influences. Notice, several Scripture readings are located near the beginning, the sermon toward the middle, and the Lord's Supper celebrated weekly (or at least frequently) near the end.

In contrast, the thematic service has its roots in the evangelistic crusades of Moody/Sankey and Sunday/Rodeheaver. The crusades incorporated a song leader, a gospel choir sitting directly behind the pulpit, and special music immediately before the message. The message was the centerpiece of the event—the items before the message were considered the preliminaries.[2] Free-flowing praise, on the other hand, arose during the 1970s.

Whatever style or style mix you choose, protect your fundamental priorities: Keep prominent the congregational singing, the offering of prayers (widely neglected), and the reading of Scripture (also widely neglected).[3]

Let's begin with liturgical services, keeping in mind that liturgical worship is *not* inherently less spiritual than thematic or free-flowing worship.

Liturgical Services: Isaiah 6 Model

In liturgical services, the church year (Advent, Christmas, Epiphany, Lent, Easter, and Pentecost) and the lectionary (predetermined, systematic Scripture readings for the entire year) drive the service. The pastor does not freely select his own sermon topic; it is drawn from one of the three Scripture readings—the Old Testament, Acts or the Epistles, and the Gospels. As we saw in Webber's liturgical model (chapter 4), the theophany of Isaiah 6, also called the "Divine-Human Model," provides a pattern for organizing the overall service that is compatible with our psychological makeup:

Praise	I saw the Lord seated on a throne, high and exalted. . . . "Holy, holy, holy is the LORD Almighty; the whole earth is full of his glory." (vv. 1, 3)
Confession	"Woe to me! . . . I am ruined! For I am a man of unclean lips, and I live among a people of unclean lips." (v. 5)
Forgiveness	Then one of the seraphs flew to me with a live coal. . . . With it he touched my mouth and said, ". . . your guilt is taken away and your sin atoned for." (vv. 6–7)
God Calls	"Whom shall I send? And who will go for us?" (v. 8)
Commitment	And I said, "Here am I. Send me!" (v. 8)

The transcendence comes first. Once the greatness of God is established, then we see ourselves as sinners in need of forgiveness. An angel takes a live coal from the altar and touches Isaiah's mouth,

79

pronouncing his sin "purged." God calls, "Whom shall I send" (sermon) and Isaiah responds, "Send me" (response of commitment). In the dismissal, the people are sent to live out the gospel in their communities.

Robert Webber, an evangelical Episcopalian, advocates the following standard order of service based on Isaiah 6:[4]

I. The Preparation (Six Elements)
   Opening Hymn
   The Call to Worship
   The Invocation
   The Acknowledgment of God [Transcendent Praise]
   The Confession of Sin
   The Words of Forgiveness
II. Scripture Reading, Preaching, and Response to the Word
III. Lord's Supper
IV. The Dismissal [Commitment]

Observe first that the confession and words of forgiveness occur early in the service, clearing the way for joy in worship. Second, time is given for response *after* the sermon.

In this format, the people sing an opening hymn. There is a call to worship (e.g., Ps. 95:1–2) and a prayer calling on God to make himself present. The acknowledgment of God extols his transcendent nature (not his intimacy). After the words of confession and forgiveness, readings from the Old Testament, the Epistles, and the Gospels are given. After the sermon, the offering and announcements, the recitation of a creed, the Lord's Supper, and the benediction occur.

Contrast with Thematic Service

By way of contrast, in thematic services the announcements and the offering usually precede the sermon, a single Scripture passage is read, no creed is confessed, communion is not observed weekly, and the service comes to an abrupt end after the sermon. Pastors like their sermon to be ringing in the ears of the people at the benediction.

In the liturgical model, revelation precedes response. The first part of the service is weighted toward revelation (Scripture), the closing part to response, with various "chains" of revelation and response occurring along the way. Take, for example, the chains of revelation and response in the first part of the 1662 Anglican prayer book order of worship:

Revelation	Reading of Psalm
Response	Singing of Gloria Patri (Glory be to the Father)
Revelation	Old Testament Reading
Response	Te Deum (a "Glory to God" statement)
Revelation	New Testament Reading
Response	Nunc Dimitus (Now let Thy servant depart, Luke 2:28–32)

Hustad's Variation on Isaiah 6

Hustad adapts the liturgical order of service for mainstream evangelical practice.[5] He suggests a simple prayer of confession and the use of Scripture for the words of forgiveness:

Confession. "Our Father, we thank you that, no matter how often we have failed you and others in the year that is past, today—and each day—we can begin afresh. . . ," or, "Father, we come to you today asking that we might receive that refreshing of forgiveness. . . . We confess that too often we have loved things and used people and we need your forgiveness. . . ."[6]

Words of Forgiveness. "If we walk in the light, as he is in the light, we have fellowship with one another, and the blood of Jesus, his Son, purifies us from all sin" (1 John 1:7), or, "If we confess our sins, he is faithful and just to forgive us our sins, and to cleanse us from all unrighteousness" (1 John 1:9 KJV).[7]

Hustad's Isaiah 6 Order of Worship

Spiritual Goals	Order of Worship
Awareness of God	Hymn: "To God Be the Glory" (Crosby-Doane)
Confession and Forgiveness	Opening Prayer (Invocation, Confession, Assurance of Pardon) Greeting/Welcome Hymn: "Break Thou the Bread of Life"

(continued)

Hustad's Isaiah 6 Order of Worship (*continued*)

Spiritual Goals	Order of Worship
God Speaks to Us	Scripture Reading
	Choir: "We Praise Thee, O God"
	Sermon
We Respond	Hymn (Invitation): "Stand Up, Stand Up for Jesus"
	Offering (Solo): "Wherever He Leads I'll Go"
We Celebrate	Lord's Table (bread, cup)
We Pray	Pastoral Prayer and United "Amen"
	Doxology and Benediction

"Break Thou the Bread" foreshadows the Scripture reading, and the choir number, "We Praise Thee," follows it as a response to revelation.

Note that several responses occur after the sermon: the congregational song, the offering, a solo, and a pastoral prayer. Though exceptional for evangelical services, the pastoral prayer placed near the end of the service observes "the normal pattern of all Christian liturgies."[8] Responses after the sermon build around what we have learned about God. This practice also accords with the sequence in Acts 2:42: "They devoted themselves to the apostles' teaching and to the fellowship, to the breaking of bread and to prayer."

Liturgical and Free-Church Formats Compared

Liturgical and free-church formats have both strengths and weaknesses. The liturgical service imposes discipline and a logical framework to the weekly service and adheres to the church year. It contains fixed prayers. In contrast, the thematic service emphasizes impromptu prayer—people learn how to pray spontaneously. Prayers for needs in the congregation, outreach, and missions often predominate, whereas prayers of confession may not occur.

The liturgical service calls for many short, dialogical responses. For example, the leader says, "Lift up your hearts," and the people automatically respond, "We lift them up to the Lord." The people respond, "Thanks be to God" (after Scripture), "Lord, have mercy" (after intercessory prayers); and when the minister says, "The Lord be with you," the people rejoin, "And also with you." On the down side, these predetermined responses may feel stiff to some churched and nonchurched participants. In thematic services, spontaneous amens may punctuate the service. People feel free to react at any point, not just when the worship book or folder calls for a response.

In addition, the liturgical service employs lectionary Scripture readings, and the sermon is drawn from those readings. An obvious benefit of this practice is that it discourages partisan, hobbyhorse preaching. It prevents leaders from centering on a few favorite passages for Scripture readings Sunday after Sunday.

On the other hand, the minister in the thematic tradition can choose any sermon topic for the day or prepare a series on a book from the Bible. The pastor is free to address the people wherever they need help the most.

Thematic Worship Planning

Thematic worship has been the favored design of perhaps the majority of evangelical churches. Pastors want the freedom to choose their sermon topics and sermon series. And they want the service planning to center around the sermon. This good intention (i.e., a thematically integrated service), Hustad maintains, can be carried too far:

> There is a concept of worship order held by some evangelicals, which sees "unity without diversity" as the guiding principle. If the morning sermon is about "faith," every hymn will support that subject—"Faith of Our Fathers," "Faith Is the Victory," "Have Faith in God," "O for a Faith That Will Not Shrink," etc. This practice reveals that the sermon and its response are the only significant acts of worship for those planners. The wise and humble pastor will acknowledge that on some occasions a praise hymn, or the prayer of confession or of intercession, or the choir anthem may meet the spiritual needs of some people more than the homily.[9]

Must the sermon be the highlight of the service every Sunday? That is a commonly held evangelical belief. The following deficiencies may also accompany free-church worship: (1) lack of planning, (2) too little time devoted to prayer, (3) insufficiently prominent Scripture reading(s), and (4) meager congregational response opportunities. The thematic service, however, has proven to be tremendously effective over the years and will continue to be a powerful, much-used concept.[10] Ronald Allen and Gordon Borror encourage evangelicals to enjoy their freedom and not be locked into any ordering of service events.[11]

When planning a thematic service, the pastor and worship leader need to communicate early in the week. Consider this logical sequence of questions:

1. What is the *target* of the service? Where is the pastor headed? What response, what outcome, is desired? Planners need more than the Scripture passage for the day. Allen and Borror suggest obtaining the sermon outline:

   The best way to begin is with the sermon topic or outline. . . . An obvious burden for a pastor, he must notify his other service participants in advance. But it will be well worth the trouble. The point of the hour will be so clear, even before the message, that all involved in a well orchestrated effort will be a part of the success and the blessing! . . . All musical input must help build the case.[12]

2. What are the *givens?* Congregational praise, Scripture reading(s), and prayers all seem foundational. So keep these prominent. Other considerations include greetings, testimonies, announcements, the offering, and musical expressions.
3. What *resources* are available? Would any of these—a prayer of encounter and intercession (corporately or in small groups); a fresh testimony from someone; an interview; a solo; a choir number; a letter, book, newspaper, or cassette tape excerpt; a reader's theater; a banner; or a pantomime—serve to enhance the service?
4. What *sequence* of events would give the service a logical progression and be psychologically sound?
5. What *title* or *captions* would integrate the service?

Greater freedom entails greater responsibility. Pastors in the thematic tradition must not squander their freedom. They need to be committed to clear service objectives, aware that worship services are dramatic events, and they need to be more open to collaborative planning than their liturgical brothers and sisters.

Developing Procedures for Free-Flowing Worship

In open or free-flowing worship, predetermined understandings between leaders are vital—particularly in relation to the *procedures* employed in the outworking of the service. "Open worship" means worship where "rather than keeping strictly and exclusively to the pre-planned program [note: There is preplanning], all the participants are seeking to be led creatively by the Spirit into a flow of events unique to that group of people at that point in time."[13] The format seems akin to Paul's description of *koinonia* worship at the house church in Corinth: "When you come together, everyone has a hymn, or a word of instruction, a revelation, a tongue or an interpretation. All of these must be done for the strengthening of the church" (1 Cor. 14:26).

Graham Kendrick admits, "The job is often done badly. . . . [There] is all too often a suspicion of advance planning, firm leadership and efficient organization."[14] Advance preparation is necessary. Kendrick, a guitarist, says:

> I find it necessary to prepare a list of songs complete with number and key, and position it on a clip-board in front of me. This functions not only as a reminder of the numbers . . . but as a reminder of the breadth of choices available.[15]

In open worship we must "expect the unexpected" and "be free to alter or abandon the plans we have made. . . . Leading worship is leading people . . . standing before God on their behalf seeking their health and welfare. . . . It is a process of active faith to lead people by following the Spirit."[16]

Kendrick emphasizes the importance of maintaining a discerning approach: "We need to develop a sensitivity as to when something 'jars' against the spirit within us or disturbs our peace. . . . [Discernment] comes through experience and the practice of spiritual sensitivity over a period of time."[17] He urges leaders to be alert to opportunities for ministering to people the very moment they have shared. "It is remarkable how we quickly move on to the next item on the agenda, when the obvious thing to do would be to stop and take action immediately!"[18]

Moreover, in open worship, leaders need a sense of derived authority: "Jesus recognized . . . [that authority] was derived from being under authority (Matt. 8:9), and being submitted to one another (Eph. 5:21)."[19] Leaders must develop behind-the-scenes interpersonal trust in one another and have the security of ground rules:

> It helps a great deal for there to be a set of ground rules generally understood by everybody and in detail by the leaders. For example,

there are questions of who acts in a crisis. . . . I remember occasions when I have been leading and something has unexpectedly happened that was beyond my "jurisdiction" or ability to cope with. It has been a great relief to myself and to everyone else when another leader has stepped forward and dealt competently with such a situation. . . .

The degree of genuine caring that the leader displays is crucial to the kind of response he gets back . . . the degree of care taken "behind the scenes," developing among the leadership a quality of friendship and functional interaction frees people from worry, fear, uncertainty and unhelpful interruption as they worship.[20]

Usually the problems encountered are not dramatic. A simple but sensitive redirection of the service may be needed:

Sensitivity must be shown to the person who makes a faulty contri-bution in sincerity and good faith. . . . [The leader should be positive and not "put down" the person, saying rather,] "We seem to be mov-ing toward intercession here and it is tremendously important to pray for Mr. Smith's gout, but I feel that at this moment we should be taking note of our earlier exhortation to give the Lord a rich offer-ing of thanks and praise, so let's sing. . . ."[21]

Kendrick maintains, "If, however, a dangerous or hurtful thing has been said, then it should be refuted and corrected immediately or else the meeting may never recover."[22]

Though Kendrick advocates less structure than found in the "man-aged flow" of the Wimber five-phase and Cornwall Journey into the Holy of Holies models, he would probably feel a kinship with these service formats. He understands that not all worship teams are com-fortable improvising, and premade plans are difficult to abandon. Yet true open worship insists on the freedom to abandon plans and follow the Spirit.

Astonishing Variety of Pauline Worship

If we look at the extraordinary variety of elements that appear in Pauline worship, it seems clear that Paul was drawing on synagogue and temple influences as well as the body-life metaphor of the church that so captivated him. As you look through the list of Pauline elements provided in the chart below, some may be familiar to your weekly wor-ship practice and some may be foreign. Try to imagine attending a

Pauline worship service—for many of us this would be a stretching experience! This recognition alone should teach us to be more charitable to other worship traditions.[23]

Variety of Elements in Pauline Worship

Opening and closing benedictions	1 Cor. 1:3; 16:23
Doxology and acclamation	1 Cor. 15:57
Liturgical prayer	2 Cor. 1:3
Spontaneous prayer	1 Cor. 14:14–15
Hymns, psalms, spiritual songs	1 Cor. 14:26; Eph. 5:19; Col. 3:16
Praise, singing, thanksgiving	1 Cor. 14:15
Responsive amens	1 Cor. 14:16
Physical prostration	1 Cor. 14:25
Holy kisses	Rom. 16:16; 1 Cor. 16:20; 2 Cor. 13:12; 1 Thess. 5:26; 1 Peter 5:14
Public reading of Paul's letters	Col. 4:16; 1 Thess. 5:27
Prophecy, revelation, discernment	1 Cor. 12:10; 14:6
Tongues and interpretations	1 Cor 14:27
Instruction, preaching, edification	1 Cor. 1:17; 14:26; 15:14
Healing	1 Cor. 12:9, 28, 30
Breaking of bread	1 Cor. 11:20–34
Baptism	1 Cor. 1:13–14
Use of Maranatha, an Aramaic liturgical form	1 Cor. 16:22
Collection	1 Cor. 16:1

Surprised by Convergence Worship

In the new worship, the liturgical, thematic, and flowing praise formats sometimes converge. Robert E. Webber calls this confluence of disparate worship traditions "convergence worship." Churches today are more aware of other traditions and more inclined to draw on aspects of them. Even divisions between Protestants and Catholics are not as strong as they once were, as the following story demonstrates.

A professor friend talked me into going to a citywide Catholic Renewal Conference held at the Anaheim Convention Center, a stone's throw from Disneyland. About eight thousand people were present. I sat amazed as the people fervently sang Catholic songs, Protestant hymns, Maranatha! and Integrity praise choruses, the Lord's Prayer, and—would you believe—evangelical choruses from the 1960s with such enthusiasm you would have thought they were "hot off the press." A worship team, comprised of several singers and a supporting cast of professional-quality instrumentalists playing synthesizers, guitars, and percussion, led the worship. The worship style combined the liturgical and flowing praise formats.

After the service I got up enough nerve to go to the stage and talk to one of the instrumentalists. I told him I was a Protestant observing the event and was really surprised that Catholics had such a skilled rhythm section and band. He pulled me aside and whispered: "The singers are Catholics, but all of us playing instruments are Protestants—we lead worship at various Vineyard churches in the area. We were hired for the event." They weren't Catholics at all! This cross-fertilization of worship styles and personnel would have been unthinkable a couple of generations ago. I also couldn't help but comment, "These Catholics are learning our hymns and we are forgetting them."

Suggestions for Small- to Medium-Sized Churches

Whatever your style or tradition, the following practical suggestions may be appropriate when designing the service. I offer them as something to think about.

1. *When communicating the sermon content to worship planners, merely telling them the scriptural reference is usually not enough.* A short paragraph on the central thrust of the sermon, prepared one or two months in advance, though, is invaluable. If such direction is unavailable, insufficiently clear, or, because of the nature of the topic, difficult to act on, worship leaders can lead the congregation in Godward praise. Godward praise complements almost any sermon.

2. If the prelude is not meaningful (people are late, talking), here are some options:

Retain the prelude but reorganize it. Five minutes before the service proper, stop the prelude. Have your pastor announce the preparation for worship, read a Scripture call to worship, and remain on the platform. Continue the prelude for another five minutes before the opening event. By doing this, you place the prelude within the body of the service, elevate the significance of preparation, provide an incentive for the prelude instrumentalist, and eliminate the need for negative comment from the pulpit regarding talking or lateness.

Disband the instrumental prelude. Have a five- to ten-minute preservice of praise choruses led by the worship team. Your worship bulletin could alert guests to the preservice sing. Or as an alternative, use this time to introduce or rehearse new hymns or choruses, alert the people to unusual features in the service, and establish a tone of worship.

Accept the talking and play an instrumental praise tape as background music. Begin the service with announcements and a Wimber-type invitation phase.

3. *Consider placing the announcements/welcome at the beginning or end of the service, but not in the middle (it kills the flow).*

4. *Remember, the main reasons for announcements are to* (a) create a climate for ministry, (b) share concerns, and (c) establish a "family" environment.

5. *Introduce guest musicians during the welcome and announcements.* This helps the flow and prevents them from being perceived as entertainment.

6. *If your offertory time is not meaningful*—the service seems to stop, or the piano, guitar, or worship team offertory is not being listened to—use that space for a vocal solo, for a memorized congregational song, or for learning a new hymn or chorus. Play through the song while the offering is being taken, then have the people join you. This works best when the words are sung from memory or shown on a screen. Then the people do not have to juggle hymnbooks and offering plates at the same time.

Hymn texts can reinforce the action of giving. Hymns like "We Give Thee but Thine Own," "We Praise Thee, O God, Our Redeemer," "The Wise May Bring Their Learning," "Come, Ye Christians, Be Committed" say in words what the people are doing. This is an elegant way of underscoring meaning.

7. *In general, discourage the practice of lengthy, flow-killing, verbal introductions to special music;* rather, encourage musicians to "let their music do their talking."

8. *If you desire but can't seem to find enough time for free-flowing praise,* try (1) starting a praise preservice, (2) merging your singing

into the offering, (3) lengthening the service, or (4) timing the parts of the service for a month to discover where the time is going.

A pastor of a large Los Angeles church shared this story with me while we were having breakfast at a restaurant. It underscores that we learn by doing. His son came back from the library all excited:

Son: "I've learned how to swim, Dad. I can do it!"

Dad (amazed): "Great! How did you learn it?"

Son: "From a book in the library." (Son gets down on the floor and demonstrates how it's done.)

The pastor told me, "Later in the day at the pool, it was all gurgling."

That is the way it is with the material in this chapter. It needs experiential outworking. Try some of the ideas and remember that more than one trial run may be necessary.

Worship both reveals and forms our identity as persons and communities.
C. Welton Gaddy, *The Gift of Worship*

Questions for Reflection and Discussion

1. When planning services, are pastors more content-oriented and musicians more feeling-oriented?
2. Would giving time for response after the sermon fit into your service?
3. Would you feel comfortable with a time of confession and words of forgiveness during your service?
4. Regarding inappropriate responses in "open worship," what procedures could be put in place in anticipation of problems?
5. Compare the merits of liturgical, thematic, and open worship.
6. Evangelicals are criticized for being antiliturgical and antiaesthetic. Is this warranted?

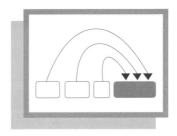

DRAMA, SCRIPTURE, TECHNOLOGY

Authentic worship begins with exalting God, but it is not complete until it issues into the action of reaching people.
                    Gary Hardin and Martin Thielen, *Authentic Worship*

Without question, television, computers, and the Internet are commanding our attention and dramatically impacting our society. After being immersed in these media during the week, our people come to church with quite different expectations than they did in the past. We are a more visually oriented society. Therefore, we must be open to new ways of using the new media and dramatic action in our services, especially when these can contribute positively to authentic worship. And make no mistake about it—worship involves drama!

Heaven's Worship

Think of this: God, the consummate Creator-Artist, thought of drama first.[1] The Book of Revelation has the look of a media event. We read of God seated at his throne, of elders wearing crowns and falling prostrate, of white raiment and golden sashes, of thunder, lightning, hail, torches, trumpets, harps, palm branches, of a wedding supper, of hair as white as wool and eyes that burn like a blazing fire.

Have you ever wondered how evangelicals, suddenly transported to heaven, might react to the dramatic action in the Book of Revelation? The transition could be difficult. Some of us might have salty responses.

> Imagine the criticisms God would receive from Evangelicals like us who arrive in heaven and find the roar of the congregational response too loud, the thunder and lightning too unsettling, the four living creatures too weird, the incense too strange, the white vestments too showy, the thirty minutes of silence too long, the prostration too embarrassing, the tabernacle furniture too Catholic, the endless undulations of "Holy, Holy, Holy" around the throne too mysterious, or phrases like "We give thee thanks" too liturgical, stilted, and confining![2]

The words "we never did it this way before" will take on new meaning! I challenge you, read the Book of Revelation again—this time from the point of view of worship. It looks like a dramatic media event. Revelation worship balances proclamation through words with proclamation through symbols.

The use of symbols has not ceased! The Judeo-Christian God is a symbol-making God. Symbols provide a vehicle for joy, for multilevel communication, and for commemoration. The Maker of all things beautiful will forever be the lover of light, color, sound, drama, and ceremony. "He who was seated on the throne said, 'I am making everything new!'" (Rev. 21:5).

Drama in Our Worship

Many evangelicals don't seem to realize that worship is drama no matter what format we use. The issue is not whether we're going to have drama, but what kind of drama we're going to have. The essence of drama is action. We can have either visible drama with external action or mental drama as we listen to a sermon or a story. What are some of the visible possibilities? Common examples of visible drama in worship are baptisms, the dedication of babies, altar calls, processionals, the offering, the lighting of an Advent candle.

The Lord's Supper is the highest visible drama in worship. In communion we reenact a drama that consists of an extended action: The elements are taken, blessed, broken, distributed, and consumed. The drama of participation in the Lord's Table can be heightened a number of ways. One idea is to invite the people to come forward and receive the elements. Another is to choose a family to walk the aisle with the elements and present them to the minister and elders. In small groups, the people can stand in a circle and receive the elements from each other. Some churches follow that with a time of sharing and prayer.

At a student-led chapel of two thousand people at Biola University, the students erected a large, wooden cross at the front. They handed out a few threads of wool to each of us as we entered. In a dramatic act at the conclusion of the service, they invited everyone to come and throw their threads at the foot of the cross, a symbol of releasing their burdens and sins to the Lord. Many did, and many wept, as the song "It Is Well" was sung by the congregation:

> My sin—O the bliss of this glorious tho't—
> My sin—not in part, but the whole,
> Is nailed to the cross, and I bear it no more,
> Praise the Lord, praise the Lord, O my soul!

At Good Friday services, some churches have handed out nails and have invited the people to come forward and nail their sins to a wooden cross while singing "It Is Well" during a silent communion service or a service of darkness. We can learn to respond during worship with our hands, feet, nose, and mouth. It can do us good to break from a verbal, mind-oriented form of worship.

We have not talked about the short dramatic vignettes that are typical in seeker-sensitive services. A scene in a coffee shop (or some other place) is often set on the platform. The drama functions to pose a situation, raise questions, establish tension and relevancy to life situations, leaving the preacher to answer or resolve some issue (see endnote for resources).[3]

I hope I have whetted your appetite!

Reading Scripture

The reading of Scripture corporately as a congregational act is becoming rare in churches on the West Coast. It's usually not a significant part of services these days. My personal conviction is that the reading of Scripture can be the most powerful communication of all. Remember, Paul himself charged Timothy: "Until I come, devote yourself to the public reading of Scripture, to preaching and to teaching" (1 Tim. 4:13).

The use of "responsive readings," however, may not always be adequate for today's worshiper. Therefore, here are some creative ideas for corporate Scripture reading.

Scripture during the Sermon

Pastors, this could make your sermon more interactive! Occasionally invite the congregation to read Scripture with you in the middle of your sermon. Rather than read it yourself, ask them to read along with you. It's an especially viable option if you can display the words on a screen via computer-generated images. No time is lost waiting for the people to look up verses, and you can put up any translation you wish.

Fonts for a Dynamic Response

One way to avoid wordy explanations and communicate instructions visually is to use fonts to improve response. Fonts are especially helpful in antiphonal readings. If the following were printed in your worship folder, what would it communicate?

Praise the Lord
Praise the Lord
Praise the Lord
Praise the Lord

Praise the Lord!
PRAISE THE LORD!
PRAISE THE LORD!

Yes, the larger fonts suggest a louder response, and the bold face type indicates the congregation's response. Phrases like "Glory to God!" "He is coming!" and single words like "Amen" also work well with this technique.

Three Repetitions

We sometimes forget that the psalms were written specifically for public worship. They contain ideas we could use today. Here's an idea that comes straight from the poetry of the Psalms: Use three repetitions for emphasis.

Let the heavens rejoice,
Let the earth be glad;
Let the sea resound, and all that is in it.

Psalm 96:11

In the example below, the congregation could recite the boldface and the worship team, choir, or pastor could read the rest.

Ascribe to the LORD, O families of nations,
Ascribe to the LORD glory and strength.
Ascribe to the LORD the glory due his name.

Psalm 96:7–8

Flexible Interaction

A variation on this same idea is to let the bold print be performed by the choir or the congregation:

As servants of God we commend ourselves in every way: in great endurance; in troubles, hardships and distresses . . . beaten, **and yet not killed,** sorrowful, **yet always rejoicing;** poor, **yet making many rich;** having nothing, **and yet possessing everything.**

2 Corinthians 6:4, 9–10

This technique not only relieves boredom but engenders a more *intimate, flexible interaction* between the leader and congregation, and it can reinforce the meaning of the text. When bold type is employed in paragraph form, line headings indicating who should read ("Leader" or "All") may be superfluous:

After the death of Moses the servant of the LORD, the LORD said to Joshua the son of Nun, Moses' aide: "Moses my servant is dead. Now then, you and all these people, get ready to cross the Jordan River into the land I am about to give to them—to the Israelites. I will give you every place where you set your foot, as I promised Moses. . . . **No one will be able to stand up against you all the days of your life. As I was with Moses, so I will be with you; I will never leave you nor forsake you.**

"**Be strong and courageous,** because you will lead these people to inherit the land I swore to their forefathers to give them. **Be strong and very courageous.** Be careful to obey all the law my servant

95

Moses gave you; do not turn from it to the right or to the left, that you may be successful wherever you go. **Do not let this Book of the Law depart from your mouth; meditate on it day and night, so that you may be careful to do everything written in it.** Then you will be prosperous and successful. Have I not commanded you? **Be strong and courageous. Do not be terrified; do not be discouraged,** for the LORD your God will be with you wherever you go."

Joshua 1:1–3, 5–9

The congregation or choir can read the bold print. Where there is punctuation, instruct everyone to take a breath. This will improve the reading by keeping everybody together.

Children Reading Scripture

If you want children to read Scripture along with adults—and understand it—then consider using the Children's International Bible, which has a grade six vocabulary. It has short sentences:

So then, get rid of all evil and all lying. Do not be a hypocrite. Do not be jealous or speak evil of others. Put all these things out of your life. As newborn babies want milk, you should want the pure and simple teaching. By it you can grow up and be saved.

1 Peter 2:1–2

Character Lines

A technique used in reader's theater involves using *character lines.* That is, employ a different reader for each character in a story—for example, Mary, Pilate, Christ, and angels in the Easter story. Or use two readers for one person—one for the dialogue lines, another for inner thought lines. "He said/she said" lines can be left in and spoken by a separate reader (narrator). A reader's theater based on the Easter story is available in appendix 4 of my book *People in the Presence of God.*

Effects That Startle and Surprise

At our church on Pentecost Sunday we had "Peter" and "two disciples," dressed in traditional garb, walk down the aisle and act out the scene in Acts 2:5–42. The person playing Peter memorized the sermon

(vv. 14–36) and preached it to the awestruck congregation. The choir and other readers were involved in the reader's theater (below) that preceded Peter's entry.

The Roman numerals refer to Readers 1, 2, and 3. Have the choir enter only on the bold print in the last paragraph. This results in an arresting, rapid-fire effect, which conveys a feeling of the unexpected, which is appropriate for Pentecost Sunday.

I. So when the disciples met together, they asked Jesus,

II. "Lord, are you at this time going to restore the kingdom to Israel?"

I. He said to them:

III. "It is not for you to know the times or dates the Father has set by his own authority. But you will receive power when the Holy Spirit comes on you; and you will be my witnesses in Jerusalem, and in all Judea and Samaria, and to the ends of the earth."

I. When the day of Pentecost came, they were all together in one place. Suddenly a **sound** like the blowing of a **violent wind** came from heaven and **filled** the whole **house** where they were sitting. They saw what seemed to be **tongues** of **fire** that separated and came to **rest** on **each** of them. All of them were **filled** with the **Holy Spirit** and began to speak in other **tongues** as the **Spirit** enabled them.

Acts 1:6–8; 2:1–4

This piece takes a minimum of rehearsal but has a maximum effect. The last paragraph should be read briskly. Practice it during a choir rehearsal. Choirs will perform the bold print *without straggling readers* if you instruct them to read the plain text silently (moving their lips) and give voice only on the bold print.

Reader's theater is flexible in regard to time and space; it can take two or ten minutes. It is especially useful for heightening interest on festive occasions. Readers may be placed in any configuration, in any location in the worship space—even in the audience. Fashion your own homemade material.[4]

Read a Whole Book Sunday Morning!

Our pastor informed our worship committee that he was planning to present a series of sermons that would take our church, chapter by chapter, through the entire book of 1 Thessalonians. As a precursor to his series, we created a worship service, the Sunday morning prior to his first sermon, in which the whole book of 1 Thessalonians (three chapters) was read congregationally from beginning to end. We punctuated the reading with prayers, hymns and choruses, the welcome, and the offering. We employed individual readers, old and young, in addition to the whole congregation.

We had an "appearance" by Paul. After a time of corporate prayer, he slipped in and appeared on the platform dressed in sandals and a robe, writing on a desk with a quill in his hand. Simultaneously, a pre-recorded tape ran with scratching sounds and then the voice of Paul reading 1 Thessalonians 2:17–3:13. "Paul" left secretly during the prayer for the offering. At the end of the reading, we invited the people to share what they got from the reading, using a roving mike.

The service was an astonishing success. Our pastor was extremely pleased. The service provided an overview of his series. Moreover, we reminded our people that Paul had charged the early church to read his letters in church publicly. And we did!

Computer Presentation Software

Wireless microphones, video clips, computer presentations, and lighting systems are becoming normative in many contemporary worship services. The public is accustomed to them and expects them today. The number of things worship production crews need to know has quadrupled! For up-to-date information on these areas, consult *Worship Leader Magazine* for music-related technologies, and *Church Production Magazine* for audio, video, and lighting technologies.[5] This section, however, concentrates on one area only, computer presentation software, a technology for churches of all sizes. Some computer projectors weigh less than five pounds and are effective even in new church starts, meeting in homes or hotels.

Only a few years ago it was commonplace to see overheads and slide projectors displaying hymn and chorus lyrics. Today those technologies are being retired, and sophisticated computer projectors are being employed to display hymn and chorus lyrics, announcements, ministry opportunities, testimonies, Scripture readings, sermon notes, video clips or movies, and spreadsheets for church business meetings.

Some software programs, like *Worship Builder* and *Worship Leader,*[6] take advantage of the strengths of the Microsoft PowerPoint engine and incorporate worship-related features. *Worship Builder,* for example, has a number of preset libraries—song, sermon, announcement, drama, song sheet, presentation, and order of worship—in its streamlined program. It automatically builds points, scales graphics to the right size, stores files systematically for retrieval, and provides a usage report so you can know when you last used a given song.

A number of similarly designed products have also entered the market to date.[7] These programs feature, variously, up to six Bible translations including Spanish, 21 worship songbooks, 17 hymnals, graphic backgrounds, 3,000 songs, and almost all have the ability to locate hymns or choruses on the fly with hot keys and can be navigated with programmable bookmarks.

When pastors use computer projection with their sermons, they can change the slides themselves with a hand-held remote control, or have an individual in the projector booth work the slides while following the sermon notes. Pastors will need to provide their notes a week in advance to allow time for the presentation to be built. Printouts of the presentation, up to six slides per page, can be made available to the pastor to review prior to the sermon delivery, and can be filed for future reference.

In preparing computer presentations for sermons, the most common mistake is to put too many words on the screen. David Russell advises that short, content-loaded statements with active verbs are most effective.[8] Put the framework of the sermon on the screen, not the details. The pastor should preach the details—that way the congregation will be listening to him or her, not trying to read a lot of information while the pastor is speaking. Look at magazine advertisements and TV commercials to learn how to be a good presenter of visual material.

In my university teaching, I've discovered that graphics, especially those of a conceptual nature, are more effective than words. They are also more difficult to think up! Don't select people to create your PowerPoint presentations because they are "techies." Choose people gifted in graphic design—artists with aesthetic sensitivities, if at all possible. Pictures and clip art are available at retail stores and on the net.

When shopping for a computer projector, ask your dealer to demonstrate the unit at your church. The brightness of the projector, expressed in lumens, is a key factor. The lumens must double for there to be a significant difference in brightness. For example, there would be a significant difference in the brightness of 1,000, 2,000, and 4,000 lumens. On the other hand, a lumens rating that differed by only 500 would not be significantly brighter. The projector should be bright enough so that you don't have to dim the sanctuary lights. The darker the screen area, the less washed out the color will be. You may need to rearrange your lighting so that stray light does not fall on the screen. You will need a high-resolution projector—a VGA resolution of 640 by 480 is insufficient. Never use the built-in projector speakers for the audio; use your speaker system in the sanctuary.

One large screen at the center of your church platform is preferable to two—one on either side—if your architecture allows for it. It results in more unified participation and less polarization of the congregation.

Churches with a significant number of young people will find presentation technology to be especially important—virtually essential. As you can tell, I have a positive attitude toward the potential of technology. There are those, however, who are not as positive.[9]

> There is a sense in which we may think of the whole life of the Universe, seen and unseen, conscious and unconscious, as an act of worship, glorifying its Origin, Sustainer, and End.
>
> Evelyn Underhill, *Worship*

Questions for Reflection and Discussion

1. Does worship in the Book of Revelation have the look of a media event? Explain.
2. What do advertisements suggest is most important for your PowerPoint slides—framework or detail?

INSPIRING THE PEOPLE'S SONG

But this I know: when the Holy Spirit of God comes among us with His anointing, we become a worshiping people.
A. W. Tozer, *Whatever Happened to Worship?*

This chapter is about improving response, particularly congregational response, in worship. All around the country there are pastors and musicians who really care—care enough to do the things advocated in this chapter. Devotion to our Lord impels them to go the extra mile, do the psychologically sensitive thing, and learn the strategic techniques.[1] Let's explore what pastors and musicians can do to improve response. [Pastors, the first and third sections of this chapter may be most helpful to you.]

What Can Pastors Do?

A worshiping pastor will seek to develop a worshiping church. The pastor's responsibility (which is so important) is to oversee, to set the tone and direction, to encourage the proper attitudes and conditions, and to be visibly supportive. Pastors should pursue the following goals.

1. *Link Sunday morning music to lifestyle worship.* The offering of our lives in service to God each day is our lifelong calling. Sunday morning worship is the *continuation* of that calling. Encourage not only strong singing but a *life* of praise and worship.

2. *Ensure that God is the primary object of worship, not the music.* God should be primary—not the music performance, style, or instru-

mentation. In our era, people equate worship with music: If the music is good, then the worship is good. We are in danger of becoming neglectful of other worthy activities such as prayer and Scripture reading. Therefore, teach your people to offer up worship in all parts of the service—during the prayers, the Scripture reading, the offering, the sermon. Release a spontaneous prayer in the middle of your sermon occasionally. Also teach the people that some songs are sung prayers.

3. *Ensure that the people's singing gets priority over individual or group performance.* The people's praise is paramount; protecting that ought to be one of your fundamental responsibilities. Most music directors would subscribe theoretically to the notion that the congregation is the first and most important choir, but if you look where they put their energy, you'll find it seldom goes into improving congregational response.

Don't be fooled! You can't expect to develop a strong singing church if you don't work at it and allow time for it. When we fill up the service with special music, the choir, or the worship team, to the point that we neglect the congregational response, we are teaching our people to be spectators.

4. *Communicate the purposes of congregational song to all.* Choruses and hymns help us express our deepest thoughts and emotions to God, serve to unite congregations, express and inspire prayer, teach fundamental doctrines, and draw people into the presence of God. Faithfully reinforce, underscore, state and restate these and other purposes until they take hold in the people.

5. *Insist on a variety of musical materials.* "Let the word of Christ richly dwell within you . . . teaching and admonishing one another with *psalms and hymns and spiritual songs*" (Col. 3:16 NASB). If the early church had a variety of materials, why should we accept the poverty of *only* hymns, *only* choruses?

6. *Nest new hymns and choruses*—that is, encourage worship leaders to work on and continue to review new songs until they take hold. Then move on to another cluster of materials. If you are committed to a new song, have it reinforced every Sunday until it acquires the status "very familiar"; then place it into your rotation. This method is superior to a scattered approach where *all* songs are chosen because they fit the theme of the day and then are dropped for months or years. Balance a sensitivity to the theme with the need for reinforcement. Nesting promotes understanding and memorization.

7. *Paraphrase hymns and choruses.* Paraphrasing new or difficult worship songs (just before singing them) is more helpful and less boring than merely reading stanzas. Meanings can be embellished in fresh ways; abstruse language can be clarified and feelings brought out. Use paraphrased songs in your prayers. This way of praying means that worship does not stop; it continues during your prayer. Take, for example, the hymn "Jesus, the Very Thought of Thee" (Caswall-Dykes):

> Jesus, the very thought of Thee
> With sweetness fills my breast;
> But sweeter far thy face to see
> And in thy presence rest.

Just before singing this hymn, improvise a prayer that expresses the lyric in your own words. Your opening line could be: "Jesus when I (we) think of you...." Elaborate on how sweet Jesus is and how wonderful it is to rest in him. Or have the congregation read your paraphrase printed in the worship folder or displayed on the screen:

All:	Jesus, just to think of you brings the Adoration of our inner beings. But far greater will be our adoration When we see you face-to-face And can rest in your presence.
Women:	It is impossible to sing with our voices, To hold you in our hearts, or even to remember Having heard a sweeter sound than The blessed Name of Jesus, our Savior.
Men:	You are the hope of every repentant heart, The joy of all those who yield to you. Your kind compassion is known to all who fall; Your goodness is felt by anyone who seeks you.
All:	Jesus, be to us our only source of joy. You, Yourself, are our great reward! And Jesus, we want you to be our glory Now and throughout eternity.[2]

Now sing it! The reading above is essentially a written prayer. The hymn text will have more significance now, because the people have had time to dwell on it.

103

A more challenging example is the great hymn "Immortal, Invisible." The words are complex and the ideas tumble out so rapidly that people usually miss much of its impact:

> Immortal, invisible, God only wise,
> In light inaccessible hid from our eyes.
> Most blessed, most glorious, the Ancient of Days,
> Almighty, victorious—Thy great name we praise.

If you precede this hymn with an improvised prayer in which you clarify the difficult words and concepts while extolling the character of God—how he exists without beginning or ending, how he cannot be seen with our naked eyes yet dwells in celestial light, surrounded by flashes of lightning—the lyric can be sung by all with more understanding. In your prayer be sure to use some of the words in the text so that a clear connection is established. Also express genuine emotion.

Paraphrasing lyrics is a skillful way to help people meditate on and drink in the full meaning of weighty texts without being boringly didactic. Worship continues as you pray and teach. The technique is also subtle, because the people are not aware that, in addition to praying, you are preparing them to experience a magnificent lyric. You must try this! This is an important tool for making blended worship meaningful.

8. *Arrange for testimonials.* Incorporate a "What this hymn means to me" feature occasionally in your service. Invite someone to share (see student responses in chapter 1).

9. *Share hymn stories* (see chapter 1). Hymn stories are valuable motivators, especially for the youth. Buy Kenneth W. Osbeck's *101 Hymn Stories.* It's also a great resource for sermon illustrations. Also see *The Worshiping Church: A Hymnal,* worship leader's edition, which contains a historical sketch of each hymn (865 sketches in all).[3]

10. *Encourage the purchase of hymn and chorus books and CDs for home use.*

11. *Eliminate wordy, intruding hymn announcements.* In some churches the music stops after each piece and the leader explains how each song fits into the theme. I have not found this enticing. Use words sparingly. Avoid intrusions by listing page numbers on an overhead or printing the lyric in the worship folder. Short, road-mapping comments, however, can be helpful. Pastor Paul Anderson reports that his elders continually encourage him to tell the people what is happening. He suggests the following: "Take them there, but tell them as they go where they are going. Not a lot of words, just a line to connect two

songs together, or a sentence before singing in the Spirit. It can help lift the fog and give people permission to enter."

12. *Model spirituality.* When I was a teenager, I'd bicycle to church to practice on the grand piano. As my pastor went in and out for appointments, he'd often stop by and say "Hi!" or wave to me. When he left, he was often singing a hymn, and when he returned he'd be singing another spiritual song. When preaching, he quoted hymns by memory, just as he did Scripture. That's musical leadership! Have hymns and choruses nurtured you? Let your people know.

13. *Prepare for spiritual warfare through worship.* This point has tremendous potential. When we think of spiritual warfare, we think of putting on the armor of God as described in Ephesians 6. But we often don't see Ephesians 6 as a continuation of Ephesians 5.

Clint Arnold shared with me, "I used to see worship in individualistic terms. Now I see it as a corporate act in which we arm each other for the struggles and temptations of life."[4] Arnold believes that worship leaders, teams, and choirs have an important role to play in preparing and equipping their brothers and sisters to live an overcoming life. In worship we arm ourselves with the Spirit and the Word of God, which are embedded in psalms, hymns, and spiritual songs. These songs "stick" with us during the week; they "dwell" with us and help us during the day.

In Ephesians 6, Paul exhorts us to put on the armor of God and to pray. Arnold maintains: "We need to add worship to that list! We have not related Ephesians 6:10 to 5:19 and 3:16. When Paul says in 6:10, 'Finally, be strong in the Lord' and 'put on the full armor of God,' we need to see the word 'finally' as having continuity. We need to see the armor as related to what he was talking about before. Be filled with the Spirit by speaking to one another with psalms, hymns, and spiritual songs [Eph. 5:19]. Be strengthened with power through the Spirit in your inner being so that Christ may dwell in your hearts [Eph. 3:16–17]. Or, again, in Colossians 3:16, which says, let the word of Christ richly dwell in your midst by teaching and admonishing one another with psalms, hymns, and spiritual songs. We need to see Ephesians 6 in light of the whole letter."[5]

Many of us have not thought of Christian warfare this way. Put on the armor—clothe yourself with a wise song! Worship teams and choirs are more than performers. They have a vital equipping role. Impart these ideas to your worship team and congregation.

14. *Share* Wesley's Rules for Congregational Singing *(1770).* They're valuable for inspiring response. Be proactive! Project them or print

them in your bulletin and read them together. Brace yourself; the text is "salty." Imagine gapped-toothed miners hearing these words and falling in line! Says John Wesley:

> *SING ALL.* See that you join with the congregation as frequently as you can.
> *SING LUSTILY,* and with good courage. Beware of singing as if you were half-dead or half-asleep; but lift up your voice with strength.
> *SING MODESTLY.* Do not bawl, so as to be heard above or distinct from the rest of the congregation—that you may not destroy the harmony—but strive to unite your voices together so as to make one clear melodious sound.
> *SING IN TIME.* Whatever time is sung, be sure to keep with it. Do not run before and do not stay behind it; but attend close to the leading voices, and move therewith as exactly as you can; and take care not to sing too slow. This drawling way naturally steals on all who are lazy; and it is high time to drive it out from among us, and sing all our tunes just as quick as we did at first.
> *SING SPIRITUALLY.* Have an eye to God in every word you sing. Aim at pleasing Him more than yourself, or any other creature.[6]

You can be sure your efforts will be appreciated by your worship leader. "What a team we are!" she or he will be thinking as you read "Wesley's Rules" together with your people. Tom Kraeuter makes an incisive observation:

> I have had the opportunity to visit churches where it was obvious that the pastor had not yet grasped the importance of his leadership in worship. In those churches, even though they may have tremendous, high-caliber musicians, the worship time was lifeless. The people had not understood the significance of worship because the pastor had not.[7]

What Can Musicians Do?

I can think of at least seven things musicians can do to inspire the people's song.

1. *Make the learning of choruses and hymns enjoyable.* This is critical. There is much learning to be done because most young people have little acquaintance with hymns, and the older people do not know the choruses. Most people learn tunes by rote, therefore *repetition* is

106

vital. Planning ways to showcase the tune in a variety of settings *before* attempting to engage the congregation in singing is invaluable—it increases receptivity.

Let me explain. Effective learning may occur by listening and then later by singing. If I want to introduce a new hymn or chorus, I play it the week before during the offering. When the congregation hears a new hymn or chorus played or sung gorgeously, they become aroused and their readiness to learn increases. When they start thinking, "Isn't that a beautiful tune!" that's a turning point. So do everything possible to make the tune enticing *before* the people begin to sing it.

Ways to learn by listening. (1) Let a CD player, live singer, or instrumentalist play the tune beautifully as part of the prelude, special music, offering, or postlude for one or more Sundays; (2) have the choir perform the song; (3) read or paraphrase it; (4) communicate in the church bulletin interesting details about the song's composition; (5) have a singer or choir sing the first two stanzas and then invite the congregation to join in. Again the goal is for the congregation to have such a positive experience that they will *want* to sing it.

Preparing to teach new songs. When you are about to present a new song, think through your strategy for introducing it. Do a trial run at home exactly as you plan to present it. Talk and play it through out loud. Anticipate problems—"winging it" could be disastrous. Don't teach a song you don't know. Memorize it. Close the book and test your memory.

Lining out new songs. When lining out hymns or choruses congregationally, reduce explanation to a minimum, maintain the musical momentum, and repeat difficult phrases. Keep your presentation flowing. Say to the people, "Repeat after me," and have them echo you. You may not want to use any accompaniment at this stage, or the keyboardist could play simple octaves. Pitch the tune low to maintain a relaxed atmosphere.

Introducing one song. Introduce no more than one new song at a time. It is better to teach a new song at the beginning of a set and reinforce it at the end than to teach it in the middle when the people have already entered into worship. That's distracting and breaks the flow.

Introducing songs prior to the service. If possible, introduce new songs prior to the Sunday morning service: (1) in home Bible studies or Sunday school classes, (2) during a Sunday evening given over to praise, (3) during a two-to-five-minute preservice warm-up. It builds momentum.

2. *Pitch songs intelligently.* The right pitch is not always the key in the hymn or chorus book. The right key results in a solid response from

people with both high and low voices and captures the mood and function *of the moment.* No one key can suffice for every situation. Variables, such as the acoustics, the confidence of the people, the time of day, and the context, enter in. Are the people coming out of a time of quiet prayer?—then pitch it lower. Guitarists, use your capo if necessary.

 Some hymnbooks (e.g., *The Baptist Hymnal*) pitch tunes in different keys. An annotation at the bottom of the page indicates where a lower or higher version can be found. Clever! Photocopy and tape these versions together so you have two choices.

If your church sings feebly, try using a lower key for a limited time. Lower keys are less strenuous and more inviting. A leeway of two to four semitones often exists on the lower end of songs. The pitches A and B-flat below middle C are singable if they don't need to be expressed forcefully. Keyboardists may have to write out the entire transposition—*but do that!* (Electronic keyboards can transpose with the flick of a switch. Try that.)

If response remains anemic, as a last resort, drop the instruments and the worship team for one or more songs, and let the people sing a cappella. This takes courage, but it results in a restored sense of responsibility by the people.

 Allow for early service warm-up. If your service begins early in the morning, allow the voices to limber up by lowering the key one to three semitones for the opening hymns and choruses.

Build forward momentum by modulating. Pitching the song lower than written and raising the key a half step once or twice can add a sense of forward direction and excitement. Use this device on stanzas where it will have the greatest effect. For example, with "May the Mind" (Wilkinson), modulate on the words "May I run the race," but don't overuse this technique!

Seek restful feelings during times of prayer and adoration. If your song emerges out of a time of corporate prayer, relaxed singing at low volume is often desirable. Choose a low key. It makes no sense to strain for high notes when you are trying to communicate restfulness. *A low key equals restfulness.* In these circumstances, soft, expressive singing is much preferred to loud singing. Switch on the chorus button on the digital piano for more ambience, and choose a darker piano sound or a Rhoades preset.

Avoid vocal fatigue. If the tune has several high notes in a row (a high tessitura) and few low notes, vocal fatigue may set in after a few stanzas, particularly for men. They may resort to singing an octave lower. To reduce fatigue, pitch the tune lower initially, then raise it for the last stanza. For example, "All Creatures of Our God and King" (in E-flat) has several high E-flats. Ask your accompanist to learn this piece in C, D-flat, or D, and raise the key to E-flat for the last stanza.

Obtain feedback. Listen to the congregation as you lead. Stop momentarily and evaluate. Are men singing an octave lower? Are people cutting out on the high notes? Is there depth to the worship? Ask for feedback from the worship team and pastor.

3. *Get the men singing.* Instill in men the idea that it's not sissy to sing. David, Israel's greatest warrior, was also their greatest singer. Men should sing for the sake of their children and for the reputation of God's name. What does listless singing communicate? Are we not telling others through our voices that we don't really believe in God? That the God we serve is flat and bland—nothing to be reckoned with? How false! Our God is a God of surprises, unimaginable gentleness, and—above all—someone to be feared and respected. Transcendent worship should reflect that.

To get the men singing, consider this strategy. Rehearse the women and men separately for two to five minutes before the service starts. Keep it short. If you accomplish only a little each time, be happy with that. Avoid negative comments. Since it is more difficult to get men singing, concentrate on the women first. When the men hear the women improve, it will become an incentive for them to match it. Here are two ideas for getting a joyful noise out of the men.

- Have the men sing the melody and the women a descant. Practice "Seek Ye First the Kingdom of God" or "Sing Alleluia to the Lord" before the service.[8]
- Teach all the men to sing the bass part in "All Hail the Power of Jesus' Name" (Diadem). Say, "Repeat after me," and then sing (line out) measures 13^3 through 17^1.

If the key of B-flat is too high for the sopranos, try it in A or A-flat major. Break down the bass part into three learnable segments (see p. 110). Practice it for two or three minutes each Sunday for two weeks with the men seated. Response may be poor at first; then have them stand on the third week.

I tried this. The instruction to stand came as a surprise. Some women smiled and poked their husbands in the ribs! But what a change it made

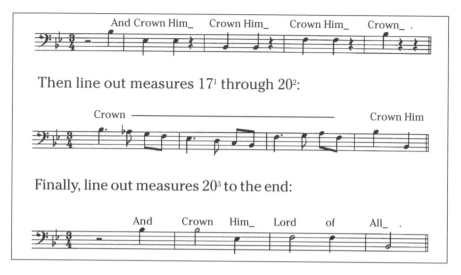

Then line out measures 17[1] through 20[2]:

Finally, line out measures 20[3] to the end:

as men all over the church stood: Response improved dramatically. The next Sunday we had the altos sing their part. The Sunday after that we had everyone sing the piece in three part harmony (the bass part was miked in the worship team). The result was fantastic! People were buzzing about it after the service. That effort, though, took a month of practice. Try the same procedures with "Wonderful Grace of Jesus" and "God of Great Wonders."

Remember, it takes time. Don't force or labor it. If you need to, back off and pick it up a little later. Having an initial success is the important thing!

4. *Employ a worship team to improve response.* Worship teams provide stability for the worship leader and support for the congregation. When worship leaders are "down," team members can "lift them up." A team approach can improve ideas during rehearsal and assist with evaluation after the service.

If you are a small church, do the following as your bare minimum. Practice *well before* the service begins. A weeknight rehearsal is essential too. Perform a sound check on every mike. Meet separately with your core musicians first—the keyboardist, guitarist, bassist, and percussionist—an hour and a half before the service. Check for agreement on all the chords and review the tempos. Practice the rhythmic feel where necessary and rehearse the transitions between songs. Then invite the other musicians and singers (an hour before the service) to do a run-through on the platform of the key pieces, focusing on the basic shape as well as specific details, including the synchronization of the projected words.

Model an attitude of calmness and confidence before the service. Avoid hurrying about. Have prayer with the team at least fifteen minutes before the service. When worship teams pray together, they bring power and unity to the service. Kneel together in private before going on the platform.

5. *Impart musical shape and variety.* Use your singers and instrumentalists to impart musical shape and variety to the congregational singing. Having someone sing or play a stanza alone can accomplish several important functions. A mood can be set and emotion generated. The congregation can relax its voice and have time to meditate on the text. A stanza can be repeated if the text is dense with meaning. Where several pieces are in a set, a soloist can help smooth transitions, thus contributing to the sense of flow. Moreover, when soloists are integrated into congregational song, they function more as servants and are less likely to be perceived as entertainers. Here are a few more ideas.

Choose soloists who personally identify with a song. For example, have a woman who has recently given birth sing stanza two of "Because He Lives" ("How sweet to hold a newborn baby"). This can have a riveting effect!

Choose songs that have great theology or inherent drama. For example, the carol "I Heard the Bells on Christmas Day" has the line "and then in *my* despair . . . there is no peace on earth I said." That stanza is much more dramatic as a solo.

Encourage spontaneity!—include an unplanned solo occasionally (if performers are comfortable with that). As the individual steps to the mike, say "Congregation on stanza three" to indicate the soloist will perform stanza two alone. Without missing a beat, the singer (or instrumentalist) will begin on time and the congregation will enter on stanza three. After your congregation experiences this several times, they will immediately "read" the situation.

6. *Employ choreographed hand movements.* When we get our bodies into the act of worship, a new dimension can result. "Won't the people resist?" you ask. I have yet to find resistance to the hand movements to the following piece, "Holy Holy Holy" (see endnote for text and music).[9] When the people understand the *meaning* of hand gestures and sense there is a reverential purpose to what they are doing, a positive response ensues. The instructions below are included so

you can get an idea of how you might talk your way through the meaning of the gestures as the people perform them.

First, teach them (line out) the melody in a low key (B-flat).

Second, focus on the hand movements. Speak gently to the people: "Do what I do. Strive for flowing movement." Have them say the words (not sing) as they imitate your flowing gestures.

"Holy Holy Holy is the Lord of Hosts. By putting our hands over our chest we are saying, 'Lord apply your holiness to my life. I want to be holy.'

"The whole earth is full of your glory. Feel the downbeat on the word *whole* [demonstrate that a couple of times]. Now we raise and circle our arms. Three times. The whole earth is full of God's glory.

"Holy is the Lord. Gradually raise your hands above your head. Now form praying hands. Look up. Our eyes are looking up to God. He is our source of holiness. Let's linger for a moment, arms extended. [Pause.] Now, let them gently fall."

Third, proceed to the next stage. "Now, let's sing the tune twice *with* the motions." Sing the tune first in B-flat: for the repeat, modulate to C. "We'll begin *very* softly. On the repetitions of the line *The whole earth is full of your glory* let the volume build, then let it subside on the last line." The surging bass part in the music arrangement (see note 9) will help secure that effect.

The result should be one of real reverence. I've used this piece just before the closeout of the Wimber model (see chapter 3). For other examples, see my book *People in the Presence of God.*

Here are a few more guidelines for encouraging the people's song:

- Have a positive attitude.
- Stand for praise, sit for adoration.
- Conduct praise with your hand, adoration with your voice.
- Don't close your eyes too much while leading—be aware.
- Perk up dragging songs with a percussive touch.
- Practice the hymns and choruses during choir rehearsals.
- Let the choir/worship team sing in the aisle for processionals.
- Plan a "Hymn of the Month," a "Hymn Sunday," or "Hymn Festival." The pastor can preach on a hymn text. A good series of messages can result.
- Keep records. Record the date each song was sung.[10]

7. *Musical contrast is essential!* Jeff Baxter, a highly sought-after, triple-scale studio musician, was called in for a three-hour recording session. He looked over the music, took the money, and without performing said, "I'm outta here!" Evidently, after looking over the score, Baxter felt his conclusion—that the recording would be better off *without his instrumental input*—was worth 750 dollars to the producer. His experience in hundreds of studio sessions led him to that judgment.

We need this kind of insight in worship! It would be good if musicians would say from time to time, "I'm outta here," and offer *not* to perform on every number. The malady is widespread in our churches: Everyone wants to play—all the time. And it makes musical contrast almost impossible to achieve.

Contrast is so essential! Talk to your musicians! Educate them. Point out that *in symphony orchestras not everyone plays all the time.* Employ all your musicians only for loud, exalting pieces, and use just a few for intimate songs. Why must the organ play for every piece? The same instruments, the same synth presets, the same dynamics for each number is a deadly combination. Mindless performance breeds mindless singing! I can't emphasize this enough—people need contrast!

Guitarists and keyboardists, be aggressive! Take some risks. In many cases you will be the emotional center of the song service. If you don't feel anything, if you don't have strong convictions about the songs you're playing, the people won't either. Sit down and write on a piece of paper your identity as a church musician: "I help to bring people into the presence of God; I help the service flow; I open up the meaning of hymn texts; I am a triumph maker." Statements like these can bring integrity to your role.

Leaders, Protect Each Other!

> Each of you should look not only to your own interests, but also to the interests of others.
>
> Philippians 2:4

Let's look at an area where pastors could understand musicians better—and musicians, pastors. Let's compare the task of delivering a thirty-minute sermon with leading a thirty-minute worship set in the free-flowing style.

Imagine a contemporary format: The worship leader is leading from a keyboard or a guitar, assisted by two or more vocalists, a bass, and a percussionist or someone using a drum machine.

For the pastor, the sermon is a solo effort; but for the worship leader, the worship is a team effort. The pastor has control over every part of his delivery, while the worship leader is dependent on the skill level of volunteers who may perform wrong notes and rhythms; may show a lack of phrasing and articulation, an insensitivity to dynamics, an inability to find the rhythmic groove, an incapacity to modulate between stanzas or create transitions between pieces; or may be unable to improvise in different music styles. Obviously the skill level of members in the group may vary greatly.

While many pastors are minimally dependent on technology, worship leaders are highly dependent on an array of technology—mikes, monitors, synthesizer patches, projected lyrics—and their proper sequencing and timing. The miking, mixing, and sound levels of monitors, particularly, often cause untold frustrations for the musician. I hear these voiced continually and emphatically. Musicians need to hear each other in the worship space to be a good ensemble.

The Sound Booth and Church Acoustics

Seek for your sound booth a person who knows the sound board technically and has a musical ear. That combination is rare. Individuals are often strong in one area but not in both. So place your most musical person in the sound booth. If you're a large church, hire a knowledgeable person to ensure that the sound quality is consistent from service to service. If you're working the sound board, take off the headphones when determining the volume level and equalization.

Church acoustics may be a problem that no one but church musicians recognize. Preachers can be relatively comfortable in any number of minimally reverberant spaces, but a good music space requires a longer reverberation time than does a space for speech. Good acoustics result from informed, architectural designing.[11] I rarely find new church buildings that have good acoustics for congregational singing.

The following conditions make singing difficult: thickly carpeted floors, cushioned seats, curtained backdrops, low ceilings, seats positioned under balconies, and acoustical tile. They stifle the natural resonance and amplification of the human voice and can discourage (even cripple) congregational response. Musicians end up not being able to hear one another. Sounds do not sparkle, blend, and fuse. Feeling alone and missing the supporting sound around them, people sing more self-consciously, tentatively. There is little joy in corporate singing. Such acoustics dampen the energy people bring to the service. *In such*

114

spaces, worship leaders labor against unyielding, enormous odds. Frequently in new mega church structures the acoustics are so bad that only a tiny percentage of the people even attempt to sing!

Pastors, do you want a preaching space? That's simple. Or do you want a worship space? That's complex. Consider this when you are building. Your chief musician does—or should!

Feeling Inadequate and Vulnerable

As for the matter of response itself, the preacher usually does not require an overt response every Sunday, but the worship leader requires one every time. And that response is measurable by everybody. That puts extra pressure on the worship leader. People can *pretend* to be interested in the sermon, while in the privacy of their minds they are thinking of the grocery list or the lawn that needs watering. But with worship leaders, there are *no pretensions.* Feeble singing is observable by all, and it is unsettling! It directly reflects on the musician's ability to spark interest. Further, if attendance is sparse and the seating scattered, response is adversely affected.

 Many other factors work to break down the confidence of worship leaders. Worshipers may criticize their music style (timing, pacing, tempos, amount of chorus repetition, the amount of talking done), and how their personality comes through (in dominating or less obtrusive ways).

Regarding the exertion of personality, the real issue is not how much but when. To lead worship, establish control at the outset. As the people settle into worship, however, relinquish some control so as not to be a dominating, visual presence. As the service moves toward intimacy, let the congregation focus on God without distraction. You may need to reassert yourself again for the closeout number.

Recognize also that the worship leader is uniquely subject to the immediacies of the moment and the collective consciousness of the congregation—sometimes they're up, sometimes down for apparently unaccountable reasons. The result? This often-repeated soliloquy as the worship leader sits down and reflects: "It wasn't happening today. I may have led them in singing, but I did not succeed in leading them to worship. Response was really off."

Pastors often feel the same way. A pastor read this quote and responded, "Sometimes, Barry, I'm thinking this through my sermon—'I'm not connecting. Boy, the people are down today.'" Pastors take congregational response very personally too.

Encouraging Each Other

For worship leaders, the shaping of congregational song is uniquely *embodied* in their personality and style. They need to be covered—not left open to the criticism of the congregation. Pastors, protect your musicians' self-esteem with words of encouragement. Keep your worship leader from being destroyed by criticism or self-doubt. Worship leaders cannot help but fail occasionally.

And musicians, return the favor—protect your pastor! What pastor, coming down from the platform, does not often feel vulnerable? What pastor does not think about illustrations and transitions that could have gone better—not to mention his awesome accountability before God to help the people grow spiritually? What pastor doesn't receive criticism for long sermons, redundancy, and alleged insensitivity? Because, as a musician, you understand the pressures of performance and ministry, your support of your pastor can be particularly comforting.

Most musicians (and I suspect many pastors too) are perfectionists. Guitarists and keyboardists spend their time trying to perform passages smoothly and with better phrasing. Soloists try to improve their tone. Worship teams and choirs polish their diction and refine attacks and releases within the pressing time constraints afforded them. Self-criticism can be tremendously tenacious, because musicians always feel they could have done it better. Often they are satisfied with a tiny portion of their work and disappointed (even disgusted) with the rest.

In some congregations there is undue pressure for leaders to produce emotional highs every time—the "Can you top this?" syndrome. No matter what happens in the service, it is not enough! We need some healthy realism. Worship involves response but not necessarily an emotional catharsis every Sunday!

The worship leader should not attempt to create, induce, or worse yet, command the presence of God. That is what the prophets of Baal tried to do on Mount Carmel. Who are we to think we have the power to order around the Almighty? If the worship leader succumbs to this pressure and begins to manipulate the people, the pastor or a worship committee member must apply loving correction, interceding with honesty and insight. Again, pastors often feel subject to similar pressures and may also need some honest feedback from the worship leader or elder board.

Body Language

The body language that both musicians and pastors display publicly is terribly important. It can support or undercut everything. Reviewing music scores and shuffling papers or sermon notes should be left for some other time, for they undermine the respect for leaders and detract from the sense of transcendence we so much want to obtain. Gum chewing, fidgeting, slumping in seats, and gawking at the congregation during worship services is also inappropriate. Musicians should set a good example in sermon listening—and pastors in hymn and chorus singing. Total attentiveness and delight in God's presence should be our constant intention. Leaders must model good churchmanship.

Worship is the total response of each individual to the call of God.
Austin C. Lovelace, *Music and Worship in the Church*

Questions for Reflection and Discussion

1. What hymn or chorus could benefit from a paraphrase?
2. Is there one correct key for a hymn or chorus? Discuss.
3. "The worship leader is uniquely subject to the immediacies of the moment and the collective consciousness of the congregation—sometimes they're up, sometimes they're down." Share examples and discuss.
4. How can you use your hymnal in your devotions this week?
5. How can you hear criticism of your worship leading or preaching without becoming defensive?

PART 2

PRESSING ISSUES

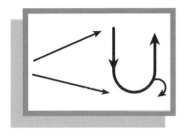

IS WORSHIP A PERFORMANCE?
THE CONCEPT

To perform is to do something complicated or difficult with skill in public with a view toward serving and ministering.

Studio recording musician Tom Keene shared his concerns about worship leaders and recording artists with me after a Sunday night church meeting. He's turned off: "I see worship leaders doing things just to be clever. They're 'pushing buttons,' drawing attention to their expertise and exceptional skills—not leading worship. In the evangelical scene we've gone through this phase of big endings and high notes.

"Christian professional artists are trying hard to be hip. They put on 'fun' concerts, make all the funny faces, do all the gyrations of rock stars, bump into the bass player, act out all the 'accepted' rock and roll gestures, and deliver emotional highs for every concert.

"These artists have painted themselves into a terrible corner, pandering to the self-indulgences of their audiences. What will be the next high? When you take your clothes off? Performer egos are rampant. It trickles down, and now we have the local church clones infected with the same 'Can you top this?' attitude.

"Then they wonder why the pastor is upset! This stuff is meeting nobody's needs. It's amateurish to the pro musicians, and the older people are mortified by it. When will worship leaders and Christian music artists learn to feel as much rewarded by having an ovation as

121

having nothing at all? If you have one standing ovation after another, you have no standing ovations.

"I'd just like to sit down at the piano and share some music with the people, listen to each other and God, not necessarily expecting, or having anyone expect from me, a tremendous high."[1]

The reality is, though, people *are* attracted in great numbers to hear the good performers, the skilled speakers and musicians. We *are* inclined to buy into the entertainment syndrome and exalt the Christian performer, preacher, or musician. This ought to make us uneasy.[2]

When performers are exceptionally good, it is not easy to distinguish the genuinely motivated from the fraudulent: "People think they may be able to discern if a minister or musician is genuine, but they probably cannot if that person is highly skilled. They need to ask if he lives what he preaches and inquire how he is doing in his home life."[3]

Reloading the Word *Performance*

The idea of worship as performance is troublesome. A right attitude toward performance, therefore, is *foundational* to ministry. Pastors, musicians, and the people perceive the idea of performance differently. For example, the people distrust it, musicians value it, and pastors deny it (deny that they are performers). The people are right in wanting sincerity. The negative connotations associated with the word *performance* have caused many Christian leaders to jettison the term from the pulpit altogether. Most leaders would rather use the words "participating in" worship rather than "performing" worship. Similarly, many pastors feel more comfortable using the terms "executing" or "delivering" the sermon rather than "performing" the sermon. Even more unacceptable, however, is to call a Christian concert or a musical at church a "show." Concern for the appropriateness of this kind of language is proper.

Pastors, nevertheless, need to understand that in their relationships with musicians, the word *performance* simply will not go away. For musicians, it's a word they have used throughout their training and they will *continue* to use it in their conversations with choirs, soloists, and worship teams—and perhaps even in the pulpit. It's also a word employed in our most recent and widely read Bible translations, and it has something positive to teach us, as we will see.

Speaking as a musician, let me state boldly that I believe worship has a strong performance dimension—when the concept of performance is properly understood and applied. I know this may sound like heresy to many, but hear me out. Since the word will not go away, I propose to reload its meaning for the purpose of forming bridges of understanding between musicians and pastors. We need a level playing field where we understand what is meant by different terminology. Often we fight without knowing what we fight about.

Kierkegaard and Performance

Although evangelicals would not endorse all aspects of Kierkegaard's theology, in recent days they have been influenced by his statement that in corporate worship

- the people should be the *performers* of worship
- the pastor and worship leaders the *prompters* of worship
- God the *audience*[4]

To grasp his concept, consider a football stadium in which the people are on the field, the pastor and worship leaders prompt the people (as player-coaches), and God is the audience in the stands. The value of this formulation is that it stresses active, major participation by the people. It is a corrective to many churches where the people take their

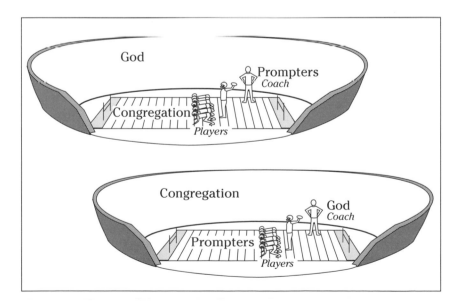

seat, drop some coins into the offering, sit back and expect to be entertained by the choir and an interesting sermon. It also questions contemporary praise formats where the band leads and the audience listens and enjoys.

Did you notice that the way Kierkegaard uses the word *perform* creates no problem for us at all? Why is that? It is because in this context we (the people) are performing "to God." We are not performing for human applause. God is the audience, and that changes everything. The "to the Lord" principle is Kierkegaard's exclusive focus.

Helpful though this focus is, it is an oversimplification of the actual dynamics involved. In reality there are *two audiences* (God and the people) not one. God is not only the audience, he also *initiates* the worship process. God reveals himself to us and we respond to him. Scripture clearly teaches that worship is response. The picture becomes even more complex when we consider the worship leaders. They bear the responsibility of being both *performers and prompters* of worship—again, more like player-coaches—and that makes everything more challenging.

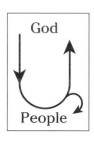

The Unseen Prompter

The role of the prompter is crucial in leading worship, as the following remarkable story illustrates. The opening of San Francisco's opera season was an hour away when disaster struck. The lead tenor, about to sing the demanding role in Verdi's *Othello,* lost his voice. A worldwide search began to see if one of a half dozen tenors knowing the role could come and save opening night.

Curtain time was delayed three hours. Rumors were rampant that none other than Placido Domingo was being flown in from New York by private jet. They proved true, and Domingo sang, without rehearsal, an opera he hadn't sung for a year.

When asked how he did it, he said, "I couldn't have done it without the help of the prompter."

The prompter sits hidden from the audience in a tiny box attached to the stage floor. His head and upper body are above the stage; his lower body is below floor level but above the orchestra pit. At times he comes close to being trampled by the performers.

His job is arduous. He cues every singer and knows the mind of the conductor, the weaknesses in each opera, and the individual stumbling

124

blocks of each performer. If trouble comes, he must unscramble it. *When his job is well done, it normally goes completely unnoticed by the audience.*[5]

The prompter's task corresponds to the role of keyboardists, guitarists, worship leaders, and pastors in a worship service. What is most important is the meeting of the people with God. The prompter removes distractions and helps secure that meeting.

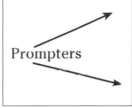

Performance *in Webster's Dictionary and the Bible*

Note the dimensions of the word *performance* that Webster's dictionary underscores. To perform means "to carry on to the finish . . . to carry out or execute some action, engagement, or the like; to do something with special skill; also, to show off; as, to perform on the piano. . . . Perform usually refers to processes that are lengthy, exacting, or ceremonial, or to deeds that are striking."[6] Components of this definition relate strongly to worship practice.

Although Webster's refers to "showing off"—the negative aspect—more importantly it brings out something that interests artists: skill. Whereas the people are particularly sensitive to one's motivation in performance, musicians are particularly focused on the details that make a performance noteworthy. *Musicians equate performance more with quality and excellence than "showing off."* They cannot easily "turn off" this orientation. Listen to conversations among musicians and you will find they keep circling back to the issue of quality and standards.

But how does the Bible use the word *perform* in relation to worship? Does it reveal any additional dimensions? Yes. The Old Testament word translated *perform* is often associated with obedience in carrying out some work, duty, or command. The context often takes the form "they *shall* perform" (NASB): "All that is to be done, they *shall perform*. . . . All their work, *shall be performed* at the command of Aaron and his sons" (Num. 4:26–27 NASB; see also Num. 8:22). The word *perform* is also associated with artistic skill: "See, the LORD has called by name Bezalel . . . to make designs . . . and in the cutting of stones for settings, and in the carving of wood, so as to *perform* in every inventive work" (Exod. 35:30, 32–33 NASB).

A unique biblical emphasis not found in Webster's is the association of performance with "serving" and "ministering":

[The priests] shall *perform* the duties . . . to do *the service* of the tabernacle.

Numbers 3:7 NASB

Now these are those whom David appointed over the *service* of song. . . . and they *ministered* with song . . . and they *served* in their office according to their order.

1 Chronicles 6:31–32 NASB[7]

[The levitical priests] are to come near my table to *minister* before me and *perform my service.*

Ezekiel 44:16

In the last quote the words *minister, perform,* and *service* occur together in a single verse. Here is the most important point in the chapter: I believe these three words are practically interchangeable and that the idea of connecting serving and ministering with performance is immensely helpful in clarifying the biblical attitude toward performance.[8] When we picture these three words together, a healthy perspective on performance emerges. So when you use the word *performance* in public worship, include the words *serving* and *ministering* in the immediate context.[9] The negativity associated with this term will be muted . . . hopefully.

Operational Definition of *Performance*

Drawing from Webster and the Scriptures, then, here is my attempt to *reload* the term *performance* and to offer an operational definition for corporate worship:

> To perform is
> to do
> something complicated or difficult
> with skill
> in public
> with a view toward serving and ministering.

Two aspects of this concept that are unique to Scripture and *not specified* in Webster's are "in public" and "serving and ministering." Now let us examine in sequence the parts of this definition, bearing in mind three groups of people—the pastor, the worship team, and the congregation.

To Perform Is to Do

Worship is a verb; it's active. There is a task to do, a service to render:

> Come, let us worship and bow down;
> Let us kneel before the LORD our maker.
>
> Psalm 95:6 NASB

> Ascribe to the LORD the glory due his name;
> bring an offering and come into his courts.
>
> Psalm 96.8

These are clear-cut performance statements. Though we are powerless to effect inner transformation ourselves, we can place ourselves before God. We can bow, kneel, give glory, and bring an offering. We can wait before him.

The chart below summarizes the kinds of prayer postures found in the Bible. Notice, the greater the body movement, the greater the frequency of occurrence. This is the opposite of the use of prayer postures in mainstream evangelical church culture.

Prayer Postures

Posture	Meaning	Frequency in the Bible
Bowing the head	Submission	4
Standing	Respect	6
Lifting the eyes	Looking to the source of blessing	9
Kneeling	Humility	12
Hands lifted	Expectancy, servitude	14
Prostration	Awe in the divine presence	28

We should not think of these postures as merely customs of a bygone era. They're of timeless value. I challenge you to test their relevance in your personal worship.

Some evangelical worship traditions, when analyzed, stem more from European than biblical tradition. Nowhere in Scripture, for example, do worshipers close their eyes and fold their hands in prayer—

that's unbiblical (I'm teasing!). On the other hand, forms of worship that are modeled in Scripture (i.e., raising of hands) can raise eyebrows and become subjects of controversy. But the data is incontrovertibly clear: The raising of hands is a normal part of Hebrew practice, not a Pentecostal phenomenon. We need incisive teaching on this from the pulpit—or even a paragraph in the bulletin would be helpful.

What does the raising of hands mean from a biblical point of view? What did it mean to the ancient Hebrews? Lifted hands could mean the taking of an oath: "But Abram said to the king of Sodom, 'I have raised my hand to the LORD, God Most High, Creator of heaven and earth, and have taken an oath that I will accept nothing belonging to you'" (Gen. 14:22–23). Lifted hands were symbolically related to lifted prayers: "May my prayer be set before you like incense; may the lifting up of my hands be like the evening sacrifice" (Ps. 141:2). Lifted hands could mean a lifted heart. When the Hebrews prayed at the evening sacrifice, they offered incense. As their prayers rose to God, the incense also rose. Lifted hands indicated their hearts were rising to God just as the incense ascended: "Let us lift up our hearts and our hands to God in heaven" (Lam. 3:41).

The raising of hands also expressed the meaning of yearning and thirsting for God: "I meditate on all your works and consider what your hands have done. I spread out my hands to you; *my soul thirsts for you like a parched land*" (Ps. 143:5–6). You get the picture! The psalmist imagines himself like the ground (or a plant in the ground) that needs watering. As the plant stretches and strains to receive the rain from heaven, so worshipers lift their hands to say symbolically, "Let your dew fall on me. Water me, Lord. My soul thirsts for you." Without the dew and rain, the plant would shrivel and die. It's a powerful image of the worshiper wanting, needing God.

Moreover, recall that the wings of the cherubim in the Holy of Holies hovered over the mercy seat. For some, the raised hands of worshipers today image those wings. An evocative passage in 1 Chronicles says the Lord "dwells between the cherubim, where His name is proclaimed" (13:6 NKJV).

Must everyone raise their hands in worship then? No. The practice of raising hands is *modeled not mandated in Scripture, permitted not forced or coerced.* The Scriptures don't command it; they permit it—even encourage it by modeling it. Shouldn't we then permit it too?

128

- Test this practice in your closet prayers first before performing it in public. See if it aids your personal prayer.
- Be patient with yourself and give yourself time to become comfortable with it.
- When you become comfortable privately, you may feel more at ease raising your hands publicly.

Raising our hands doesn't make us more authentic worshipers. Rather, it points to the fact that the body is an important element in worship expression. Even Paul refers to the principle: "I want men everywhere to lift up holy hands in prayer, without anger or disputing" (1 Tim. 2:8).

To Perform Is to Do Something Complicated or Difficult

As Webster's has indicated, to perform means to do something complicated, lengthy, and exacting.[10] The drama of worship in the tabernacle and temple, for instance, actively involved the people. Males presented, placed their hands on, slaughtered, skinned, and washed the lambs; but today prescribed tasks for the people are often missing. The pastor's role is exacting, the worship team's role is absorbing, but rarely is attention given to the response of the people. The people listen to the worship team!

Activities that involve the congregation in sustained, disciplined participation are essential. How can this be addressed? One way is to *teach the people to become a congregational choir.* Establish achievement goals for them. Use ideas given in chapter 7—rehearsing unfamiliar choruses and hymns before the service begins, or teaching a descant, learning to sing antiphonally, practicing a bass part, memorizing a Bible verse—the people can acquire the expectation that they have real (not token) work to do each Sunday.

Congregations need to be truly *exercised* with solid tasks that focus their attention on God, that place them before him, so that he really has them and can minister inner transformation to them. The Scriptures say, "Exercise yourself rather to godliness" (1 Tim. 4:7 NKJV). That is our part. As leaders we need to ask, "Am I truly placing my people before God this morning? Am I *training* them to attend to him?"

The Challenge: Two Audiences, Not One

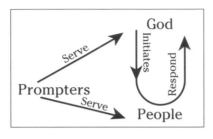

While the congregation's role is often undeveloped, the pastor's role meets Webster's criteria. It is invariably lengthy, exacting, and personally absorbing.[11] What makes this role absorbing? Consider this: Pastors have *two* audiences to attend to—God and the people. It is difficult to focus on the Lord and on the leading and preaching at the same time, as pastor Ben Patterson painfully shares:

> I can get so preoccupied with trying to get the congregation to worship that I don't worship. . . . Instead of the sermon being itself an act of worship, it becomes a performance . . . that succeeds or fails, . . . in either case a *performance for the people*. Whatever the reason, Sunday mornings before worship are often the least prayerful day of the week for me. I hope what I have done Monday through Saturday will make up for that lack. . . . The more thought my staff and I put into planning worship . . . the better able I am not to worry about worship details on Sunday. The less worried I am, the more able I am emotionally to worship as I lead in worship.[12]

Talk about this tension with your team. Teach them to become responsible to both audiences: God should be the primary audience, yet the congregation can be an intimidating secondary audience.

Ministering and Worshiping Simultaneously

Sometimes the way overheads or computer-projected lyrics are managed is distracting. I often say to individuals working these media, "Watch me. Don't get lost in worship. It is more important that the whole church worships *without distraction* than that you and I worship. We are giving ourselves for the people."

In fact this is a good principle for every leader. *Worship in private first.* You may not be able to do so satisfactorily in public, because when you are a leader, you must first and foremost give yourself for the people. I can't stress this enough, especially for the musicians. *Undistracted worship by the congregation depends on your reliability as a musician.* You must be prepared to sing the first word in the next chorus, beat the next beat, or play the next chord. If you have excess energy and attention, then worship! This may seem callous, but it is a practical reality. Again, in this sense, worship is a performance.

Don't misunderstand! By all means, worship as completely as you can. Leaders who want their people to be hungry for worship should eat themselves! Encourage the worship team to model worship in their facial expressions and demeanor. And in general, *the better prepared you are, the freer you will feel to worship.*

One way pastors may worship more genuinely during the service is to delegate to others tasks they often perform, such as the reading of Scripture, various prayers, the announcements, welcome, or the offering. They are then able to relax and enjoy God's presence before preaching.

Developing a Sense of Flow

Those who read Scripture and pray need to be aware of how their part contributes to the larger whole. When participants understand they are coming out of and going into something, they learn to contribute to the *flow* of the service—another performance dimension.

Services that have an improvisational feel are, if anything, more demanding. Leaders must select and rehearse their songs to the point that their performance is fluent, not strained. They need to have enough reserve energy to be aware of what is happening. Guitarists and keyboardists must not only play but listen.

Worship leaders cannot close their eyes in worship for extended periods of time. They must be alert, aware. This is absolutely vital! How well are the people singing? Where is their point of greatest need? In order to listen carefully, keyboardists or guitarists may need to cut back their dynamics momentarily. Leaders need to be free to adhere to only part of their preplan, be able to respond to the momentum generated, and follow the leading of the Spirit. They need to cultivate a sense of timing and proportion. A particular number may be dropped, a chorus added or repeated, or silence may be required, depending on the real-time situation.[13]

We have now dealt with two parts of our operational definition:

1. To perform is to do
2. To perform is to do something complicated or difficult

We are unequally gifted and cannot equally achieve. . . . But all artists can be better than they once were. This is excelling.
Harold Best, *Music Through the Eyes of Faith*

Questions for Reflection and Discussion

1. Should the word *performance* be avoided in the pulpit?
2. Are ministry, serving, and performing related concepts?
3. How could a sense of flow be improved in your worship service?
4. What realistic achievement goals would you establish for the congregational choir in your church?

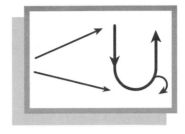

IS WORSHIP A PERFORMANCE? THE IMPLICATIONS

To perform is to do something complicated or difficult with skill in public with a view toward serving and ministering.

So far I have discussed Webster's definition of *perform* and the unique dimensions Scripture brings to the word, and I have offered an operational definition of *performance*. We learned that the Hebrew word for *worship* has a strong "doing" dimension. We underscored the need for solid congregational tasks, the challenge of two audiences, and the importance of maintaining a flow to the service. Let's explore more dimensions of the word *perform* as it relates to worship.

To Perform Is to Do Something with Skill

Performance contains the dimension of skill. *Skill,* a word frequently used in the Old Testament,[1] has a New Testament counterpart—*giftedness.*

When selecting people to read Scripture, choose gifted readers. Choose people who are skilled at communicating what is on the page and who value God's Word enough to do the reading well. Time spent coaching individuals in public reading and prayer is time well spent. Recall the request of the disciples: "Lord, teach us to pray." It's a less overt form of discipling. As designated people read and pray, a process of modeling occurs from which everyone benefits. It's also a tangible witness to the nonchurched that not only the pastor but also the people have a living, demonstrable faith.

Demands for Quality

Lyle E. Schaller, well-know church consultant, says to midsized churches (churches in the 100- to 250-people range), "Act your size!" A church of 150 people is in reality a complex organization. When churches reach this critical mass, *growth is strongly tied to excellence in performance.* But the reality is that unchurched persons stepping into our churches are often bored with our worship. Unconsciously, they compare what they experience with television—quick-paced sound bites assembled by slick production crews.

Consider the concerted effort required to produce a single newscast. Gone are the days when the weatherperson "lectured" with chalk in hand; now the public is treated to a "presentation" (note the difference) with computer graphics, nature scenes, satellite pictures, and a running dialogue interspersed with humorous one-liners dreamed up by staff writers. The next time you see the credits scrolled at the end of a program, remember that people come to your worship service with similar unconscious expectations.

We might not like this state of affairs, but it's a reality we must face. True, there is no way a small- to medium-sized church can fully compete (and I don't think people's expectations are *that* high), but we must make *some* cultural adaptation. *We must strive for excellence.* I am disturbed, for example, when I hear musicians say when a musical number is ragged from inadequate rehearsal, "It doesn't matter; the people will never know the difference."

This kind of talk is destructive. First, it simply is not true. *People notice and appreciate quality.* They know when something has been properly rehearsed, though they may not be able to analyze the details that made a performance outstanding. Second, when we are careless, we are the losers. We suffer a loss of personal integrity. Third, carelessness undermines faith. Our work, because it is not an honest effort, cannot be truly offered in faith.

Exercising Our Skill with Wisdom

The Old Testament concept of skill is broader than we usually understand it; it embraces the big picture and includes *wisdom.* I learned something about this during my teens when I was the pianist for evangelistic teams doing citywide campaigns. Being young and exuberant, I would perform dazzling runs on the keyboard during the congregational singing. One day an evangelist took me aside. "Barry," he said gently, "have you noticed the people have been a little lost?" That hurt a little, but I got the point. What I was doing was distracting.

We need wisdom when we exercise our skill. Good technique is not so much virtuosity as it is being responsible or *response-able*—having the ability to do *what* needs to be done *when* it needs to be done.[2] Under certain conditions it's appropriate to exercise the full range of our skill; but there are other times when *restraining* our skill may be wiser. For example, during songs of adoration and intimacy, playing too many notes on the keyboard, guitar, or percussion instruments only distracts; what is important is delicacy of touch and beauty of tone and phrasing. On the other hand, passages of awesome transcendency may demand many notes and wide spacing that cut through to the people with authority, power, and energy.

When the sermon, prayers, and song service function properly, we should not be conscious of the prompters. Remember our football analogy—the coaches "prompt" from the sidelines, and are only secondarily "players." I like to think that the song service, if done well, will blossom like a rose. It will open up so naturally and develop so easily that the people might be inclined to say, "I could have led that! There's nothing to it!" It's marvelous when services appear to take off on their own; and more than anything else, we are aware of the presence of the Lord with us in power and beauty. Amazed, we exclaim in awe to ourselves, "I couldn't have done this! This is not my doing!" Is this not precisely what Paul valued? Read carefully; Paul did not put his *confidence* in technique:

> And when I came to you, brethren, I did not come with superiority of speech or of wisdom, proclaiming to you the testimony of God. For I determined to know nothing among you except Jesus Christ, and Him crucified. And I was with you in weakness and in fear and in much trembling. And my message and my preaching were not in persuasive words of wisdom, but in demonstration of the Spirit and of power, that your faith should not rest on the wisdom of men, but on the power of God.
>
> 1 Corinthians 2:1–5 NASB

> We . . . who worship by the Spirit of God . . . put no confidence in the flesh.
>
> Philippians 3:3 NASB

Does this mean we should not pursue excellence? Not at all! The eighth chapter of Romans and the thirteenth chapter of 1 Corinthians contain passages of soaring eloquence. The key is not to *trust* in eloquence. Place your faith in God, not technique! Nonetheless, C. S. Lewis contends (and I think Paul would agree), "When Christian work is done on a serious subject there is no gravity and no sublimity it cannot attain."[3] And technique does contribute to sublimity. The writer of Psalm 45 was conscious of possessing technique: "My heart is stirred by a noble theme as I recite my verses for the king; my tongue is the pen of a *skillful* writer" (Ps. 45:1).

To Perform Is to Do Something in Public

I have asked mature Christians who do professional concert work and play in services, "What is the difference between performing at a concert and playing at church?" A thought-provoking response I repeatedly hear runs something like this: "I see no difference. As a Christian performer, all of life should be an offering of worship." Along this vein C. S. Lewis said: "Boiling an egg is the same process whether you are a Christian or a Pagan."[4] Insightful analogy! Yet in the church we must insist that a performance not distract, but serve the whole. And the force of human personality must also serve the goal.[5] Consider Peter: "Clothe yourselves with humility toward one another, because, 'God opposes the proud but gives grace to the humble'" (1 Peter 5:5). Performers must humble themselves before the presence of God; this is only proper. Only then can God, by his grace, feel free to work powerfully through us. When we humble ourselves in the act of performing, we may actually experience our spirit and those about us being lifted up.[6]

Performance: A Function of Size

Size makes for differences in standards. The larger the church, the higher the performance standard required; the larger the membership, the greater the need for a *quality* ministry of music.[7]

The tabernacle or temple liturgy, for example, was conducted by "professionals," specialists called priests and Levites. They had only one job; fortunately, they had sufficient numbers so that they could specialize. On the other hand, small churches with fewer than a hundred regular attenders have meager resources and often require one person to do several jobs. As a result, they are more people-oriented than performance-oriented. Generalists do the work, so people have a greater tolerance for uneven skill.

But we must be sensible. *As your church grows, be prepared to specialize.* Some don't, and they plateau. Schaller addresses this problem frankly:

> The biggest barrier to mission and outreach . . . is the tendency for the members of the middle-sized congregation to see it as a small church and to engage in counterproductive behavior. This widespread tendency has three common results: (1) first, and most serious, it creates a self perpetuating low self image of modest expectations based on a perception of inadequate resources and limited potential; (2) it offers a limited range of programs, often experiences an excessively high turnover in ministerial leadership; it rarely challenges the members to reach their full potential, and it frequently is underorganized; and (3) the combination of these first two tendencies has turned out to be the most effective single approach to turning the middle sized congregation into a small church.[8]

Schaller has a good line for midsized churches: "In a congregation as large as this, surely with God's help we can do it."

Viewing Pastors and Musicians as Fellow Performers

As I have already argued, pastors and musicians *are* performers— both have a performance orientation and temperament. Repeatedly I've heard pastors say something like this during the course of the service, "I don't feel ready to preach yet; let's have another song." Yet they deny they are performers! And they sorely miss preaching when they don't do it for several weeks.[9] To be on the sidelines is painful for both. In this sense pastors have more in common with musicians than, say, Christian education directors.

Moreover, both musicians and pastors minister publicly and must learn to expect public criticism—sometimes withering criticism.[10] Weekly public scrutiny exposes their warts to all. Both suffer by being compared to every TV evangelist and recording artist. Both may also err in their sense of dramatic timing: The musician needs to place the chorus or solo in the right place; the pastor must relate the appropriate illustration at the right moment. Both must find ways to transition smoothly. Musicians and pastors, in my opinion, tend to be compulsive. After ministering, their eyes glaze over. They try to "stop the tape" running in their heads—"this could have gone better; that was good"—as they mentally rehearse how their part in the service went.

Ego problems also go with the turf. Jealousy is for each an insidious, ever-present temptation, especially when comparisons are made of pastors to pastors, music directors to music directors, or when the pastor is compared to the worship leader in the same church. *We are so sensitive!*

What if the music tops the sermon? When musicians receive rave compliments, they should take the initiative to clarify to the pastor that they are not trying to upstage him or the Word, but they wish to make a strong contribution to the worship. A pastor will greatly appreciate the musician's sharing humbly but frankly his or her heart on this matter. For reasons like these, pastors and musicians put a high premium on working with someone who is emotionally secure.

To Perform Is to Serve and Minister

In the biblical perspective, to perform is to serve and to minister. How can pastors and musicians train themselves for unsullied service? If musicians and pastors would regularly engage in forms of service that are little esteemed and concealed from public view, they would not only become aware of their true state of humility but also go a long way in learning genuine godliness.

Richard J. Foster has observed that the flesh "screams against hiddenness. It pulls and strains for honor and recognition."[11] Dallas Willard encourages leaders to place their public relations department in the hands of God:

> If you want to experience the flow of love as never before, the next time you are in a competitive situation, pray that the others around you will be more outstanding, more praised, and more used of God than yourself. Really pull for them and rejoice for their successes.[12]

I love that quote. It's easy to read but difficult to practice in everyday life, especially for musicians and pastors, who frequently find themselves in competitive situations.

Service in *small things* can also discipline ego urges. Showing tiny courtesies, learning to listen attentively, visiting shut-ins and the elderly, driving individuals without rides home after practice, helping with the church janitorial chores occasionally, and being willing to assist others with trifling matters can help prevent inflatedness. Jesus said, "Whoever wants to become great among you must be your servant, and whoever wants to be first must be your slave" (Matt. 20:26–27). Recall the reason why Paul said he was given "a thorn in the flesh": "to keep me from exalting myself" (2 Cor. 12:7 NASB).

Yet have you observed how the phrase "anointed worship leading" is employed today? Its reckless use trivializes the concept and exalts individuals. Moreover, some leaders use the phrase "Do not touch the Lord's anointed" to place themselves beyond the pale of criticism, rendering themselves unaccountable to anyone.

On the flip side, though, is unjust criticism and, even worse, innuendo and slander. These can destroy people. Therefore, refusing to be party to gossip is an elixir of true ministry (and longevity!). In fact guarding the reputation of others is a form of ego training. Richard Foster tells of serving at a church where the staff had a policy of not allowing people to speak disparagingly of one pastor to another. "Gently but firmly," he said, "we would ask them to go directly to the offending pastor."

Self-Examination for True Service[13]

Self-Righteous Service	True Service
comes from human effort	comes from divine urges
frantic, anxious	dependent on God
seeks titanic, impressive ministry (big crowds)	welcomes all opportunities (large or small crowds)
craves applause	content with hiddenness
concerned with results	leaves the results with God
concerned with reciprocation	delights only in service
picks whom to serve (the high and powerful)	serves enemies as well as friends (servant of all)
serves when the "feeling" is there	serves when the "need" is there
uses technique for ego enhancing	submits technique to function
must perform (even if destructive!)	can withhold service and wait in silence
exposes frailties of other leaders	covers frailties of others
fractures community	builds community

Let us examine our motives for service to discover whether we are serving God and others or ourselves. Asking if we would be content to serve in ministry that is unrecognized and unappreciated, that is hidden, will help to reveal whom we serve. When any leader discovers that his or her service is self-serving, that person needs to repent and humbly seek God's direction in any future use of his or her gifts.

Questions for Reflection and Discussion

1. Do you feel a "pang" if you do not perform music or deliver sermons regularly? Are you a performer?
2. To what extent should worship leaders exert their personality in the worship service?
3. Should performance standards be related to church size?
4. In competitive situations, do you pray that others will be more outstanding, more used of God than you?

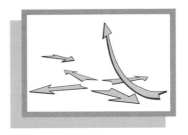

WORSHIP: CHRIST'S ACTION AND OUR RESPONSE

The real agent in worship, in a New Testament understanding, is Jesus Christ, who leads us in our praises and prayers, "the one true minister of the sanctuary." . . . He is the high priest who, by his one offering of himself on the cross, leads us into the Holy of Holies, the holy presence of the Father, in holy communion.

Jesus comes as our brother to be our great high priest, to carry on his loving heart the joys, the sorrows, the prayers, the conflicts of all his creatures, to reconcile all things to God, and to intercede for all nations as our eternal mediator and advocate.

James B. Torrance,
Worship, Community and the Triune God of Grace

As a worship leader, I've always been concerned about the response of the people. Will they enter in? Will both young and old participate wholeheartedly? Will the service encourage a rich, fully orbed response? Valid questions. I'm slowly coming to the realization, though, that I've been too response driven. My understanding has been inadequate. I've needed a clearer, more useable perspective of *Christ's action* in worship. Perhaps you sense a need along with me.

The topic of the first half of this chapter has not received much ink in recent days. Though it connects worship to the very heart and soul of the gospel, it apparently has yet to capture the attention of worship leaders in any significant way. There is an urgent need to reverse this. Derived from the Book of Hebrews, this chapter is intended to serve as a corrective for others like me. If we are not careful, our worship may become (unwittingly) too focused on the self. Consequently we may be missing opportunities for real growth.

In this chapter we will explore both sides of the coin—Christ's action and our response in worship. First, we will look at the continuing role of Christ our high priest and how our dwelling on the work of Jesus Christ can lead to confident worship. Second, we will look at worship "as a response" in more depth, particularly drawing from Old Testament worship.

These topics could make a *great* sermon. Concentrated teaching from the pulpit may be the most effective way to refocus our perspective. This chapter seeks to elevate the leadership role of Jesus Christ in our thinking of worship and ground worship more securely in the biblical words for worship.

Worship as Christ's Action

Jesus Christ, our worship leader! I first became aware of this wonderful concept in a little volume on the Book of Hebrews by James B. Torrance, *Worship, Community and the Triune God of Grace.*[1] It may be an unfamiliar thought to you. I can attest firsthand that the concept can cause a major paradigm shift in one's thinking! I had read Hebrews many times before but failed to relate it to my worship leading in any way that really made a difference. At long last I am finding paths for growth and development, the full implications of which I am still working out. Let's begin with "Christ our worship leader." How does this idea play out in the Book of Hebrews (particularly) and in the Book of Revelation? In what ways could it change our perspective of Christian worship?

Jesus Christ, Our Worship Leader in the Book of Hebrews

Jesus Christ is both the receiver of worship as a member of the Trinity, and the offerer (or leader) of worship as humanity's representative before God. In the Old Testament, priests had the responsibility of leading their people in worship and representing them before God. In the Book of Hebrews, we see Christ as our high priest, ministering on our behalf, and as our leader, representing us before the Father. Not at all peripheral, the concept of Christ as our high priest is at the heart of the book. It occupies a central place in chapters 3 through 10 and 12. Without Christ's work, the rationale underlying Christian worship would completely collapse. Christ is the *only* one who can stand on our behalf before the Father.

142

Jesus is our leader by virtue of the fact that he is our forerunner, entering into the presence of God for us, offering himself as a permanent sacrifice and interceding for us in his continuing role as our high priest.

A forerunner functions as a scout or pioneer and precedes those who follow later. Christ is our "forerunner" (6:20 NASB). Remember? Jesus said to his disciples, "In my Father's house are many rooms. . . . I am going there to prepare a place for you." Thomas asked, "How can we know the way?" "I am the way," Jesus said. "No one comes to the Father except through me" (John 14:2–6). Consider this. As our way into the Holy of Holies, Christ has preceded us and has entered into the very presence of God on our behalf:

> We have a great high priest who has gone through the heavens, Jesus the Son of God.
>
> Hebrews 4:14

> He entered the Most Holy Place once for all by his own blood.
>
> Hebrews 9:12

> [Christ] entered heaven itself, now to appear for us in God's presence.
>
> Hebrews 9:24

He offered himself as an eternal sacrifice, provided for the purification of sins on the basis of his blood, and established a permanent priesthood. His sacrifice was better than all the animals, and it was permanent:

> Christ . . . offered himself unblemished to God, a spiritual and eternal sacrifice.
>
> Hebrews 9:14

> After he had provided purification for sins, he sat down. . . .
>
> Hebrews 1:3

> Because Jesus lives forever, he has a permanent priesthood. Therefore he is able to save completely . . . because he always lives to intercede for them.
>
> Hebrews 7:24–25

Note, he "always lives to intercede" for us. Christ has a *continuing* ministry as our high priest. Torrance remarks, "Too often we have neglected the continuing priesthood of Christ."[2] In fact Scripture employs the present tense, "we have," to indicate his continuing role: "*We have* such a high priest, who has taken His seat at the right hand of the throne of the Majesty of the heavens, a *minister* in the sanctuary, and in the true tabernacle, which the Lord pitched, not man" (Heb. 8:1–2 NASB). The word "minister" comes from the Greek *leitourgos,* indicating a service of worship, from which we get our word *liturgy.*

When Hebrews states that Christ "lives forever to plead with God" (7:25 NLT), it is a clear recognition of his continuing role on our behalf. Moreover, the statement is consistent with what we read elsewhere, for before the crucifixion in his high priestly prayer to the Father, Jesus intercedes for us saying: "I pray for them . . . protect them by the power of your name. . . . For them I sanctify myself, that they too may be truly sanctified" (John 17:9, 11, 19).

The role of Jesus Christ is basic to major areas of worship experience. Torrance maintains: "We cannot have a true understanding of worship, prayer, baptism, and the Lord's Supper without a New Testament understanding of the priesthood of Christ."[3]

Jesus Christ, Our Worship Leader in the Book of Revelation

Jesus Christ assumes at least three leadership or priestly roles in the Book of Revelation. He walks among the churches (lampstands), testifies (or sings) before heaven's assembled congregation, and advances to the throne and takes the scroll from the hand of God. Let's expand on this.

In the Book of Revelation, we see Jesus depicted in heaven with a sash around his chest, walking among the lampstands, not unlike an Old Testament priest in the temple:

> I turned around to see the voice that was speaking to me. . . . among the lampstands was someone "like a son of man," dressed in a robe reaching down to his feet and with a golden sash around his chest. . . . In his right hand he held seven stars, and out of his mouth came a sharp double-edged sword. . . . The seven stars are the angels of the seven churches, and the seven lampstands are the seven churches.
>
> Revelation 1:12, 13, 16, 20

Is Christ exercising vigilance over the churches, symbolized by the lampstands? It appears so. Christ's role as our worship leader becomes even more specific, for in heaven he leads us, his brothers and sisters, by voicing public praise to God's name: "I will declare your name to my brothers; in the presence of the congregation I will sing your praises" (Heb. 2:12). William L. Lane views Christ here as our exalted Lord, "who as the singing priest leads the redeemed community in songs of praise."[4]

Similarly, in reference to this passage, Calvin describes Christ as "the chief Conductor of our hymns."[5] Could this be Christ's song of vindication over death as our risen Savior? Again, it seems so.

At the most crucial point in heaven's worship, Christ, the agent and leader of heaven's worship, performs what no one else can do. Christ advances to the throne, takes the scroll from the hand of God, and breaks the seven seals. This liturgical drama centers on his singularly heroic, visible action, and it results in a new song in honor of the Lamb:

> Then I saw in the right hand of him who sat on the throne a scroll with writing on both sides and sealed with seven seals. And I saw a mighty angel proclaiming in a loud voice, "Who is worthy to break the seals and open the scroll?" But no one in heaven or on earth or under the earth could open the scroll or even look inside it. . . .
>
> Then I saw a Lamb, looking as if it had been slain, standing in the center of the throne, encircled by the four living creatures and the elders. . . . He came and took the scroll from the right hand of him who sat on the throne. And when he had taken it, the four living creatures and the twenty-four elders fell down before the Lamb. . . . And they sang a new song:
>
> > "You are worthy to take the scroll
> >   and to open its seals,
> > because you were slain,
> >   and with your blood you purchased men for God
> >   from every tribe and language and people and nation."
>
> Revelation 5:1–3, 6–9

The contrast is enormous. We lead worship at our churches, but our Lord leads in the heavenly sanctuary. But there is more—Christ our leader imparts confidence to us in worship.

Confidence in Worship

When worshipers dwell on the completed work of Christ, they gain confidence to draw near in worship. What an enormous insight! Before entering into worship, have you ever helped your people reflect on this thought? The writer of Hebrews says: "Therefore, brothers, since we have *confidence* to enter the Most Holy Place by the blood of Jesus . . . let us draw near to God with a sincere heart in full assurance of faith" (Heb. 10:19, 22). We enter on the basis of his blood. Our hope is anchored (a strong image). It reaches right through the curtain and into the Holy of Holies. It is anchored or fixed, as it were, in the very reality and presence of God: "We have this hope, a sure and steadfast anchor of the soul, a hope that enters the inner shrine behind the curtain, where Jesus, a forerunner on our behalf, has entered" (Heb. 6:19–20 NRSV).

We draw near in confidence knowing Christ is a "merciful and faithful" high priest, who has "been tempted in every way, just as we are." He calls us his "brothers and sisters" (that's powerful!) and is able to "deal gently" with us. His blood cleanses our consciences "from acts that lead to death, so that we may serve [worship] the living God."[6] Moreover, God sends the Holy Spirit, the Spirit of Christ, who "helps us in our weakness" (NRSV), and "intercedes for us with groans that words cannot express" (Rom 8:26).

These strategic truths are confidence builders for all worshipers. Now let's think through the idea of response in worship, staying within the context of the Book of Hebrews.

The Starting Point of Worship

Frequently we are inclined to conceive of worship as our response to God—*our* response, *our* decision to worship. Worship boils down to "us and God." The human-Godward movement in worship is often viewed as wholly ours. If we are not careful, we can short-circuit grace when we think this way.

In reality, ours is not the only human-Godward movement. Jesus Christ himself performs the primary human-Godward role. Christ's gracious initiative is *the* crucial Godward action in worship. Christ, in his sinlessness, rises from the dead, enters the Holy of Holies, represents us before the Father, and intercedes for us, "uniting us with himself in his life in the Spirit" and "drawing us into the very life of God."[7] Think about that! Our response, then, is really *a response to his response* already effected, which is "continually being made for us."[8] When we begin to think in this way, the starting point of worship becomes less "our experience" and more the work of Christ, the true agent of our worship. We are drawn away from any narcissistic preoccupation with self and toward a Christ-centered (other-centered) worship, which is more biblical and healthy.

WORSHIP: CHRIST'S ACTION AND OUR RESPONSE

Practical Applications

Worship leaders, how effective have we been in instilling thoughts like these in the teaching opportunities we have between musical segments and throughout the service? What energizes our worship? Have we acquainted our people sufficiently with Christ's action in worship? How would we, personally, go about integrating the theology of worship into our worship practices?

Here are a few creative suggestions on how you might employ this material in a "teaching moment." Vary these ideas to fit your context. Near the beginning of your service, lead your people in a time of reflective prayer (sometimes called a "bidding" or "guided" prayer): "As we are entering into worship this morning, we do so with thankful hearts and with confidence because of what Jesus Christ has done for us. Jesus, the leader of our worship, has entered the Holy of Holies in heaven on our behalf to represent us before the Father. Hebrews tells us our hope reaches right through the curtain and into the Holy of Holies. It is anchored in the reality and presence of God. Take a moment now and thank God for the reality of his presence (pause). Take a moment for silent prayer right now to thank Jesus for entering the Holy of Holies on our behalf (pause). Try to imagine yourself entering into the Holy of Holies with him (pause). Tell God your hope is anchored in the reality of his existence and presence today" (pause).

After guiding your people in this prayer, you could offer an impromptu, summarizing prayer to Jesus, thanking him for being our great leader. Or you could conclude by talking through this passage from Ephesians 2:4–7: "This passage from Ephesians confirms the amazing truth that we are already seated in the heavenlies with Christ. That is what Paul teaches. He writes:

God, who is rich in mercy, made us alive with Christ even when we were dead in transgressions. . . . And God raised us up with Christ and seated us with him in the heavenly realms in Christ Jesus, in order that in the coming ages he might show the incomparable riches of his grace, expressed in his kindness to us in Christ Jesus.

"In light of this, as we continue in worship this morning, I invite you to journey with us into the Holy of Holies to meet the risen Christ."

As a worship leader, you could attempt something more dramatic: "I have an announcement to make this morning. I am not your worship leader. You may see me standing before you this morning, and I may give directions and lead with my hands and voice, but I am not your worship leader. Our true worship leader cannot be seen. He is here, but invisible to our eyes. He rose from the dead and ascended into heaven to represent us before the Father. He intercedes for us this very moment—right now—before the throne of God. Our worship leader is none other than Jesus Christ the Lord. Apart from him there would be no worship. Christian worship, as we know it, would completely collapse.

"As we enter into worship this morning, remember, Christ is your leader, not me. Because of what he has done and is continuing to do on our behalf, we have something to sing about. We have someone to sing to." Then sing "Jesus Is King" (excerpt below):

> Jesus is King and I will extol Him,
> Give Him the glory, and honor His name.
> He reigns on high, enthroned in the heavens,
> Word of the Father, exalted for us.
>
> We have a hope that is steadfast and certain
> Gone through the curtain and touching the throne.
> We have a Priest Who is there interceding
> Pouring His grace on our lives day by day.
>
> Wendy Churchill
> ©1981 Springtide/Word Music, U.K.

For another exercise, ask your congregation to imagine being in heaven and hearing Jesus testifying, voicing public praise before the Father and the redeemed community. Imagine being there as one of the worshipers and responding along with the innumerable host of heaven. Then sing together the chorus "Thou Art Worthy."

In other words, fasten on any strong idea from the above paragraphs. Bring it before your people. Memorize what you are about to say so that you don't have to look at any notes. Pastors could have a sermon on "Jesus Christ, Our Leader" and follow that with a time of worship. Spend some time thinking about how you might implement these concepts. I've barely scratched the surface here!

Jesus Christ, Our Model for Leadership

Now let's look at Jesus Christ from a slightly different perspective, that of being our model for leadership. In a culminating passage in the

148

Book of Hebrews, the theme of Christ as the "author" and "perfecter" (or completer) of our faith resounds powerfully. We see the struggle and triumph of Christ. Once again Christ's ultimate objective is restated: to seat himself at the throne of God as humanity's representative, and to provide, as a consequence, a means of access for us into the very presence and life of God:

> Therefore, since we have so great a cloud of witnesses surrounding us, let us also lay aside every encumbrance, and the sin which so easily entangles us, and let us run with endurance the race that is set before us, fixing our eyes on Jesus, the author and perfecter of faith, who for the joy set before Him endured the cross, despising the shame, and has sat down at the right hand of the throne of God.
>
> Hebrews 12: 1–2 NASB

The phrase "Jesus, the author and perfecter of faith" is "remarkable for its conciseness and rich suggestiveness."[9] Bible translations and commentators acknowledge that the word translated above as *author* can be rendered as *leader* (as in the NAB rev. and NLB translations), adding further support to our stress on Christ as our leader. Other versions translate it variously as *pioneer* (NRSV), "the one who *leads*" (NJB), and the one "who is the *leader* and *source* of our faith" (New Amplified). The NASB submits the word *leader* as an alternative. This emphasis is also held by commentators Buchanan, for whom the word carries the meaning of "initial leader," "primary leader," or "chief leader";[10] and Lane, who prefers the word "champion," believing it better nuances the sense that Christ is both a leader and a "model for imitation."[11] Lane renders the passage as follows: "Let us run the race prescribed for us, fixing our eyes on Jesus, the champion of faith, and the one who brought faith to complete expression" (Heb. 12:1–2).[12]

That considered, what sort of a worship leader would Christ make today? Putting it most simply, "What would Jesus do?" What qualities would he model for us? In what ways would we want to imitate him? Again, Hebrews offers us some solid direction. We learn that Christ identifies completely with his people; he calls them his brothers and sisters. He leads them "gently," since he is well acquainted with their weaknesses. After all, he too understood firsthand what it meant to be "tempted" and to "suffer." Aren't these some of the foundational sensitivities and attitudes that all worship leaders need? It takes deep insight, however, to apply these thoughts meaningfully to our ministry.

Worship as Our Response

Now let's turn the coin over and explore worship more thoroughly as a response to God. First, we will look at worship *as an action,* such as singing, speaking, bowing down, prostrating, and confessing with our lips. Second, we will focus on worship *as a complete surrender* of ourselves to God and his will. In this second sense, *anything* we do could be worship if it is done in obedience to him.

Tom Finley, professor of Old Testament at Talbot School of Theology, wrote me this note after reading this part of the manuscript: "This is an *important* section. We need *scriptural* support to give us permission to involve our bodies in worship. Too many still identify bodily expression with 'Pentecostal' worship."[13]

Old Testament worship has a powerful response orientation. Jack R. Taylor writes that Davidic praise is "always active, assertive, demonstrative and open. It is not passive, presumptuous, undemonstrative, or secretive. Whenever it is mentioned, movement, action, and songs are seen and heard."[14] Doesn't that sound oddly contemporary? "Davidic praise" is far removed from the comfortable pew of noninvolvement. Perhaps the most extravagant image of utter abandonment in worship we have is the image of David leaping and dancing as the ark was carried into Jerusalem.

Secular concerts have extravagant images too. Have you noticed how people applaud at rock concerts? The picture that comes to mind is a sea of raised hands undulating high over hundreds of heads.

What about our churches? In visiting 120 churches in the past four years, I could not help but be impressed with how rapidly the raising of hands in worship has become commonly accepted—even in some of the most conservative churches on the West Coast of North America. In many churches in the United States and Canada, it is no longer uncommon to see at least a few hands raised in worship at some point in the service. Our entire worship culture is in transition. We are becoming, in some respects, more Hebraic.

A Holistic Response

What is Hebraic worship like? Hebraic worship encourages a full response from *the whole person.* In the Old Testament "there is no systematic distinction between the material and the immaterial, the physical and the spiritual."[15] Rather, it acknowledges the "interrelatedness

150

of the physical and the spiritual."[16] Human beings, soul and body, are an indivisible totality in Hebrew thought.

Not so in Greek thought! For the Neo-Platonist philosopher Plotinus (who died in A.D. 270), the body was considered a "barrier or impediment" to the spiritual. He spoke of the soul as "deeply infected with the taint of the body," and as being immersed in "filth" and "daubed" with the "mud" of the body: "The nature of the body, in that it partakes of matter, is an evil thing . . . a hindrance to the soul in its proper act."[17]

In contrast, Hebraic worship depicts the flesh as *yearning for God* and as *singing for joy* to him:

My soul thirsts for Thee, my flesh yearns for Thee, in a dry and weary land.

Psalm 63:1 NASB

My soul longed and even yearned for the courts of the LORD; my heart and my flesh sing for joy to the living God.

Psalm 84:2 NASB

Worshipers, as depicted in the Old Testament, were free to worship God with their total beings—mind, emotions, will, personality, body, and senses—without the negative connotations of Greek dualism intruding. The New Testament projects a similar emphasis, for Paul exhorts us, "Glorify God in your body" (NASB).

This is good news for musicians, for I contend that musicians naturally tend to approach worship less theologically, less cerebrally, and more from the human side of emotion and affective response than do pastors. This may be due in part to the fact that musicians spend so much time trying to find the right piece, the right key, the right ordering of events, the right musical expression or feeling for a given moment. It is not surprising that Don Hustad, noted worship author and musician, defines worship in terms of response, as "any and every worthy response to God," whereas the theologian-scholar Ralph P. Martin defines worship in terms of the Trinity, as "the adoration and service of God through the mediation of the Son and prompted by the Spirit."[18]

An Attitude and an Act

Worship in Scripture is "both an attitude and an act."[19] The various words associated with worship in the Old Testament depict the atti-

151

tude of the people toward God and the nature of their approach to him. To worship is to seek God with one's whole heart, to inquire *(darash)*, to come and enter *(bo)*, to approach *(nagash)*, to draw near *(qarab)*, and to offer a sacrifice. Words like *seek* and *draw near* convey a sense of intimacy and relationship in Old Testament worship, not merely an obligatory observance of ritual: "But as for me, it is good to be near God" (Ps. 73:28).

Hebrew worship is very closely associated with feelings. The emotions of fear and reverence *(yare)* are frequently expressed—sometimes they border on terror and dread. Incidentally, fear and reverence also continue to resonate in the New Testament: "So worship God acceptably with reverence and awe, for our 'God is a consuming fire'" (Heb 12:28–29).[20]

To worship God is to prostrate *(shachah, segid)* oneself before him, to give homage, to bow down—to grovel, and even to wallow, as before royalty. Subservience and a sense of personal unworthiness are also part of the dynamic Old Testament picture.

Obedient Service

In the Old Testament, to worship also means to serve *(abad)* or work for God, to obey his divine commands as part of one's total lifestyle. For the priests who served in a specialized manner, it meant to "attend" or to "minister" *(sharat)* to God in the temple ceremonies, and to perform blameless service to him with integrity. The same terminology is applied to angels serving God.[21]

Comparing Worship in Old and New Testaments

That is the overall portrait of the worship terminology in the Old Testament. But at this point, let's tighten the focus of the Old Testament terminology and extend the discussion to the New Testament. Here are some crucial questions we will ask: What are the *primary* emphases of the worship terminology in both Testaments? How do the Old and New Testament words for worship *compare?* Are their meanings *similar* or *different?* Let's attempt to answer these questions.

Prostration, the Main Idea

The two words used most often for worship in both the Old and New Testaments emphasize: (1) the body bowing or prostrating, as the dom-

152

inant image for worship; (2) service to God, as a lifestyle of worship. The emphases are strongly established in both Testaments.

The primary word that defines worship in the Old Testament makes explicit reference to the body. *Shachah,* translated "worship" in the NASB eighty-one times, means literally to "bow" politely or respectfully, to "prostrate oneself," to "make obeisance," or to "bend low."[22] Worship has a profound physical dimension in Hebrew culture: "Ezra praised the LORD, the great God; and all the people lifted their hands and responded, 'Amen, Amen!' Then they bowed down and worshiped *[shachah]* the LORD with their faces to the ground" (Neh. 8:6). Worship includes the prostration of both the heart and the body. It "emphasizes the way in which an Israelite fittingly thought of his approach to the holy presence of God. He bows himself down in lowly reverence and prostration."[23] Prostration means to touch one's forehead to the ground (see Gen. 42:6), a gesture representing absolute submission.[24] The Old Testament word for worship is not primarily propositional. It is visual, gestural, and attitudinal:

> King Hezekiah and the officials ordered the Levites to sing praises to the LORD with the words of David and Asaph the seer. So they sang praises with joy, and bowed down and worshiped *[shachah]*.
>
> 2 Chronicles 29:30 NASB

> Worship *[shachah]* the LORD in holy attire;
> Tremble before Him, all the earth.
>
> Psalm 96:9 NASB

Visible actions, trembling feelings, and joy are evident above.

Proskuneo, the Greek counterpart of *shachah* in the New Testament (translated "worship" fifty-one times in the NASB), has the same basic meaning with the same overtones of "submissive lowliness and deep respect." *Pros* means "to turn toward," and *kuneo* means "to kiss." Kissing here mainly refers to kissing the feet (as in an act of prostration before a great one), signifying humility, subjection, and submission, not intimacy (as some teach).[25]

We simply cannot do better than to meditate on these words if we want to be instructed by the biblical attitude to worship. To worship is to fall down before God and to offer him the respect due our Maker: "O come, let us worship *[shachah]* and bow down: let us kneel before the LORD our maker. For he is our God; and we are . . . the sheep of his hand" (Ps. 95:6–7 KJV).

The dominant prayer posture in the Book of Revelation is prostration. When the apostle John sees Jesus Christ, he falls down in worship: "Among the lampstands was someone 'like a son of man.' . . . When I saw him, *I fell at his feet* as though dead" (Rev. 1:13, 17). The quotation is not atypical. *Proskynein* occurs twenty-four times in Revelation and is regularly coupled with the verb "to fall down" (4:10; 5:14; 7:11; 11:16; 19:4).[26] Should this data have significance for worshipers today? I think so.

I have seen my own university students, while in the act of leading worship, spontaneously fall to their knees. It has stirred and moved me. It was real. Pastors could do this too! It's been said, "The pastor should be the most radical worshiper in the church." The people should be able to look up to their pastor and say, "Now there is a real worshiper of God!"[27]

I see no biblical reason for evangelical leaders to be squeamish about bodily expression in worship, as long as it is not distracting or ego-centered. The body can teach us something about worship. Try kneeling or prostrating yourself during your private devotions. Experiment. Physical involvement can enrich the experience of worship—it should not be despised. Prostration is embodied prayer. Kneeling is one of the clearest and most telling ways to express reverence to God. Kneeling attacks our prideful nature. As expressed previously, Davidic praise is not "secretive."

Another Old Testament word strikes the second major emphasis of this section, the crucial emphasis of serving God obediently in a *lifestyle of worship.* The Hebrew word *abodah* is translated "worship" (thirteen times in the NASB); it means to "serve" or "work." Its Greek equivalents *latreia* and *latreuo* have the same meaning and are translated as "worship" (six times) and "service" (twenty times) in the NASB.[28] *Latreuo* is often used for cultic service. *Latreia* is used in explicit reference to a sacrificial lifestyle of worship in this well-known passage: "I urge you therefore, brethren, by the mercies of God, to present your bodies a living and holy sacrifice, acceptable to God, which is your spiritual *service of worship*" (Rom. 12:1 NASB).

It is surprising to note that in the chart below the gestural pair of words (*shachah* and *proskuneo*) occurs in the Bible at least twice as frequently as the propositional pair (*abodah* and *latreia*). We must conclude that worship involving the body is as meaningful as verbal proclamation.

Hebrew and Greek Words for Worship and Praise

Words	Frequency	Meaning
shachah (Heb.)	81	to bow, prostrate
proskuneo (Gr.)	51	to turn toward, kiss (prostrate)
abodah (Heb.)	13	to serve, work
latreia, latreuo (Gr.)	26	to serve, worship

My sense is that the dominant image of worship in Scripture—prostration and all it entails—is not emerging with sufficient force and clarity in the books of worship I have read. That is why I have given it such prominence in this chapter.

A Comprehensive Worship

When individuals worship comprehensively, both verbally and gesturally, worship takes on an added dimension and significance from a psychological standpoint:

Meaning involving several senses is obviously more vital than meaning involving only one. . . . Normally, the meaning of a thing thought is less powerful than the meaning of a thing heard, which in turn is less powerful than the meaning of a thing seen as well as heard.[29]

Ultimately God will require a comprehensive form of worship. Worship expression involving "seeing" and "hearing" will be unmistakably clear and integrative, involving both symbolic and verbal communication:

That at the name of Jesus every *knee* should bow,
in heaven and on earth and under the earth,
and every *tongue* confess that Jesus Christ is Lord,
to the glory of God the Father.

Philippians 2:10–11

Worship in heaven encompasses the total person. Knees and tongues preach and proclaim.

Almighty One! I bend in dust before You;
Even so veiled cherubs bend;
In calm and still devotion I adore You,
All-wise, all-present Friend.

Sir John Browning

155

Paul's Worship Terminology

In the New Testament a strong emphasis emerges for worship as an everyday commitment of one's total life to God and others.[30] Christ, the obedient "Adam," is our leader and perfectly models a lifestyle of worship, doing his Father's will in everything, and living consciously in his Father's presence. We, following in his footsteps, should always be at worship too! A life of sacrificial obedience in all of life, as a result of a renewed mind, becomes the New Testament measure of acceptable worship (Rom. 12:1).

The Torah and the system of sacrificial worship in the Old Testament ends and is fulfilled and replaced by Christ-centered, Spirit-energized worship.[31] Christian worship is now "by the Spirit" (Phil. 3:3).

The worship terminology of the Old Testament remains foundational but is transformed and renewed. There is continuity with transformation. For example, in reference to the body in worship—as we saw in chapter 8—Paul says: "I want men everywhere to lift up holy hands in prayer, without anger or disputing" (1 Tim. 2:8).

Lifting up "holy hands" most certainly refers back to Old Testament practice. Though Paul, a Hebrew, undoubtedly raised his hands physically in worship, raised hands in this verse become a visual image (metaphor) for holy living. On another occasion, Paul employs a word used most for cultic service, *latreuo,* to describe his life work of preaching: "God whom I serve *[latreuo]* with my whole heart in preaching the gospel of his Son, is my witness how constantly I remember you in my prayers at all times" (Rom. 1:9). Paul gives his preaching ministry, therefore, "a novel significance when he describes it as the means by which he worships or serves God."[32]

Similarly, Paul transforms Old Testament terminology when he views himself as discharging a priestly duty to the Gentiles, though he ministers not in a sacred temple but in the public marketplace: "God gave me to be a minister *[leitourgos]* of Christ Jesus to the Gentiles with the priestly duty of proclaiming the gospel of God" (Rom. 15:15–16). Or again, Paul regards his service of worship as a "drink offering" (Phil. 2:17), a "libation" poured out on the top of a sacrifice, given for the Gentiles, both an Old Testament and a Greek image.[33]

For Paul, serving God in the whole range of relationships and responsibilities believers have to one another is a response of worship. A monetary gift given to him becomes a "sweet aroma" of worship, a metaphor associated with Old Testament sacrifices. *Leitourgia,* formerly a term for expressing specialized ministry by priests to the Lord, now expresses the sacrificial care rendered by one believer to another—in this case Epaphroditus to Paul: "because he [Epaphroditus] almost died for the work of Christ, risking his life to make up for the *help [leitourgia]* you could not give me [Paul]" (Phil. 2:30).

More important, Paul teaches that Christians—not some sacred place—are now the temple of God, God's dwelling place (1 Cor. 3:16), yet another transformation. Similarly, "Touch no unclean thing" (2 Cor. 6:17), a ritual command strictly observed in the Old Testament, becomes an ethical command for Christians to live a holy life. We see, then, that Old Testament terminology, though foundational to Paul's writings, is transformed and renewed. Paul's emphasis is on a total lifestyle of worship.

I can summarize this chapter in one sentence. *Christ's action* is to redeem his brothers and sisters and lead them into the very presence of God; *our response* is to fall flat on our faces in worship!

The Issue of Priority

In preparation for the next chapter, I want to conclude with the question, What priority should worship receive in the church? There is a growing recognition that the object of evangelism is to produce worshipers.[34] During the past decade, corporate worship has assumed more importance in the minds of pastors and worship leaders everywhere. An increasing number of writers, theologians, and researchers of worship are taking the view that worship should receive priority over teaching, evangelism, and fellowship. This seems to be a relatively new emphasis for evangelicals.

Bruce Leafblad writes, "If God comes first in our lives and first in our churches, then worship must come ahead of everything else we do. Worship is that process in which we make God first in our lives."[35] He reasons as follows:

1. The great commandment—"Love the Lord your God with all your heart" and "your neighbor as yourself" (Luke 10:27)—puts the love of God first.
2. Our referents for God describe him in terms of worship. The biblical words for God—both the Hebrew word *Elohim* and the Greek word *Theos*—mean "an object of worship."

157

3. Worship is a priority in the Old Testament. The first four commandments of the Decalogue have to do with worship (Exodus 20), and one of the chief struggles of the Old Testament prophets was to keep Israel's worship uncorrupted by foreign gods.
4. The Westminster Shorter Catechism answers the question, "What is the chief end of man?" with, "To glorify God and enjoy Him forever."
5. Worship is the central issue in the Book of Revelation. When teaching and evangelism end, worship continues.[36]

Jack Hayford also assigns to worship the top priority: "I am totally persuaded that worship is the key to evangelism as well as to the edification of the Church."[37] "Our first sacrifice ought to be the sacrifice of praise . . . our first work ought to be the humbling of ourselves in His presence."[38] He sees evangelism as a "by-product . . . nourished through worship and fellowship"[39] and views worship "as a key to the release of the church's power":

> We present ourselves in worship purposing to provide a place for God to make an entrance among us, to shape us, to work among us and through us.
> God's revealed will in calling His people together [in worship] is that they might experience His presence and power—not as a spectacle or sensation, but in a discovery of His will through encounter and impact. . . .
> I am troubled because, for the most part, believers gathering for worship generally do not expect God to be present in a distinct and profound way or do anything especially discernible. He [God] wants a place to display His presence, His love, His power, and *Himself.*[40]

Hayford's priorities are clear. Ministry to the Lord comes first, then ministry to the saints, and finally ministry to the world.[41]

Peter, the head of the apostles, identifies worship as the ultimate goal of the church:

> You also, like living stones, are being built into a spiritual house to be a holy priesthood, offering spiritual sacrifices acceptable to God through Jesus Christ.
>
> 1 Peter 2:5

But you are a chosen people, a royal priesthood . . . that you may declare the praises of him who called you out of darkness into his wonderful light.

1 Peter 2:9

And in Paul's writings, the ultimate goal of evangelism is a life of sacrificial worship: "God gave me to be a minister of Christ Jesus to the Gentiles . . . so that the Gentiles might become an offering acceptable to God, sanctified by the Holy Spirit" (Rom. 15:15–16).

> *Worship is not passive, but is participative*
> *Worship is not simply a mood; it is a response.*
> *Worship is not just a feeling; it is a declaration.*
> Ronald Allen and Gordon Borror
> *Worship: Rediscovering the Missing Jewel*

Questions for Reflection and Discussion

1. How did the concept of Jesus Christ, our worship leader, impact you?
2. How can response-driven worship leaders become more biblical in their worship leading?
3. Young people are attracted to the physical side of worship. Is this legitimate? Explain.
4. What priority should worship receive in the church?

159

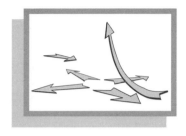

WORSHIP THAT MODELS
THE PURPOSE OF THE CHURCH

*To worship is to quicken the conscience by the holiness of God,
to feed the mind with the truth of God,
to purge the imagination with the beauty of God,
to devote the will to the purpose of God.*

William Temple

Worship should be "determined by the nature of the church," says David B. Pass.[1] That's the foundational premise behind this chapter. How should worship function within the church? What purposes should it address? What could it look like today? These are questions we'll explore. I also want to furnish many practical examples for implementation.

We will assume that the Greek terms *kerygma, koinonia,* and *leitourgia,* which characterize Pass's model of the New Testament church, address the basic purposes of the church.[2] They have the following meanings:

- *kerygma:* to proclaim
- *koinonia:* to fellowship
- *leitourgia:* to serve (minister or worship)

Let's look at the first basic purpose of the church, *kerygma.*

Kerygma

Kerygma has to do with preaching and proclaiming the message of Jesus Christ. It calls people to faith, to conversion, to discipleship. It is translated "preach" in this passage: "Jews demand miraculous signs and Greeks look for wisdom, but we *preach* Christ crucified" (1 Cor. 1:22–23). See also 2 Timothy 4:17. *Kerygma* originates with God: "For what I received I passed on to you as of first importance: that Christ died for our sins according to the Scriptures, that he was buried, that he was raised on the third day" (1 Cor. 15:3–4).

Kerygma convicts and calls for repentance. It tends to be hierarchical: Someone preaches while others receive the message, or someone sings while others listen. *Kerygma* was demonstrated at Pentecost when Peter "raised his voice and *addressed* the crowd" (Acts 2:14), and when Cornelius said, "Now we are all here in the presence of God *to listen* to everything the Lord has commanded" (Acts 10:33).

The Kerygma *Worship Service*

A *kerygma* service may include preaching, teaching, evangelism, or outreach. It emphasizes communication from the *one to the many*. The apostle Paul, for example, encouraged numerous *kerygma* contributions from individuals to the group: "When you assemble, *each one* has a psalm, has a teaching, has a revelation, has a tongue, has an interpretation. Let all things be done for edification" (1 Cor. 14:26 NASB). From this verse one could conclude, by extension, that solos[3] and small group musical presentations—especially those having a proclaiming or teaching function—would meet with his approval.

Kerygma has both strengths and weaknesses relative to worship. On the plus side, integrity can emerge in the act of proclaiming truth. In performance-oriented services, the pastor comes to preach, the band to play, and the worship team/soloists to sing. Skilled staff members lead public prayer, read the Scriptures, take the offering, and make the announcements. The look of excellence and professionalism pervades the service as it unfolds dramatically—there is a script (order of service), a performance of that script, and lighting and staging may receive attention. Moreover, *kerygma* communication can also occur when *all the people* proclaim the Word of God by means of song: "Let the word of Christ richly dwell within you, with all wisdom teaching and admonishing *one another* with psalms and hymns and spiritual songs" (Col. 3:16 NASB).

Professionalism is not bad in itself, but when performers fail to see themselves as offerers of worship, and when the congregation fails to become engaged, a great danger looms.

Many times a performance orientation produces an audience of religious onlookers with a passive mentality. The people come to hear a presentation and be entertained. Everything is done *to them*. The audience sits in their padded seats and listens as the worship team sings for 10 or 15 minutes. Almost nobody sings. Those with specialized gifts *dominate* the service. Only those miked up front have a significant role.

The drive for high standards occupies the head musician, who functions more as music director than as worship leader. An unhealthy tension often exists between production and mentoring. Production values receive priority (i.e., rehearsal, refinement), and little attention is given to the spiritual growth of the participants. Accountability and the spiritual disciplines are shortchanged.

On the congregational side, there is not much emphasis on the people singing "to God" or responding in prayer. Response to God is not at the forefront, is not articulated by the leadership, and is not perceived as vital by the people. When the people leave, they talk about what they received from the service, how they were inspired, and especially, *how well the pastor, choir, or band did their job.*

When this happens, Dianne Bowker notes, the service is not a true *kerygma* service.[4] The goal of *kerygma* is conviction and change. True *kerygma* engenders a response from the soul.

If I seem excessively negative, not all of these features characterize all performance churches. Yet if we are honest, they typify too many large-sized, consumer-oriented churches today. Some have learned the bitter lesson that their college students and Gen-Xers may not be very interested in the "big people's church" if it emphasizes performance and production at the expense of genuine involvement. Gen-Xers want church to be real—they are seeking real relationships and a real encounter with God. Meeting with God ought to be more important than "watching a show."

But is all proclamation that has a strong performance dimension bad? No!

Kerygma *Music*

To help our understanding, let's first consider the parallelism between the ministry of music groups and the preaching ministry (see the figure on page 172). In the preaching ministry, the pastor stands

163

before the people and proclaims the Word. Due to his specialized training and his giftedness in the art of communication, he has been set apart to perform this service. He exegetes the passage, consults commentaries, and delivers a message as God's representative, speaking God's words boldly. An implied hierarchy informs the event. Few in the congregation could replicate his sermon in terms of its quality or authority.

Can music-making correspond to the act of preparing and delivering a sermon? Yes, closely. Clearly, the concert format—where a soloist, specialized group, or choir performs mono-directionally to an audience—corresponds closely to the pastor's format. Music groups and choirs have their technical music scores. Due to their training and talent, they perform pieces the congregation would not attempt and with a precision the people cannot attain.

Gifted performers can proclaim the fundamentals of the faith in endlessly interesting ways, and it is precisely the core beliefs that need continual emphasis. *Let all the techniques of art serve content.* If you are a soloist or a member of a small musical group, give more thought to your role and calling as a proclaimer and a teacher. That emphasis can bring integrity to your role.

Not so long ago, it was a common assumption that every worship service should have a special number from the choir and a solo number too. Not so today! Some churches *intentionally* eliminate vocal or instrumental solos and small group or choir numbers. This is unnecessarily limiting. It confines the gifts and stewardship of the body. Moreover, this approach is not modeled in Pauline worship (1 Cor. 14:26) or in the Book of Revelation.

When accomplished musicians offer their music as a sacrificial gift to the Lord, God may choose to manifest himself in power as they serve—just as he did in the dedication of the temple:

> All the Levitical singers . . . and with them one hundred and twenty priests blowing trumpets in unison . . . lifted up their voice . . . and when they praised the LORD saying, "He indeed is good for His lovingkindness is everlasting," . . . the house of the LORD, was filled with a cloud, so that the priests could not stand to minister . . . for the glory of the LORD filled the house of God.
>
> 2 Chronicles 5:12–14 NASB

The Levitical singers and instrumentalists were musical specialists. This was their lifelong calling, their career. Years were spent in prepa-

164

ration, and they received the tithe just like the priests. By God's design, the Levitical musicians had a formalized role in the temple institution. Altogether they constituted a force of 4,000 musicians, with 288 master teachers dispersed among 24 groups. This institution wasn't a human invention. "'All this,' said David, 'the Lord made me understand in writing by His hand upon me, all the details of this pattern'" (1 Chron. 28:19 NASB).

Like the Levitical musicians of the Old Testament, highly skilled, spirit-endowed musicians should be encouraged to serve today. In fact in some situations the ministry of choirs and special groups may be best realized when they are used as "specialists." When they are freestanding and not limited by involving the congregation in their music-making process, they are freed to proclaim the truth with a greater diversity of style and genre. This implies a certain functional *separation* from the congregation, as in the case of the Levites. The soloist, choir, or group performs (ministers), God makes his presence felt, and the people meet God.

An additional dimension needs emphasis if we are to catch the full picture of *kerygma* communication. *Kerygma* includes evangelism. Paul anticipates that visiting unbelievers will be converted during worship services:

> If an unbeliever or someone who does not understand comes in while everybody is prophesying, he will be convinced by all that he is a sinner and will be judged by all, and the secrets of his heart will be laid bare. So he will fall down and worship God, exclaiming, "God is really among you."
>
> 1 Corinthians 14:24–25

Fee writes: "This suggests that some expressions of prophecy, besides being directed toward believers for their edification (v. 3), are also directed toward the unbelieving. . . ."[5]

In general, we should expect evangelism to be the by-product of a believer's worship service. But whenever evangelism is the focus of a service, as in a "special" evangelistic emphasis, *whatever* style communicates the gospel should be acceptable—even "rap" in some churches—so that "by all possible means" we "might save some" (1 Cor. 9:22). We should be willing to set aside our preferences and traditions in order to allow God to work freely.

Koinonia

This section on *koinonia* worship, a hallmark of the Pauline churches, should be especially valuable for small or midsized churches. Large churches can also benefit. William Lock asks, "Isn't *koinonia* significant no matter what the church size?"[6]

Koinonia addresses a basic purpose of the church. It involves communicating one with another, establishing and enhancing relationships, and maintaining community and unity in the body of Christ. *Koinonia* is translated not only as *fellowship* but as *partnership:* "I always pray with joy because of your *partnership* in the gospel" (Phil. 1:4–5). Shared feelings, giving and receiving, equality and reciprocity all characterize *koinonia.* It encourages, nurtures, comforts, and affirms: "If you have any encouragement from being united with Christ, if any comfort from his love, if any *fellowship* with the Spirit, if any tenderness and compassion, then make my joy complete by being likeminded" (Phil. 2:1–2).

Moreover, the word *koinonia,* translated as "participation," expresses the meaning of the Lord's Table—"Is not the cup . . . a *participation* in the blood of Christ? And is not the bread that we break a *participation* in the body of Christ?" (1 Cor. 10:16). When *koinonia* is translated as "contribution," it is referring to giving financial help to the Christians in Jerusalem (Rom. 15:26).

Koinonia happens in an informal, relaxed, family atmosphere. It occurs in the ordinary activity of eating together (Acts 2:46). It flourishes in a forgiving community: "Be kind and compassionate to one another, forgiving each other, just as in Christ God forgave you" (Eph. 4:32). Touching—greeting someone with a handshake or a hug, affirming someone with a pat on the back—is a nonverbal means of expressing *koinonia. Koinonia* addresses the needs of those who are "hurting, lonely, who find it hard to trust others and God."[7] Each person is a full participant, ministering and receiving ministry: "Its parts should have equal concern for each other. If one part suffers, every part suffers with it; if one part is honored, every part rejoices with it" (1 Cor. 12:25–26).

Koinonia recognizes a plurality of leadership and exercises the gifts of the spirit for the common good: "When you come together, everyone has a hymn or a word of instruction, a revelation, a tongue or an interpretation. All of these must be done for the strengthening of the church" (1 Cor. 14:26). Most naturally expressed in small, intimate groups, *koinonia* is where maximum participation of the people prevails.

The Koinonia *Worship Service*

Koinonia worship is uniquely a Pauline conception—I call it "Pauline worship." It is body-life worship in action. The church as a body was Paul's dominating, overarching metaphor.[8] Pauline churches were house churches of probably 30 to 50 people—small groups that allowed for participation. Today the trend is toward large churches. Even so, both small and large churches urgently need to facilitate body-life interaction.

A *koinonia* service may resemble a family get-together or even correspond to a TV talk show. It's more of a hands-on service. Today's *koinonia* service could even feature wireless, open-mike sharing from the congregation. But, as Craig Erickson explains, the intent is not just to create an informal, "folksy" feeling:

> The purpose of spontaneity is a very specific one: the edification of the church, the building up of Christ's body (1 Cor. 14:26). A true charism is given for the service of the community. It is bestowed in the interest of others. . . . All spontaneous involvement must flow from the Spirit's ministry to edify the church.[9]

The ministries of exhortation and admonition by individuals to the congregation ought to be valued. Spontaneous and prepared contributions should be encouraged. Chuck Smith Jr. notes, "The more people participate, the more likely a part of them will open up to God."[10] In *koinonia* worship, no one person tends to dominate; communication is more omnidirectional, with the Holy Spirit leading everyone.

There are many ways to obtain a sense of *koinonia* in services. A small group or Sunday school class could read the Scripture for the day. A family could quote the Scripture reading by memory, each member taking a verse. A responsive reading could be shared by everyone over thirty or under thirty years old. The pastor could ask a layperson, during an interview, to help illustrate his sermon.

One church collects short audio or video "thankfulness clips" of answers to prayer, which are played between worship songs or before a time of thanksgiving. Another church has a time of congregational sharing using a roving mike after communion.

During the baptism ceremony before individuals are immersed, a church can invite a close friend to come to the mike and say a word of affirmation: "Susie, I have seen firsthand your love for Jesus Christ and for your family, and your faithful witness at work. The fruits of the Spirit are so evident in your life. I believe you are ready to take this step of baptism." Powerful!

Various kinds of "ministry time" have developed. Some churches invite the people to come to the front for prayer in the middle of the service while everyone continues to sing. A pastor comments: "Apart from the sermon, it is the single most significant thing that happens in our morning worship service. Ministry time is different from an 'altar call.' There is a process that goes on. There is a sharing of the need—a finding out of the need, before the praying and laying on of hands by the team member(s). The ministry team becomes involved. There are other benefits to our service from 'ministry time.' On the pastor's side, it breaks down the 'Thou-I' distinction between the pulpit and the people. It allows for a body feeling in the service. On the people's side it allows an opportunity for a one-on-one encounter. Most importantly, it has strengthened the faith of our entire congregation as our people have seen God work in answer to prayer."

At the Church on the Way, a mega church of over 10,000 in Van Nuys, California, during ministry time the people divide into small circles of three or four to pray for one another during the middle of the service for five to ten minutes. The leader's instructions in framing the event are critical: "We not only call upon the Lord, we expect him to do something in your life. We want you to know his love and power to you and through you."[11] He then encourages everyone to divide into groups of three or four, share prayer requests, hurts, and needs, and he quotes some prayer promises from the Word. He asks that no one be left out. To those too frightened to pray he says, "Just join in silently, but if you do, join in with your heart." Everyone is encouraged to hold hands while praying and to give heartfelt embraces afterward, thus showing mutual support. Jack Hayford, formerly pastor of the Church on the Way, reports that the unchurched "like" this part of their service and "feel the concern of the local body for their hurt." During this time, he sees some crying and others enjoying the presence of God.[12]

A Lutheran pastor explains how a "healing service" was instituted in his church. Fearful that it might be perceived as "kooky," he prepared the way with an article in the church bulletin defining healing in a broad way (i.e., body, mind, and spirit). He related to me: "That first Sunday I preached a cautious sermon on how God heals in different ways, using the Greek word *soteria* (salvation-health) as the central thought. Then my assistant and I invited people to come forward to the altar railing for prayer. To my complete surprise, 95 percent of the 275 people present came forward! Our healing service is now one of our most popular services. A team of eight ministers and people invite their friends and neighbors. Total strangers have come forward. The service occurs regularly on the fifth Sunday of the month (four or five times a year), and we print a clarifying statement in the church bulletin for that day."

The above three examples of "ministry time" deserve our attention. Many of us live in densely populated cities, yet we feel so alone, especially in times of crisis. Ministry time addresses this lack.

Koinonia worship also intersects with evangelism. Recall Paul's words anticipating the visitor who is converted during a worship service:

> If an unbeliever or someone who does not understand comes in while everybody is prophesying, he will be *convinced by all* that he is a sinner and will be *judged by all,* and the secrets of his heart will be laid bare. So he will fall down and worship God, exclaiming, "God is really among you."
>
> 1 Corinthians 14:24–25

The unbeliever is "convinced by all" and "judged by all"—not the pastor's sermon. The body-life interaction and proclamation effects through the Spirit a remarkably deep work of conviction. "The secrets of his heart are disclosed" and he cries, "God is certainly among you" (NASB). It's a classic example of an unbeliever encountering God's presence during a "believer's worship service."

God's presence is compelling! Worship leader Marty Nystrom remarks: "I've never had anybody look me in the eye and say, 'You know, I've experienced the presence of God, and quite honestly, I don't want it.'" Chuck Smith Jr. shares:

> Not long ago, I began to ask myself, "Why don't we market our unique contribution to the community—that we help people find God? Are we afraid to make this promise?" . . . There's a huge vacuum in North America when it comes to spirituality. . . . People are realizing "there must be more to life."[13]

We need to reevaluate the belief that worship and seekers do not mix. (For help on inviting unbelievers into your worship service, see Sally Morgenthaler's *Worship Evangelism.*)[14]

In Paul's scenario, unbelievers not only experience God's presence, they encounter a community at worship. They see firsthand what a body of Christians looks like and how they relate and care for one another. That's pertinent today. A desire for community is high on the agenda of the unchurched.

In summary, *koinonia* worship tends to have: (1) a strong orientation to ministry to one another, (2) a less professional look, and may (3) involve small groups, (4) employ improvisational procedures, and (5) demonstrate a concern for being Spirit-directed. *Koinonia* worship is worship done *for* one another. A primary question the people ask is, "Did I give and receive ministry?"

Koinonia *Music*

How can *koinonia* be expressed musically? *Koinonia* music tends to be more congregational and more cohesive. *Koinonia* songs include: "Yes, We All Agree" (Tommy Walker), "Blest Be the Tie That Binds," and "In Christ There Is No East or West." *Koinonia* music comforts, promotes unity, and can even be provocative, like this hymn text, which employs a popular Ghana folk song melody:

Jesu, Jesu, fill us with your love,
show us how to serve the neighbors we have from you.

Neighbors are rich and poor, neighbors are black and white,
neighbors are near and far away.

These are the ones we should serve, these are the ones we should love, all these are neighbors to us and you.

Loving puts us on our knees, serving as though we are slaves,
this is the way we should live with you.

Thomas S. Colvin (words)[15]

Beyond specific examples of music, however, the act of music-making itself can be inherently *koinonian*. As music groups breathe together, build phrases, perform crescendos and rubatos, and blend their voices in harmony, such a collaboration of mind and spirit is required and such an intensity of listening and responding to each other is demanded that a baseline for *koinonia* experience is established. Furthermore, improvising in an ensemble—like a four-way telephone conversation—requires extreme sensitivity, because performers can easily "talk over" each other and clutter the texture, instead of waiting for the right moment to make "fills."

The reciprocal nature of such an ensemble relationship led James I. Packer to exclaim, "The best representation of New Testament *koinonia* I know of is New Orleans Jazz. Everybody gets a chance to solo, and when they come together—it's magic, a real oneness. Unity-in-diversity. No one person predominates."[16]

While *kerygma* communication may create a functional separation between the performer and the audience, *koinonia* bridges that gap, *bringing the performer functionally closer to the listener.* A leader may sing a verse and invite the people to sing the refrain. A performer may call for an antiphonal response. The leaders(s) may sway to the beat and invite the people to sway or link hands. A choir or brass group may be located in the audience and establish a connection by their presence there. The music itself may not have specific *koinonia* content, but the *structure* of the performance promotes and projects these values.

Leitourgia

With *leitourgia*[17] (to minister, serve, or worship), a group of individuals addresses the One in vertical praise and prayer. *Leitourgia* is used in reference to formal priestly service, ministry, or "liturgy" carried out by Moses, Zacharias, and Christ:

> He [Moses] sprinkled with the blood both the tabernacle and everything used in its *ceremonies.*
>
> Hebrews 9:21

> And it came about, when the days of his [Zacharias's] *priestly service* were ended, that he went back home.
>
> Luke 1:23 NASB

> But the *ministry* Jesus has received is as superior to theirs as the covenant of which he is mediator is superior to the old one, and it is founded on better promises.
>
> Hebrews 8:6

> We do have such a high priest [Christ], who sat down at the right hand of the throne of the Majesty in heaven, and who *serves* in the sanctuary, the true tabernacle.
>
> Hebrews 8:1–2

What Transpires during Worship Services

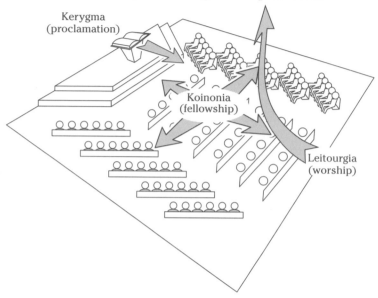

Of the three Greek words for worship, *leitourgia* is the most comprehensive and climactic. It is "the summit toward which the activity of the Church is directed. . . . For the goal of apostolic works is that all . . . should come together to praise God."[18] The most integrative of the three modes, *leitourgia* involves everyone, whereas *kerygma* especially activates specialized communicators, and *koinonia* galvanizes the people in "one-to-another" sharing. In a unique sense, *leitourgia* both includes and subsumes *kerygma* and *koinonia*.

Moreover, *leitourgia* is not limited to Sunday morning worship. *Leitourgia* expresses sacrificial service rendered by one person to another—a life of service—as in this case of Epaphroditus to Paul: "because he [Epaphroditus] almost died for the work of Christ, risking his life to make up for the *help [leitourgia]* you could not give me [Paul]" (Phil. 2:30). Sharing the gospel, supporting gospel work, entertaining strangers, and offering help to those with material needs are central to the Pauline emphasis on a total lifestyle of worship (Rom. 12:1).[19]

The Leitourgia *Worship Service*

In *leitourgia* the many address the One in prayer and praise as the people minister directly to God. The people want God; they wait on

172

God. There is reverence and there may be silence. They offer a costly response with their whole person. They have an active role—and not just musically.

In Acts the word *leitourgia* was used when the leaders of the church of Antioch were praying with Paul and Barnabas:

> While they were *worshiping* [ministering to] the Lord and fasting, the Holy Spirit said, "Set apart for me Barnabas and Saul for the work to which I have called them." So after they had *fasted* and *prayed,* they placed their hands on them and sent them off.
>
> Acts 13:2–3

Both fasting and prayer were involved. Peterson observes that the passage highlights prayer as a "priestly" activity in which all can participate.[20]

In *leitourgia* there may be prayers of confession, prayers of adoration, and guided prayers. Hands may be lifted, eyes may look up to God, and knees may bow before God. Multiple, corporate Scripture readings may be read by the people. Communion may be observed frequently.

When *leitourgia* involves a large group, more vision, more planning, more drama, more mystery, and more symbolism are required.[21] The worship in the Book of Revelation is the perfect example of this kind of worship. Whereas *kerygma* is done *to* the people, and *koinonia* is done *for* one another, *leitourgia* is primarily the response *by* the people to God. The primary question the people ask themselves is, Did I meet with God? Did I serve and minister to the Lord?

Leitourgia *Music*

Leitourgia music is directed to God. Congregational song receives priority. In our culture, hymns, gospel songs, and contemporary choruses are the musical mainstays. Joseph Gelineau expresses a powerful vision of *leitourgia* music: "[It is] music not necessarily new and surprising in its language, not necessarily too difficult to perform, but so suited to what it is celebrating that it would be an inexhaustible source of prayer, meaning and feeling."[22] What an evocative thought—a music that would be "an inexhaustible source of prayer, meaning and feeling"!

As for the choir and worship teams, in *kerygma* they are functionally separate from the congregation, whereas in *leitourgia* they join the congregation "as an indivisible part" of its praises.[23] In *leitourgia,* the choir is never just an elitist performance group (nor is it in true

173

kerygma). It is comprised of people spiritually prepared to worship. A primary purpose is to undergird and strengthen congregational singing by adding infectious visual support, volume, harmony, and by demonstrating new or unfamiliar hymns and choruses. Leitourgia choirs assist a cappella singing and perform dramatic Scripture readings. The choir assumes some of the functions of a worship team.

In *leitourgia,* the choir could be positioned at right angles to the congregation to the side of the pulpit or in the balcony. In *kergyma,* the choir is centered behind the pulpit to emphasize its declarative function. *Kerygma* is performer-oriented and emphasizes specialized groups. *Leitourgia* is participant-oriented and provides support for the congregation.

Blend All Three

The church's mission is to incarnate all three modes—*kerygma, koinonia, leitourgia*—"regularly, creatively, systematically, and carefully."[24] The "mix" of modes may change weekly, and activities in and outside the church can help address imbalances. However, we need to seek balance over a period of time. Preferably all three will function to some extent in every service.

A final suggestion. In our technological culture, worshipers have a strong appetite for change and variety. Take advantage of that. Introduce contrast to your services occasionally by generating a service that has a unique *kerygma, koinonia,* or *leitourgia* focus.

Summary of *Kerygma, Koinonia,* and *Leitourgia* Music

Kerygma Music	*Koinonia* Music	*Leitourgia* Music
proclaims God	communicates belonging	approaches and celebrates God
calls to faith	calls to love, care	calls to pray, praise
confronts	comforts, affirms	praises God
soloists, specialized group to congregation	semi- or nonspecialized group among congregation	both specialized group and congregation to God
hierarchical relationship	egalitarian relationship	integrative relationship
boldness	togetherness	jubilation
formal format	informal format	formal format

Kerygma Music	*Koinonia* Music	*Leitourgia* Music
people face forward	half or full circle	forward or circular
monodirectional	omnidirectional	bidirectional
one to many	one to another	many to God
one sings, all listen	all can sing, all listen	all sing, God listens
stylistically diverse (innovative)	stylistically relevant (midway)	stylistically familiar (learnable)
low replicability	medium replicability	high replicability
performer and listener separate	performer and listener merged	performer and listener combined
performer oriented	relationship oriented	participant oriented
proclaiming God to all	singing to one another	singing to God
"A Mighty Fortress Is Our God," "These Things are True of You,"	"Yes, We All Agree," "Make Us One," "I Have Decided to Follow Jesus,"	"Shout to the Lord," "O God, Our Help in Ages Past," "I Stand in Awe of You,"
"We Declare Your Majesty," "Our God Reigns," "I Know Whom I Have Believed"	"In Christ There Is No East or West," "Spirit Song," "Blest Be the Tie That Binds"	"All Hail the Power of Jesus' Name," "Be Thou My Vision"

And this is the happy life, to rejoice to Thee, of Thee, for Thee: this is it, and there is no other.

Augustine

Questions for Reflection and Discussion

1. Does your form of worship model the purposes of the church?
2. How could you better convey a sense of *koinonia?*
3. What's your position on worship versus evangelism?
4. What about the use of soloists and specialized groups?
5. Is *leitourgia* worship the most comprehensive and integrative of the modes? Explain.

RESOLVING TENSIONS
OVER MUSICAL STYLE: PETER

Why is the church so reluctant to enjoy the rich variety of style, vocabulary, process, shape and medium that issues from every quarter of the globe?

Harold M. Best, *Music through the Eyes of Faith*

The greatest revolution in the modern-day church is erupting in the area of worship.[1] Around the world, churches are grappling with what is "proper" in worship. Pastors I've talked with insist that music is the major, divisive issue. Music uniquely brings the issues of cultural change to a head.[2] This chapter and the one following are devoted to reducing divisiveness over music style.

The Divisiveness of Musical Style

Why is the issue of music style so divisive? First, we all have preferences, which is not a problem; however, we all too often *think of our own interests first.* This reveals several truths about us: (1) we are entertainment oriented; (2) we are not mature; (3) we are not willing to die to self; (4) we don't ask the primary questions: Is the mission of the church being well served by this music? Does it advance the kingdom?

Second, we *listen* to sermons, but we *perform* hymns and choruses. Because we are personally involved—including our bodies and even our self-identity—we are more sensitive. We want the music at our church to suit our temperament, our self-image.

Third, *music is a language*—another cause for divisiveness. We understand some music languages better than others. Through repeated exposures, we learn the nuances of certain styles and experience exquisitely rich pleasures. We want those pleasures! When we are young, our lack of perspective frequently makes us intolerant of anything not contemporary. As we become older, we grow less open to acquiring new musical languages.

Fourth, *music triggers associations.* Music has the ability to set our emotions vibrating, to stir memories, and to awaken guilty consciences. A saxophone may evoke a dance floor or New Age music. Rap music may suggest mind-numbing ghetto blasters. A hymn may trigger a longing for a departed loved one, or—boredom!

Fifth, *we are conditioned to have our favorite music whenever we want it.* At home or in our car, we pop in our favorite CD or dial in our favorite radio station and tap our feet to "our kind of music." In LA we have more than eighty radio stations! To survive, each caters to a narrow niche market. The same style—rock, country, classical, whatever—is played twenty-four hours a day.

But the attitude that we should be able to have our kind of music whenever we want it is *disastrous* when applied to the church. In the church we have both the young and the old, and people with different cultural backgrounds—churches are meant to be intergenerational and inclusive. The tendency to want to have our way all the time must be resisted.

Sixth, and more deeply, *music carries forward traditions.* To tamper with these traditions is to stir up values close to the heart.

When Traditions Are in Transition

When we read the Book of Acts, we become conscious of the early church wrestling with culture. The church was being transformed from a Jewish phenomenon into a supranational body, and this was not at all easy. At first there were mighty miracles and incredible responses to preaching; but as we follow the church's development, we see objections arise and issues becoming more complex, not amenable to simple solutions. This is the life we know so well in contemporary churches. I am convinced, however, that if we could apply the biblical principles found in this and the next chapter, much of the infighting we experience relative to music style would dissipate.

"Much" but not all! Music style is relative (I'll support that later), not absolute, and until Jesus returns, people will argue the merits of one style over another. No one universal music style exists. The music of distant cultures can be as meaningless to us as ours is to them. But we can work on and improve our attitude and understanding.

Music style, in my opinion, falls in the area Paul calls "disputable matters." Concerning these matters, he says, "Each one should be fully convinced in his own mind" (Rom. 14:5). Admittedly, we are forging into difficult water. All I ask is that you give this chapter and the next one a fair hearing.

I now invite you to feel Acts 2, 10, and 15 unfolding as a unit. See connections that can be related to music style. See real people coping and, under the inspiration of the Holy Spirit, learning to grow through live confrontations into *sensitive, nurturing individuals.* These individuals are totally inspiring. The early church underwent enormous change, and we can learn from them. Intolerance and entrenchment do not characterize their behavior.

The Case for Diversity

In Acts 2, "tongues of fire" descend on the disciples in the upper room and the Holy Spirit is outpoured—the harbinger of the "church of the nations," the contemporary church in full bloom. From this outpouring, we can learn something about the acceptability of *a Pentecost of music styles:*

When the day of Pentecost came, they were all together in one place. Suddenly a sound like the blowing of a violent wind came from heaven and filled the whole house where they were sitting. They saw what seemed to be tongues of fire that separated and came to rest on each of them [on their heads?]. All of them [the 12 apostles or 120 disciples?] were filled with the Holy Spirit and began to speak in other tongues as the Spirit enabled them.

Now there were staying in Jerusalem God-fearing Jews [note: only Jews] from every nation under heaven. When they heard this sound, a crowd came together in bewilderment, because each one heard them speaking in his own language. Utterly amazed, they asked: ". . . how is it that each of us hears them in his own native language [dialect]? Parthians, Medes; . . . residents of . . . Asia, . . . Egypt . . . Libya; . . . visitors from Rome; . . . Cretans and Arabs—we hear them declaring the wonders of God in our own tongues!"

Amazed and perplexed, they asked one another, "What does this mean?"

Acts 2:1–12

Luke reports that the gospel was preached in many native languages; he cites more than a dozen locations. This stunning passage has important ramifications for music and worship, often overlooked, that I want to develop.[3]

Here is my key point. *Many languages inevitably means many musics.* If a multilingual approach for propagating the gospel is revealed as normative, then *multistylistic music languages* must necessarily follow as inevitable.

Let me explain. Musical style is tied to language.[4] Music *tracks* language, even the syntactic and tonal patterns of language. The rhythms embedded in individual words, the pitch patterns in which people talk, the pitch glides in speech indicating surprise or disappointment—all these are absorbed by composers. They are captured and become meaningful parts of musical expression. Inescapably, the feel of each dialect and culture becomes patterned in indigenous music.

If you listen carefully to instrumental music, like the Blues for example, you can "hear" African Americans talking in the music itself, irrespective of the words. The melodies and rhythms mirror the way black speech inflections are uttered in everyday life.

Again, my point. If we accept that the gospel can be preached in any spoken language, then we must also accept that it will eventually be preached through any music. Another implication follows: Local musical dialects should not be despised. Expressions of Nashville "country music," for example, should be allowed in churches where that musical dialect pervades local culture, just as much as a southern drawl or a Bostonian accent should be accepted in the pulpit.

A Limited Vision

A curious development follows Peter's sermon, though. The release of the Spirit is not perceived as being for Gentiles. Only a worldwide harvesting of Jews is imagined (Acts 11). When Peter speaks of the promise of the Spirit being for "all who are *far off*" (Acts 2:39), it's interpreted to mean *Jews* living in far-off lands, not Gentiles.[5] In other words, for the time being, Acts 2 is a Pentecost for the Jewish world, as Acts 10 and 11 make clear.

Have you ever wondered, Why did the Holy Spirit descend with tongues of fire? Why the different languages? It wasn't because the Jews present did not share a common language. They all knew Greek, for Peter later addresses the crowd in one language (Acts 2:14). The speaking in different tongues, however, made the event *relevant and personal, culturally.* They heard the gospel personally in their very own dialect.

With our twenty-first-century hindsight, we now see the fuller picture of Acts 2—God was initiating a brand-new direction for both Jews and Gentiles. Symbolically, through the image of the tongues of fire, he was inaugurating a plan whereby the good news would be intelligibly imparted in a personal way, worldwide, through a multitongued witness. Inevitably, in the course of time, this would mean the development of a multitongued linguistic and musical witness surrounding the globe. But they didn't get it!

Pentecost for Gentiles

Then, suddenly, a remarkable Pentecost for Gentiles occurs![6] The story of Acts 10 and 11 begins with Cornelius, a nonkosher, God-fearing Gentile, who receives a vision from God instructing him to send for Peter. So he dispatches three men who arrive the instant that Peter receives a vision (the sheet of nonkosher foods). Note that Peter puts them up for the night—a taboo action for Jews. Then he leaves the next morning with six Jewish Christian companions for the house of Cornelius, where a large gathering of Gentiles is waiting to hear him preach a salvation message. While Peter proclaims the gospel, the Spirit comes on them the same way he did on the apostles. Peter stays at Cornelius's home a few days. The news soon reaches the Jerusalem church, whose members *criticize* Peter and demand to know why he went into a house of uncircumcised Gentiles and ate with them.

Now let's back up for the crucial details and some applications. Peter goes on the roof to pray at noon, becomes hungry, and falls into a trance. A sheet comes down from heaven with nonkosher animals, reptiles, and birds. A voice—not once but three times—urges Peter to eat:

"Get up, Peter. Kill and eat."

"Surely not, Lord!" Peter replied. "I have never eaten anything impure or unclean."

The voice spoke to him a second time, "Do not call anything impure that God has made clean."

Acts 10:13–15

Note the insistence of God's voice. God does not say, "You *may* eat," but "EAT!" It's a command. How unready Peter is to hear this! It goes against his conscience and fourteen hundred years of ingrained habit, tradition, and training. I don't think we have sufficiently appreciated how difficult this confrontation was for Peter. Tradition is difficult for anybody to change, in Peter's time or ours. The tension he felt is extremely similar to the tensions and insecurities musicians face in adapting to new music styles.

For just as there are varieties of foods, there are varieties of music styles. Some styles can be as difficult for us to accept and may feel as "foreign" and "wrong" to us as the foods did to Peter. This is a broad statement, and, admittedly, one difference between us and Peter needs noting: Peter was *commanded* to eat.

But just as no foods were to be unclean for Peter, so for us (theoretically) no music styles need be unacceptable. I'm convinced this is the place to begin. Other aspects are important too—the intelligibility of the style, the associations the music has, and its appropriateness for a given local church. Nevertheless, we should begin with the thought that no melody, scale, chord, rhythm, instrument, or timbre should be theoretically off-limits to the Christian composer.

Accepting People

Until the sheet with the foods descends in Acts 10, Peter works on the assumption that he should not associate, eat, or visit with Gentiles.[7] To do so would be scandalous conduct for a spiritual leader—especially an apostle. But notice the "leap" that transpires in Peter's thinking when he processes the meaning of the descended sheet. For Peter the issue is not only eating nonkosher foods, but more fundamentally and deeply it is *accepting the Gentiles as equals*. And that is the fundamental issue we need to consider relative to musical style.

The issue of style involves not only music but, more importantly, *accepting people*. Listen as Peter addresses the crowd at Cornelius's home:

You are well aware that it is against our law for a Jew to associate with a Gentile or visit him. But God has shown me that I should not

182

call any *man* impure or unclean [the issue is larger than food]. So when I was sent for, I came without raising any objection. . . . I now realize how true it is that *God does not show favoritism but accepts men from every nation* who fear him and do what is right.

Acts 10:28–29, 34–35

Who Underwent the Greater Conversion?

Peter's amazing transformation causes professor Harold Dollar (Biola University) to ask who underwent the greater "conversion" experience—Peter or Cornelius? The central challenge, he argues, was "not the reluctance of the Gentiles to respond to the gospel, but the reluctance of the Jews to preach to them."[8] It is Peter who must change his standards; it is Peter who is forced to go to the home of Cornelius.

Peter's reaction makes him an incredible model for all leaders. He was not concerned about his own preferences; he was concerned with ministry to others, and that involved theological and cultural change as well as accepting others at a deep level.

Analysis may prove that the experienced, trained musician (or any older adults), like Peter, may undergo far more trauma during change than the young people. A radical "conversion" or reorientation may be necessary.

Also, when we reject a person's music style, there is a danger that we may reject the person. Educated musicians, like myself, the musical elite, often look down on certain styles as unworthy. We do not want to be identified with them.[9] We make fun of them.

I know firsthand what it feels like to be rejected musically and (consequently) personally. I once attempted to improvise alongside some young people in a style that was unfamiliar to me. It was obvious to everyone (including myself) that stylistically I was out of sync. I had underestimated the difficulty. The result? I was ostracized by the group. Now I'm glad I experienced that feeling!

The opposite has also occurred. There have been other times when I've had to set my preferences aside and get on my hands and knees and humbly work with people with limited skills who liked music I considered trite. Feeling something like Peter in Galatians, I said to myself, "I hope my professorial colleagues don't catch me doing this. It could be embarrassing."[10] It's like playing something that doesn't suit your image. Or it's like Peter objecting, "Surely not, Lord! Nothing impure or unclean has ever entered my mouth" (Acts 11:8).

If we are to engage in renewal and reconciliation, we must make contact with people and their styles (like the early church) and be willing to risk a little embarrassment. Best echoes similar thoughts:

> We must learn to move from anger and frustration to an attitude of redemption, nurturing, and helpful intrusion, even when we are in the presence of a musical rip-off, crass commercialism, and exploitation. And in the presence of those who make music haltingly and fearfully, we must show the spirit of the one described by Isaiah as never breaking a bruised reed or extinguishing a dimly burning wick (Isa. 42:3). . . . [We must learn that] love for them precedes the music they make, no matter how bad or good it is.[11]

We must accept people where they are. Only then can we learn from one another and take the next step together.

The Prohibition Prevented Intimacy

Peter is totally honest. He had thought of the Gentiles as tainted, due to their dietary habits. Observe too the astonishment of the six Jewish Christians present when the gift of the Holy Spirit is poured out "even" on the Gentiles (Acts 10:45). As for the Jewish Christians in Jerusalem, the revolutionary thought that forgiveness of sins might extend to the Gentiles is accepted only after Peter confirms that the same signs manifested in Acts 2 were duplicated at the house of Cornelius (11:18). In his defense, Peter says, "So if God gave them the same gift [the Holy Spirit] as he gave us . . . who was I to think that I could oppose God?" (v. 17).

For Jews, eating with Gentiles was prohibited. It meant risking defilement. (Isn't that how some Christians look at some forms of contemporary music—as music that defiles!) Eating meant compromising; it meant accepting Gentiles who, because of their unclean practices, were regarded as *inferior*. The prohibition on eating together *prevented intimacy*.

Moreover, to provide lodging for Cornelius's men, as Peter does (10:23), was contrary to Jewish practice. It could be construed as fraternizing, taking a first step toward accepting them—the "slippery slope" theory. But for Peter to go further and actually stay at Cornelius's house for several more days and eat with him (10:48)—an unambiguously clear infraction—*that* required some explaining to the Jewish Christians in Jerusalem—even from the head apostle—because through that extended contact he must have become ceremonially unclean (11:2–3).

The Cherry-Red Guitar

Two applications arise from this section of Peter's story. First, if you have problems communicating with someone, consider inviting that person to your home. When Peter stayed on at Cornelius's house, it undoubtedly deepened their friendship.

Second, when I have been involved in bringing changes in worship, I have often found it necessary to be a go-between like Peter. In one case, before we introduced a bass guitar into the morning service, I informed a few elderly members, anticipating they might have objections: "In a few weeks we plan to introduce a bass guitar during the singing. I wanted you to know ahead of time. I'll get back to you. Tell me if it contributes to your worship."

When I saw the young man's guitar, I was worried. It had a shapely, cherry-red, sensuous look! I knew its appearance alone would cause a major distraction in this conservative church and we'd lose the day. So I had several of us play at low volume where we would not be readily seen—off to the side of the front row.

The day we ministered, the worship improved. The young people hadn't been singing, but the pastor (surprised) told me, "As soon as they heard the bass guitar, they started singing." Interesting!

I went back to my elderly friends. "What did you think of the bass?" I inquired. "Oh, did it happen today?" they responded. "We didn't notice, but thanks for asking!" I was greatly relieved and found out later how much they appreciated my informing them beforehand. They became allies in subsequent changes.

Antioch at the Cutting Edge

The Christian Jews, however, were not quick to share their faith with Gentiles. Gentiles, other than those at Cornelius's house, first came to hear the gospel in the following way.

Some time after Acts 10, a wave of persecution hit Jerusalem and scattered Jewish Christians across the sea. These believers preached the gospel there to Jews *only* (Acts 11:19). Some, however, came back from Cyprus and Libya (northern Africa) to the Gentile city of Antioch and began to preach to *Gentiles* there. When the Jewish Christians in

Jerusalem heard about this, they sent Barnabas to investigate this new ministry phenomenon. Fortunately, he not only put his blessing on it, but he stayed to nurture it, seeking out Paul's assistance. Amazing! Clearly the cutting edge of ministry was now abroad, not at Jerusalem. But, happily, the parent church (Jerusalem) and the outlying church (Antioch) were able to maintain cordial relations.

How could this apply to music? Changes in music style are not likely to occur as easily in established churches, where traditions are well ingrained, as in younger churches, where traditions are just beginning to develop.

Jerusalem Council Decision

We must remember that the voice commanded Peter to eat all the foods—*against his conscience!* Why? Peter is, in God's sovereignty, a model for us all, and his actions point to the direction God wants us to go today. The radical shift is confirmed by Paul's teaching:

> Everything God created is good, and nothing is to be rejected if it is received with thanksgiving, because it is consecrated by the word of God and prayer.
>
> 1 Timothy 4:4–5

> To the pure, all things are pure, but to those who are corrupted and do not believe, nothing is pure.
>
> Titus 1:15

As the church set out to implement these principles of freedom to eat and of impartiality to all peoples, it encountered problems. A major problem was Jews who attempted to impose circumcision on everyone (including Gentiles) as a condition for salvation:

> Some men came down from Judea to Antioch and were teaching the brothers: "Unless you are circumcised, according to the custom taught by Moses, you *cannot* be saved." This brought Paul and Barnabas into sharp dispute and debate with them. So Paul and Barnabas were appointed, along with some other believers, to go up to Jerusalem to see the apostles and elders about this question.
>
> Acts 15:1–2

The epoch-making Jerusalem Council convened and ruled *against* mandating circumcision for salvation: "We should not make it difficult for the Gentiles who are turning to God" (v. 19). The critical passage of a letter they sent back to the Antioch church reads:

> It seemed good to the Holy Spirit and to us *not to burden you* with anything beyond the following requirements: You are to abstain from food sacrificed to idols, from blood, from the meat of strangled animals and from sexual immorality.
>
> Acts 15:28–29

Consider the gracious responses by Peter, James, and Paul to the Gentiles:

- "we should not make it difficult" (v. 19)
- "[we should] not . . . burden you" (v. 28)
- "[we should not put on your necks] a yoke" (v. 10)

Peter frames the question in theological terms, for he mentions "faith" (v. 9) and "grace" (v. 11), whereas James emphasizes the cultural dimension (vv. 19–21). Both the theological and the cultural are important. There *was* a theological problem with circumcision as a condition for salvation because it undercut the free working of grace apart from works. And from a cultural standpoint, requiring the Gentiles to be circumcised would have caused them to undergo a nonessential, painful ritual that could have inhibited the unfettered dissemination of the good news, burdening the gospel.

Application: Do we require non-Christians to go through a "cultural circumcision" by the way we conduct worship? On nonessentials like music style, there should be no mandatory requirements. There is no one "sacred" style. Forcing a style on people is not the New Testament pattern. Even the singing of hymns, though perhaps a wise use of resources, cannot be mandated. In some cultures, Western hymns could be burdensome.

Summary of Concerns

This chapter has addressed a number of questions that deserve honest examination. Do we accept the idea of a Pentecost of musical styles? Do we denigrate local cultures, local styles? When we reject a person's style, do we also reject the person? Are we willing to undergo transformation and admit our shortcomings as Peter did? Have we imposed stylistic burdens (standards) that have impeded the gospel?[12] I leave this chapter to your conscience.

> *If healthy change is to come to a culture, it must be guided by those who are identified with it, who love it and understand it. Actually, only they are really qualified to evaluate it.*
>
> Donald P. Hustad, *Jubilate II*

Questions for Reflection and Discussion

1. Discuss: If a multilingual approach to propagating the gospel is normative, then a Pentecost of music styles should be accepted as inevitable.
2. When we reject a person's musical style, do we in effect reject the person?
3. Do trained musicians and adults undergo greater strain during change than young people?
4. Why is the issue of music style so divisive?

STYLE

THIRTEEN

RESOLVING TENSIONS OVER MUSICAL STYLE: PAUL

Accept him whose faith is weak, without passing judgment on disputable matters. . . . Each one should be fully convinced in his own mind. . . . why do you judge your brother? Or why do you look down on your brother?

Romans 14:1, 5, 10

The rapid expansion of the faith presented Gentile Christians with serious problems. People were asking if it was proper for believers to eat meat offered to idols. Just as we saw in the last chapter that Peter was a key figure God used to effect change, so now we will look at Paul as the "point man." He responds with this general principle: "Do not violate your conscience." Paul's principle is founded on the belief, as investigated in the previous chapter, that the eating of all foods is permissible.

Paul's Advice

Dialoguing with Paul, some Christians asked a question that troubled their conscience: "When we sit down to eat at someone's home, what if we are *not sure* whether the meat on our plates was offered to idols? Should we ask our hosts?" Paul advises them not to ask that question:

Someone who is not a believer may invite you to eat with him. . . . Eat anything that is put before you. *Do not ask questions* to see if it is something you think might be wrong to eat. But if anyone [any weak Christian or non-Christian?] says to you, "That food was offered to idols," then do not eat it . . . because it would be something that might be thought wrong. I don't mean that you think it is wrong. But the other person might think it is wrong.

1 Corinthians 10:27–29 ICB

But if anyone regards something as unclean, then for him it is unclean.

Romans 14:14

Until now, some people have had the habit of worshiping idols. So now when they eat meat, they still feel as if it belongs to an idol. They are not sure it is right to eat this meat. When they eat it, they feel guilty. But food will not make us closer to God. Refusing to eat does not make us less pleasing to God. And eating does not make us better in God's sight.

1 Corinthians 8:7–8 ICB

How could these verses relate to musical style? If we substituted "musical style" for "meat" in the above passage, the following loose paraphrase could result: Listen to any musical style in the marketplace without raising questions of conscience.[1] But if someone regards a music style as unclean, then for him it is unclean. When he listens to it, he feels guilty.

Another implication might be: If you like a certain melody, don't ask if a nonbeliever, a homosexual, or an adulterer composed it. If you love a certain rhythm, don't ask if it is a dance step. Don't share information with others that could cause problems of conscience.

I did a foolish thing that I sort of slipped into. I shared with a believer that a popular Christian song we sing at church was actually composed by a non-Christian, a Jewish musician who plied his gifts in a very intelligent manner.

This is how it happened. Several years ago the Jewish musician confided in a Hollywood studio-musician friend of mine that he was interested in writing Christian music. So my friend said, "Come to my church!" He came, hung around the lobby listening to how evangelicals talk, and based on what he heard, eventually published worship songs. He's made a good living.

When I told the believer this, he became troubled and later said the association of the song with the Jewish composer had tainted its value for him. On reflection, the root of the incident became crystal clear to me, and it was distressing. The piece was still good, but through engaging in gossip, I had diminished its value.

Consider a compelling point along this line. Remember the story behind the hymn "It Is Well with My Soul" in chapter 1? You'll recall that Horatio Spafford wrote the text close to the time that his four daughters died—when the *Lochearn* sank.

What I *didn't* tell you was that Spafford later had a mental disturbance "which prompted him to go to Jerusalem under the strange delusion that he was the second Messiah."[2] I wouldn't suggest you tell your congregation this part of the story! It could destroy a tremendous hymn. It turns out that Paul's ancient advice, "Don't ask," is radiant with contemporary wisdom.

Accept the Weak

Paul differentiates between the "weak" and the "strong." He advises us to treat the weak with sensitivity and he also asks the weak not to judge the strong:

> Accept him *whose faith is weak,* without passing judgment on disputable matters. . . . The man who eats everything must not look down on ["regard with contempt" NASB] him who does not, and the man who does not eat everything must not condemn the man who does, for God has accepted him.
>
> Romans 14:1, 3

The weak group described above is different from the Judaizers. *They do not wish to impose their views on others.* Rather, they want to continue on culturally as before, observing dietary restrictions and keeping the Sabbath and special days—doing the traditional things they have always done. These cultural, Christian Jews, says Paul, need acceptance too and should not be looked down on for *not* acting on the freedom they have in Christ. Paul looks evenhandedly at both the "weak" and the "strong" in disputable matters, attempting to avoid attitudes of snobbery and exclusivity.

Application: What about the people in your church who by personality are conservative and want to keep things as they have been? Shouldn't they also be treated with respect? How do you reconcile

191

these two groups—the front-runners and traditionalists, which are present in every church to some degree?

All of us are progressive in some areas and conservative in others, aren't we? Take the practice of raising hands in worship. Publicly I tend to be hesitant, though I firmly believe in its value. Isn't Paul saying by analogy that the strong (who feel free to raise their hands) should not look down on the weak (who don't)? Conversely, the weak should not condemn the strong by labeling them as fanatics.[3]

Biblical teaching relative to cultural practices is not simplistic, it's sophisticated! Scripture tolerates inconsistencies in people: Something might be right for one person and wrong for another. Fee states: "There is no objective 'uncleanness' to anything external or material," but Paul "admits to 'subjective uncleanness' to those who consider it so."[4] Thus, though Paul demonstrates sensitivity, theologically he "cuts the very ground from underneath the weak."[5]

Even though, theologically, he demolishes the argument of the weak, Paul is committed to nurturing and caring for them. He's concerned about wounding a weak conscience (1 Cor. 8:12). For some, music can dredge up feelings of remorse and memories of past sins. When a musical style has the potential to inflict hurt, cause guilt, or threaten a person's spiritual progress, we can't excuse ourselves. We must demonstrate sensitivity:

> Be careful, however, that the exercise of your freedom does not become a stumbling block to the weak.
>
> 1 Corinthians 8:9

> It is wrong for a man to eat anything that causes someone else to stumble.
>
> Romans 14:20

> Do not cause anyone to stumble. . . . I try to please everybody in every way. For I am not seeking my own good but the good of many.
>
> 1 Corinthians 10:32–33

If Paul suspects his liberty may cause his brother to stumble, he will not eat. Nor will he flaunt his freedom verbally before his weaker brother: "Whatever you believe about these things keep between yourself and God" (Rom. 14:22). That is a demonstration of Christian sensitivity!

The Only Solution

Due to the large amount of space Paul devotes to "matters of conscience," he obviously believes that sound teaching on the subject is imperative. He identifies himself with the strong, explicitly stating, "we who are strong" (Rom. 15:1). To be strong in the full sense of the word for Paul means to be able to eat all meats, yet be willing to set aside one's freedoms and preferences for the sake of one's brother or sister. Paul would like everyone to be "strong."

Several probing questions come to mind here. Do you desire to be one of the strong? Have you prayed to be one of the strong? Don't church musicians have a responsibility to teach people to be strong in the area of musical style?—some things to think about.

Paul underscores the point of view of the strong because that is what all of us should work toward:

- "Eat anything sold in the meat market" (1 Cor. 10:25).
- "Eat whatever is put before you" (1 Cor. 10:27).
- "Everything God created is good, and nothing is to be rejected if it is received with thanksgiving" (1 Tim. 4:4).
- "I am fully convinced that no food is unclean in itself" (Rom. 14:14).

Teaching the entire church to be strong (as far as I can see) is the only long-range answer to reconciling the traditionalists and the front-runners. But the process cannot be forced: "Each one should be fully convinced in his own mind" (Rom. 14:5).

Biblical Arguments for Diversity

I take the position that the Bible encourages Christians to be open to a diversity of materials. Through biblical precedent, the case for variety (in music materials) can be argued at least six ways:

1. The created order displays immense variety.
2. The Psalm texts manifest enormous stylistic diversity.
3. The early church employed a variety of materials—psalms, hymns, and spiritual songs.

193

4. The tongues of fire at Pentecost indicate that a*ll languages* (and inevitably, all music styles) can propagate the gospel.
5. The descended sheet reveals *all foods* and peoples are clean.
6. The eating of meat offered to idols teaches that bad associations (i.e., meat with idolatry) don't spoil the goodness of the materials.

Let's enlarge on the last three points. My guess is that most readers will agree that the presence of many languages logically leads to the concept of many music styles (point 4). Similarly, in Scripture the vision of the sheet (point 5) is dynamic, beginning as a food issue but ending with the acceptance of all peoples without discrimination. The extension I make here is that nonacceptance of ethnic or regional preferences in musical styles is also a form of nonacceptance and discrimination. For some, however, the music-meat analogy (point 6) may seem "thin." I see it as addressing the issue of bad associations, a central issue relative to music. It is a judgment call, and you have to decide if I've overstepped the bounds—neither Peter nor Paul make specific reference to music. In fact the way Paul argues his position and cites Christian principles guiding his response is probably more important to us today than the actual questions.

At the same time, if we accept the meat-music analogy as having relevance, we must discern its limitations. Listening to music is a more complex issue than eating meat.[6] For instance, meat sits on your plate; you decide whether or not to eat it. In a church setting, however, music is wafted in the air for all to hear. All *must* partake; we don't have earlids!

Remember what Paul said: "I am fully convinced that no food is unclean in itself" (Rom. 14:14). This raises a similar question on which learned musicians disagree: "Are the materials of music style morally neutral?"[7] I'm guessing that most people would view the structure and syntax of spoken languages (for example, Japanese or German) as morally neutral. Are music languages and musical materials (apart from words) also morally neutral? Is the musical syntax of jazz, raga, or rock music debased or neutral? With this lead-in, consider the words of Jesus:

Don't you see that nothing that enters a man from the outside can make him "unclean"? . . . What comes out of a man is what makes

194

him "unclean." For from *within,* out of men's *hearts,* come evil thoughts, sexual immorality, theft, murder, adultery, greed, malice. . . . All these evils come from inside and make a man "unclean."

Mark 7:18, 20–23

Consider Christ's emphasis on the words *within* and *hearts.* To loosely paraphrase the paragraph relative to musical style: Jesus says, "It's not the style itself that is so bad that it needs to be obliterated from the face of the earth. It's what's within our hearts that is so persistently sinful."

An Alternative View

Committed, intelligent Christians disagree strongly on these matters. Christian music professor Calvin Johansson, for example, has views very different from mine and those of Harold Best, with whom I share much in common. For example, I believe in the Bible as the authoritative Word of God and in theological absolutes but hold that art and aesthetics (including musical style) are relative. Not so Calvin Johansson:

Christians have been influenced . . . into believing there are no divine imperatives, no aesthetic absolutes or standards.[8]

Theists must be objectivists through and through. . . . All worthy art is based on God-given aesthetic principles that are laid down in creation and are cross-cultural and timeless.[9]

When music [without words] is believed to be theologically neutral, there is no compulsion to make the best music.[10]

While a C major chord [is] quite neutral, put together within a framework of like grammatical elements, [it] emerges as an entity with a point of view.[11]

Moreover, Johansson strongly questions the use of pop and rock music styles in Christian worship, believing notes, harmonies, and rhythms—note carefully, he is not talking about lyrics—can express a moral ethos and worldview:

The adoption and adaptation of secular music does not fulfill church music's overall purpose because it is incapable of doing so.[12]

195

Pop, by whatever its name, is hedonistic. . . . It seems absolutely imperative to conclude that to use pop music as a medium for the gospel message is wrong. . . .[13]

Pop music is concerned with quality, material profit, novelty, ease of consumption, success first of all, romanticism, mediocrity, sensationalism, and transience.[14]

The music of rock supports the repudiation of biblical standards by using combinations of sounds which are violent, mind-numbing, vulgar, raw, mesmerizing, rebellious, grossly repetitive, uncreative, undisciplined, and chaotic sounding. If listeners do not hear these things, it is because rock has dulled their aesthetic sensibilities.[15]

The reason the music [i.e., rock] has largely gone unchallenged is the subjective notion that the notes, harmony, and rhythm of such songs contain no worldview, moral ethos, or life outlook.[16]

In opposition to Calvin Johansson, but in agreement with David Pass, I take the view that even if a form is abused, it should not invalidate its use by others.[17] When people do bad things with a form or style, it shouldn't prevent Christians from doing good things with it. Pass contends, "Whatever style of music communicates the gospel boldly and clearly according to convergences of person, group, culture, and historical moment is acceptable."[18] Paul shares his own reasoning for *kerygma:* "that by all possible means" some might be saved. Culturally, Paul is conciliatory: "To the Jews I became like a Jew. . . . To those not having the law I became like one not having the law. . . . To the weak I became weak. . . . I have become all things to all men so that by all possible means I might save some" (1 Cor. 9:20–22).

To translate this to music style, it means that if I had the ability, I might play some Mozartian riffs to the classically oriented, crushed thirds and open-string fourths in the right hand to the country music fan, and raga pitch components (e.g., C-E-F$^\sharp$-G-B) to my Asian Indian or Turkish friends. I would play each style to the very best of my ability, appreciating the excellence that can be coaxed out of each one. In other words, we should learn to appreciate the diverse tastes within our cities and congregations and nudge ourselves toward becoming "world" Christian citizens stylistically. Moreover, hopefully we will not be merely adapting to culture but transforming it.

Along this vein, David Swanger, who has studied the process of making moral and aesthetic judgments, says there are parallels between judging moral issues and works of art. That's provocative, says Pass: "We tend to equate a certain music style with a certain morality and then pass off our aesthetic judgments as moral judgments."[19]

Calvin Johansson, however, believes that morality and music style, in fact, are intertwined:

> . . . the music [of rock] will have its lewd say regardless of text. . . . the church has naively and simplistically split asunder the medium (music) and message (text). Some Christians have embraced the music of rock (or a derived version of it) while disavowing the texts! In fact, such a split is not feasible.[20]

He advocates the need for leanness, austerity, and temperance in church music. Though his views are not in popular favor, we do well to give him a fair hearing:

> The gospel's penchant for the narrow way, the hard way, and the disciplined way, shows the need for a music which analogically and symbolically expresses these things.[21]

> In church music, rhythm is not as disciplined as it ought to be when it imparts a sense of jolly toe-tapping and swing . . . [it] takes away from the text . . . attention is riveted to fleshly response. . . .[22]

> Harmony which is lean, sparse, and rather austere is a more disciplined harmony than the lavish and rich harmonies of the super-romantics, the sweetish supper club harmonies of added and parallel seconds. . . . These do not have the bite we expect in a disciplined music.[23]

Personally, I'm not convinced by the "narrow way" argument. Rather, God as Creator exhibits astounding variety.

The chart below compares the music philosophies of Calvin Johansson and Harold Best.[24] Their differences are dramatic.

Johansson	Best
aesthetic absolutes	aesthetic relativity
universal musical principles exist	no universal music principles
music communicates a worldview	communication of worldview doubtful

(continued)

Johansson	Best *(continued)*
art expresses one's value system	no truth can be communicated without words
evaluation using norms of Scripture	evaluation using norms from music itself
character and music style coincide	character is separate from style
separation from culture advocated	reveling in cultural diversity
music induces behavior	any power of music is conferred power
rhythm has spiritual implications	no sacred/secular dichotomy
music itself can be lewd	meaning is derived from context
our path is narrow (austerity)	God creates riotously (exploration)
narrow range of styles advocated	every style useful
pop/rock and worship incompatible	any music style compatible
worship shouldn't entertain	music by nature entertains

My sympathies are with Best. With him, I also hold to the doctrine of common grace, advanced by the early Protestant Reformers. Common grace states that the rain falls on the just and the unjust (Matt. 5:45)—that God equally gifts all believers and unbelievers without discrimination. All humans are created in the image of God and by God's grace retain the image of God to some extent, despite their fallenness.

> Common grace enables unregenerate people to perform noble deeds; to express strong societal, friendly, familial, and sexual love; to submit themselves to and show understanding for moral and ethical codes . . . the doctrine of common grace helps us understand why all the music, flowing out of the creativities of a thousand cultures, subcultures, lifestyles, and belief systems, can be good.[25]

Common grace also means that Christians can enjoy the artistic contributions of non-Christians.

Is the Devil in the Music?

Is the devil in the music? It's not that simple. Where there are differences in background, exposure, and training, the potential for misunderstanding can be enormous. Graham Cray rightly asserts, "There is probably no musical form in existence which within its original cultural context does not send some messages which are in conflict with the Christian message."[26] For this reason I am disturbed when people insist that a certain beat is "of the devil" or a certain rhythm is "satanic." A specific rhythm or beat can take on different meanings in different musical contexts.

However, if a style hinders your walk with God, avoid it![27] The basic advice that Al Menconi, who counsels parents regarding the media and youth, gives seems sensible. Since the Bible does not outlaw specific music styles, he suggests that parents sit down with their children and *examine together (line by line) the philosophy behind the lyrics.* This way the issue is not so much the music style, but the *philosophy of life advocated.* Vocal music—not instrumental music—is most dangerous. Besides, most of us (even musicians) do not have the expertise to talk about music style precisely. We *are* better equipped to talk about words.

Music in the Old Testament

What about music style in Old Testament times? It may be shocking, but scholars believe Israel followed the uses and styles of her neighbors. "In the matter of her sacred song," Von Rad writes, "Israel went to school with the Canaanites. . . . [there is] nothing unique about the Psalms as a literary form."[28] Sigmund Mowinckel concludes that temple singing "can be traced back to Canaanite patterns."[29] In fact Hebrew musicians were such virtuosos that they acquired an international reputation. Foreign kings wanted them in their courts, and the Israelites gave musicians as compensation for tribute money. Clearly, their performing ability must have been comprehensive enough to cross cultural boundaries.

Old Testament music style had no harmony as we know it, no scales comparable to ours, no music notation, no rhythmic meters akin to ours. Their rhythms followed the natural pattern in the Hebrew language of constantly *varying* accents; ours tend toward *regular* pulses in two or three beats.

Here's my point. If the Hebrew music differed so greatly from ours and was acceptable to God, must we not beware of elevating any one style as intrinsically sacred? There is no intrinsically sacred style! Any given style, however, may be a happy fit as determined by a particular subgroup at a particular place and at a particular time.

Instruments and the New Testament

There is no record of instruments being used in worship in the Gospels or Epistles. Why is that? Why were instruments seemingly banned in synagogues and the early church?

Noted Jewish scholar Eric Werner answers that Greek music culture was exerting a powerful influence on Jewish culture in the time of Christ. Hellenism "had penetrated the daily life of Palestine." Jews employed Greek terms almost exclusively "for instruments, their parts, their tuning." The same instruments that Greeks used in their temple orgies, Jews used in their temple ceremonies. In revulsion, rabbis associated the instruments with immorality and banned them as unfit for the synagogues. Even instruments that had played a highly respected role in the psalter (aulos, kinnor, tympanon, and cymbals) were held in contempt. They were considered unclean because of their use in syncretistic religions. Rabbis pictured the aulos in pagan ceremonies as "full of frenzied tones." They recoiled at panpipe players "imitating" serpent songs. They imagined men called to war "in wild terms" when they saw a trumpet. Classic examples of guilt by association!

The same attitude of horror was reflected in Christian leaders like Clement of Alexandria up to the third century: "One makes noise with cymbals and tympana, one rages and rants with instruments of frenzy ... the flute belongs to those superstitious men who run to idolatry."[30]

We don't regard flute playing today as linked to superstition, but Clement did. Recall again, these same instruments were *respected* in the Psalms. How could he forget that? In the Book of Revelation even elders carry harps!

A vital point on banning instruments in worship, therefore, needs addressing. By focusing too narrowly on *only* the Gospels and Epistles for the last authoritative word on worship style, we can draw misleading conclusions. Rather, the *whole* of the Bible as well as extra-biblical evidence should be consulted. We need to see the larger context. If instruments had not become associated with pagan worship and debauchery, their use in worship never would have been questioned.

Church Music: A Functional Art?

Is *every* style appropriate for church use? "Not so," says Donald P. Hustad, noted worship author and musician. Church music should be "functional" (intelligible) and judged on whether it fulfils its "best function." "Free" or great art music may have to have restrictions within the local church:

> "Great art" in our culture . . . tends to be elitist. One of the requirements of the art music composer is that he must be free—free to communicate anything that is in his mind and heart, free even to fail to communicate (if that is his choice) so long as the work is his honest expression. Church music cannot be so "free." It must communicate the truth of God and express the response of the body of believers by whom it is used, and this means that it must have *the potential to be understood* by that particular community of faith (italics added).[31]

Scriptural support for this principle of intelligibility comes from Paul, if we view music as a language:

> Now, brothers, if I come to you and speak in tongues, what good will I be to you, unless I bring you some revelation or knowledge or prophecy or word of instruction? . . . Unless you speak intelligible words with your tongue, how will anyone know what you are saying? . . . Undoubtedly there are all sorts of languages in the world, yet none of them is without meaning. If then I do not grasp the meaning of what someone is saying, I am a foreigner to the speaker, and he is a foreigner to me. . . . in the church I would rather speak five intelligible words to instruct others than ten thousand words in a tongue.
>
> 1 Corinthians 14:6, 9–11, 19

Hustad traces the emergence of functional church music to the sixteenth-century Protestant commitment to congregational participation. As the church moved away from "art music," serious composers shifted their loyalty away from the church. By 1850 church music was more popular in appeal; it reflected the rising tides of humanism, democracy, "religion of the heart," mass revivals, choirs singing arranged hymns, and—by the early twentieth century—gospel songs.

> Consequently, it [church music] moved to the level of the worshiper who rarely frequented the concert hall. . . . Church music was now expected to be functional in the evangelical sense that everybody should share it. . . . What is performed in 99 percent of American churches today is functional church music that should not be confused with great art.[32]

Implementing Change

In Peter, Paul, James, and Barnabas, the early church experienced statesmanship-like leadership. Through the power of the Holy Spirit, these men underwent remarkable transformations. Paul, formerly breathing threats to the church, became concerned about wounding believers! Peter, raised as a strict Jew, embraced all Gentiles. James, leader of the "establishment," steered the Jerusalem church away from entrenchment. Barnabas encouraged cross-cultural ministry. These were the people God used to be shapers of change.

Peter, particularly, was put on the spot. Music leaders too may feel that way when learning new styles. Ears strain to listen, tongues stumble over rhythms, and memories overload in striving to remember new phrases. Learning new styles means becoming vulnerable. No one wants to be humiliated. The more respected we are, the more "face" we have to lose!

For these reasons, every effort must go into providing conditions where *people can feel safe to try.* Don't expose people to ridicule. Hold weakness revealed in practice in strictest confidence. Guard self-respect. Don't mimic or poke fun. Remember Paul: He didn't want to wound anyone. Affirm individuals—"we know what you're going through . . . we've been there . . . let's break the learning down into manageable steps." Also, don't force public performance until the person feels ready. If possible, do a test run.

When I was a boy, we had a magnificent evergreen tree in our front yard. One day Mom said to Dad, "The branches of the evergreen are hanging over the walkway. The tree needs trimming." Dad went out to do the job, and my brother and I went to see how he was coming along. We were aghast! My dad, normally a man exploding with creativity, had totally lost it—lost all sense of proportion. What we saw staggered us. The right side of the tree Dad left untouched, but on the left side— there was nothing! Sheared off! It was like shaving the hair off one side of your head; one side, a full head of hair, the other side, bald. Stunned, my brother, Don, and I exclaimed, "Dad! Dad! How could you do this!" We didn't know whether to laugh or cry. And it remained an embarrassing eyesore for years and years.

Today we get a bang out of telling this story about my dad, one of many, at family gatherings. But it was painful at the time.

All this to say that we need sensitivity in implementing change. Don't lop off, without careful forethought, your most prominent, cultivated branches. Don't dismantle an adult or children's choir program just because it's not the "in thing."

And this is especially important: *Don't undertake changes in worship unless there is a certain amount of calm in the church.* If your church is boiling because of some other issue, you're inviting more trouble.

If you are an established church, bring out sufficiently what is dissatisfying in order to generate motivation for change—for example, "the branches are hanging over the walkway." Or as Nehemiah proclaimed, "The walls are in ruins."

Arm yourself with some good anecdotes.[33] Humor is always helpful. And a sense of history can broaden one's perspective. These startling facts will cause your people to think before speaking emotionally, off the cuff:

- Harps were like guitars in the Old Testament.
- Asaph, David's chief musician, was a percussionist.
- Puritans in England took axes to organs, sang no hymns (only psalms), and prohibited instruments in worship (ca. 1630).
- The pope banned the piano as unfit for worship (1903).

Upon hearing these facts, I find that church folk begin to measure their words more carefully.

Consider the significant age groups in the congregation, the educational level, the size of the church, the local culture, and the unique abilities of members. For example, one reason I am personally interested in flowing praise is because I'm an improviser. The format suits my talents.

Obtain consensus. Consider the modeling of the New Testament church. A dual emphasis on listening to the Holy Spirit and applying the best of corporate judgment guided the letter the Jerusalem Council sent to Antioch: "It seemed good to the Holy Spirit and to us" (Acts 15:28).

Finally, pray about implementation long before you take action. Music directors have emphasized this point to me repeatedly.

Standards for Church Music

Consider carefully Hustad's standards for church music: They are weighty. According to Hustad, evangelicals should:

- express the gospel in a text and musical language richly understandable by the intended culture

- offer a worthy "sacrifice of praise" (our best performance) without arrogance or shame
- express the best Christian theology of each denomination or church subculture, supporting all tenets in proper balance
- support the best activities of the group's beliefs—worship, fellowship, outreach
- speak from the "whole person" to the "whole person," balancing the physical, intellectual, and emotional, while avoiding the sentimental
- be genuinely creative, shunning the hackneyed and trite as well as the elitist and abstruse

Hustad suggests that evangelicals, rather than narrowly focusing on *raising* music standards, be open to a *broader* musical experience; that is, be open to cultures other than their own, for in this way, he says, we may "get a new glimpse of God and his truth."[34]

Music in Context

I expect this chapter to raise questions. Some may echo a friend of mine who passionately responded: "Barry, I have a lot of trouble with this chapter. . . . I refuse to sing or affirm styles that trivialize the truths of the Word of God." I hope readers will not feel this way. I don't want truth trivialized either, but I do take the position that music materials are morally neutral; any style is *theoretically permissible but not necessarily appropriate*. I cannot feel free to broadside any one style—jazz, rock, rap—as unfit, as unredeemable.

Music is like putty. The meaning of every chord, rhythm, timbre is in the hands of the context. Human "associations" greatly influence our perception of contexts. Shouldn't we logically expect tremendous diversity within Christian worship? Scripture says "*all* the families of the nations will worship before Thee" (Ps. 22:27 NASB). For sources that take a different position, I urge you to check this endnote.[35]

The church has for centuries waged one brush war after another over . . . what it means to borrow styles, forms, processes, tunes, techniques, textures, shapes, gestures, and instruments from secular sources. . . . Despite the numberless instances and their seeming diversity, one common thread runs throughout. At the time of the borrowing, the war rages, often quite bitterly and divisively. Then as time passes, the war dies down. The previously condemned becomes merely questionable, if not outrightly sacred.

Harold M. Best, *Music Through the Eyes of Faith*

Questions for Reflection and Discussion

1. Is the choice of worship style as much a pastoral matter as a musical matter?
2. Is every music style appropriate for church use?
3. Is there a "sacred" music style?
4. What three ideas in this chapter impacted you the most?

PART **3**

MINISTERING WITH OTHERS

VOLUNTEER AND STAFF RELATIONS

Worship is a conversation with God and human beings,
a dialog that should go on continually in the life of a believer.
Donald P. Hustad, *Jubilate II*

"I saw him coming. Like a runaway locomotive with steam billowing in all directions, he broke through the line of departing worshipers and screeched to a halt in front of me.

"'What's the idea of changing the closing song this morning without telling me?' he demanded. 'I worked so hard to plan the music, then you had the nerve to throw in that . . . that clinker.'

"'Clinker?' I responded, trying to appear calm before the startled people around me. I was a young pastor, he a talented musician several years older than I. We had never clashed before.

"'That song was terrible. The congregation couldn't sing it. The pianist couldn't play it. The worship team didn't like it. It didn't fit in. Never, never do that again.'

"He turned abruptly and strode off, leaving me stunned as I mumbled something about the stress of ministry to the curious bystanders in the hallway. Fumbling my way to my office, I felt the blessing of the morning quickly fade. What began as bewilderment turned to seething defensiveness.

"'Who does he think he is anyway?' I thought angrily. 'I have a right to do what's best. After all, who's in charge here? I don't care if he has been at the church longer. Besides, that wasn't such a bad song. We used to sing it in seminary all the time. He should talk. The worship

209

team has been eating into my preaching time. No wonder we get out late.'"[1]

Sound familiar? Many pastors and chief musicians experience marvelous relationships. Others struggle. Yet the relationship between the music director and the pastor is of *crucial importance to the health of the entire church.*[2] Some pastors claim it is their *defining relationship!* In this chapter I hope to shed light on what musicians are like and what is involved in their work. I want to focus on some blind spots and common misperceptions where the pastor/musician relationship is liable to become strained. I will also highlight issues of leadership style, access, trust, teamwork, self-image, discipline, release time, and budget considerations, mostly taking the musician's point of view.

What Makes Musicians Tick?

Calvin M. Johansson describes the church musician:

Of necessity the church musician is a zealous, eager, and energetic worker who has little time for reflection, contemplation, and philosophic thought. What he most often craves is inspiration, new ideas, repertoire, methodological suggestions, problem solving, and technical review.[3]

Some musicians function comfortably with an authoritarian style of leadership, but most do not. Lyle E. Schaller, church consultant, believes one-third to one-half of all professionally trained ministers of worship resist the boss-subordinate leadership style.[4] Most desire a warm, egalitarian partnership with the senior pastor, perhaps more so than do other staff members.

Long- and midrange planning is extremely helpful to musicians. Musicians want regular, direct access to the pastor for the planning of Sunday worship, preferably early in the week.

As one leader expressed to me, "It's important not to have to report to a committee to get to the pastor. It's better to answer directly to him; otherwise every part of the service can be changed by some other person. At first, the pastor kept the planning of the service tightly to himself. Now that he trusts me, I generally come to him with a plan and he looks at it and makes suggestions."

Trust and loyalty are essential if the pastor/worship leader relationship is to be effective. The depth of confidence each has for the other determines each leader's ability to lead. The following categories show the variety of relationships that people have with a leader.

- Level A will die for the leader.
- Level B will fight, but not die, for the leader.
- Level C will neither fight nor oppose. This is the largest group. Their loyalty is more institutional than personal.
- Level D doubt their leader.
- Level E are antagonists who fight and erode the leader's authority and may be willing to sacrifice the institution to "get" the leader.[5]

Staff members need to be at level A or B for an effective team relationship. If musicians behave at level E, the results can be devastating. Pastors may criticize the music program to get the musician but will generally protect the remaining church structure. Musicians, however, may assault wider dimensions of church structure to get the pastor and protect only their more limited music objectives. They may be more dangerous!

How do musicians feel about teamwork? Some musicians understand better than others what is involved. Doran McCarty observes that "a leader does not announce that a collection of people is a team."[6] A group of people *becomes* a team by working together, sharing goals, and having mutual interests. Team members turn to each other for information and emotional support, and what they achieve corporately becomes more important than each member's personal agenda.[7]

Schaller observes that a large number of musicians are begrudging team members—as this vexed pastor relates:

I inherited a full-time minister of music. And I'm ready to see him move on. He's a great musician and an excellent choir director, but he also is the least cooperative member of our staff. In the three years I've been here I doubt if he has been on time more than twice. . . . It's almost impossible to get him to cooperate. . . . it took me six months to get back the right to choose the hymns I wanted with my sermons. When I talk to him, I sometimes get the feeling that he is on another planet.[8]

To musicians these may be painful, convicting words. A potentially "profitable partnership" could become a "wicked waste."[9] Don't allow that to happen!

The process of brainstorming—taking the sermon topics for the upcoming three months and generating a myriad of nonjudgmental ideas for the service—can help create a feeling of mutual ownership. Brainstorming gets everyone talking and helps everyone "buy" into planning and preparation. Even if it's not your format, occasionally generate a tightly planned thematic service. It will draw your leadership together:[10] "The more we strategize, the better we harmonize."[11]

Understanding the World of the Artist

Creative musicians are usually individualistic. As Schaller sees it, the problem is that there are two worlds: the creative-artistic world and the organizational-business world.

> The first is a world inhabited by free-spirited individuals. The second is a culture that emphasizes groups, teams, and hierarchies. The best and most effective ministers of music come from the world of the creative artist. . . . a relatively small number of ministers of music have mastered both worlds. Creative people tend to be individuals. . . . Some creative people are willing, as a price of their freedom, to visit that second world for a few hours every week for a staff meeting . . . but many cannot see the need or value of even those occasional visits. A few grew up in that second world, escaped from it many years ago, and simply cannot bear to return to it.
>
> The wise pastor (1) understands the existence of these radically different worlds, (2) recognizes and affirms the native habitat of the creative artist, (3) sees the conflict in perspective and the values between the two worlds as a natural phenomenon, not as a product of personalities, (4) is reasonably comfortable with the fact this means trade-offs, . . . (5) does not require everyone to move and operate from that second world, (6) values the creative stimulation of artists, (7) does not project identical expectations on people regardless of the world they live in.[12]

Schaller's analysis is accurate. Pastors, when your musician seems to be in the "ozone layer," don't take it too personally. Remain emotionally secure and draw your musician out.

There are further complications. Too many musicians commit moral failure while in ministry. Church musician Jim Barnett contends that evangelicals have bought into bad ideas concerning artistic personalities and have unwisely perpetuated them: "We excuse, exempt artists from discipline. We too readily apologize for their excesses, for their not leading a disciplined lifestyle. We accept the world's image of musicians."

Discipline is *required* of the worship musician. The position involves administration: Music and overheads have to be filed, phone calls have to be made, rehearsals arranged. We simply have to address our weaknesses and build on our strengths.[13]

Compliments That Count

We also need to emphasize positive models. If Christian leaders would hold high the positive image accorded musicians in the Old Testament, that could be helpful. The temple musicians are portrayed as responsible, conscientious, and intelligent. They were chosen as supervisors in the rebuilding of the walls of Jerusalem (2 Chron. 34:12–13). Hezekiah complimented them for their intelligence and "good insight" in the temple service (30:22). During the festival preparations, they were found to be "more conscientious to consecrate themselves than the priests" (29:34 NASB). One was chosen to distribute the tithe money because he was "reliable." Positive affirmations! Pastors, share this information with your musicians! Project a positive image for them.

Well-placed compliments can serve to point everyone in the proper direction. A music director wept as she shared with me the enormous impact her pastor had on the music program by the compliments he gave the choir and supporting musicians during services: "Choir, you brought us into the very presence of God today," or "All of us thank you for projecting such an unusual sense of God's greatness this morning." Have you ever complimented your worship leadership in this way?

Instead of highlighting entertainment values—"That was fabulous, let's all give them a rousing hand!"—he focused everyone's attention on the heart of the worship experience. I think that is what made this woman weep. He used compliments to focus attention on the *proper* goal. This built integrity into their role of ministry and helped each person feel all the practicing was worthwhile. In dignifying the music ministry, go public with it. Let the whole congregation know how valuable it is and why.

Musicians can also go public with their support of their pastor. Sharing, publicly and privately, how a sermon personally benefited you builds unity. Thank-you notes also go a long way in building team spirit. Don't underestimate their value!

213

Special Tips for Working with Volunteers

A pastor's relationship with a volunteer or part-timer will be different from that with a full-timer. Volunteers need training and equipping. McCarty advises, "Whatever the volunteer needs, the effective leader will contribute toward fulfilling it. That is the pay for the volunteer. . . . The leader who overlooks the needs of volunteers is borrowing trouble."[14] Therefore, if a piano needs replacing, support replacing it. If a guitar tuner is needed, share in the expense. If speaker monitors are required, advocate their procurement. *A good leader provides.*

In small churches, particularly, interest in the needs of each musician communicates a sense of belonging. Volunteers leave when they anticipate greater fulfillment elsewhere.

The Part-Time Assignment

The part-time music position poses unique pressures for pastors. One pastor related:

> It hasn't worked for me. It is almost impossible to schedule staff meetings when everyone can be there, and a couple of part-timers have been so emotionally tied to their full-time jobs they're worn out when they show up at the church.[15]

For part-timers, fashion a precisely focused assignment, not a general job description. Determine the number of hours of work expected for preparation, rehearsal, and direct church performance. Creating a praise and worship set itself can take up to two hours.

Communicate early in the week by phone, or go out to lunch together if a scheduled staff meeting does not work. Having been a "moonlighter" myself, I know how hard it is to find time to talk about anything but the urgent. Sundays come so fast and are so unrelenting that exhaustion is a common malady. But somehow, time *must* be found to discuss the deeper questions so that mutual growth can occur. Here's where previous chapters on letting Christ dwell richly, worship as performance, Jesus Christ as our worship leader, and the problems of style can be helpful as you work through the issues together. Read and discuss this book together! Devote an entire sermon to worship at least once a year.

Schaller thinks there is a limit on what you should expect of part-timers: "The best part-time staff I've worked with has been more goal-oriented than relational. Their focus is on ministry and performance, not on staff relationships."[16] Still, a warm relationship with the pastor is indispensable. Also, assist part-timers in taking seminars and workshops, or consider viewing together a video of another church's service. From time to time, release your part-timers in order to let them rest, see the service from the attender's perspective, or find out what is going on at other churches. This will help prevent staleness and promote self-development.

A Full-Time "Miracle Worker"

As for full-timers, Schaller reports there is a temptation for the church leadership to search for someone who can produce single-handedly a comprehensive music program. In other words, find a "miracle worker." A second, more realistic approach is to seek someone who can "cause" that to happen:

> This second approach is based on the assumption that it is unrealistic to expect one person to possess all the skills necessary to do everything or to relate effectively to all age groups. . . .
>
> The easiest way to distinguish between these two approaches is to listen in on the *budget* discussions. When the first approach is being discussed, the focus is on how much additional money will be required for the compensation package for a full-scale choir director. When the second approach is being considered, the discussion is on the total budget for a full-scale music program, including the salaries of several part-time directors, the purchase of additional sheet music, supplies, new instruments, organ maintenance, piano tuning, and a half dozen other items.[17]

The latter approach seems more appropriate. For example, consider Hustad's analysis of the full-time music position. The ideal music director is (1) a musician, (2) an administrator, (3) an educator, and (4) a pastor.[18] Head musicians, however, can't be expected to have the skill (or inclination!) to fulfill each of these roles equally well, although *some skill* in each area is almost a necessity. Surround your head musician with people who can address weaknesses that become evident.

Musically, church musicians must have one strong performing area (composition/arranging could be included here). Worship band leaders must provide musical direction for the various role players in order to create a tight ensemble.

Administratively, music has to be chosen, organized, and catalogued; recruitment is unceasing—people have to be called, programs planned, rehearsals scheduled and organized; the paper blizzard has to be attended to; and the machinery has to be kept oiled;[19] music budgets must be prepared and money raised for music, new technology, and instruments.

As an educator in supervising or directing a graded choir program, the music director must know something about child development processes and techniques for teaching musicianship to different age groups.

Concerning their pastoral role, the music director should be able to teach Sunday school classes if necessary and do visitation work in caring for their choir members and worship team.

How many individuals are sufficiently gifted to fulfill each of these roles masterfully? Very few! (Again, the pastor faces the same tensions.) The wise pastor will assess the gifts of individuals and gather the correct support system so they can major on what they do best. Creative types will likely need secretarial help with administration and keeping themselves organized. Musicians are sometimes expected to keep up with the responsibilities of other pastoral staff members in evangelistic calling, weddings, funerals, even preaching. *The weight of too many of these tasks can make the job next to impossible.*

The Hurting Musician

What about the inside, emotional life of the musician? Because of the nature of the "business," musicians reap strokes of adulation one moment and rejection the next. Sound familiar, pastors? Hear these words of testimony from a veteran musician whose pastor demonstrated remarkable compassion to him at a time of crisis, nursing him back to health: "He was my spiritual father. He loved me, discipled me. He loved me for more than my gifts. He listened, prayed, stood by me— literally hugging me as I would cry out my emotional hurts, having no inkling I would later be his head musician."

These are the words of the worship pastor at one of the largest churches in America, burned out after serving four years at a previous church. He was telling me how grateful he was for his present pastor. "For several months," he told me, "I just sat in the services, doing nothing, recouping, replenishing." Now healed, he continued: "I don't advocate a relationship like___and___had, who'd show up at a certain hour, do their thing, depart. It's purely professional. They don't know each other. Ministry with that kind of professionalism backfires."

216

How can pastors and worship leaders begin to open up honest communication? Pastors could ask, "What is it like to be an artist? What are the pressures of being a musician?" Musicians could ask, "What is it like to be a pastor? What are your pressures?"

This story of burnout and hurt feelings, though, is not at all uncommon as I talk to church musicians serving in churches of all sizes. It has been said that "belonging is the foundation of all motivation."[20] Yet I hear of musicians who feel used—used for their gifts—but not appreciated as persons.

Like thoroughbreds, they run hard but feel unconnected.

Or like underpaid hired hands leading choirs or teams, they take the brunt of criticism, working on budgets allowing little creativity.

Or like sweatshop workers, they grind out the same tunes at the same location, at the same time, week after week.

Some feel as triflers or distant cousins to the really important ministry going on—the bearers of low-level entertainment.[21]

Feeling used, overworked, underpaid, not paid—these are the wandering thoughts of musicians on bad days! Caring pastoral leadership can do much good in these circumstances. Unfortunately, some pastors appear insulated from and unaware of these feelings. They enter the sanctuary Sunday morning thinking, "I hope everything goes smoothly this morning. . . . Please! Please! Don't embarrass me!" Sometimes that's the extent of their concern:

> The minister is glad to have a conductor who will take the whole responsibility from his shoulders; and then, so that there be quiet in the choir and no disturbance in the congregation, he does not trouble himself any more about the matter.[22]

Where such attitudes exist, smoldering feelings can erupt. Hurting from a lack of respect, one such musician said to me, his voice choking with emotion, "I am a human being!" It's interesting that pastors experience the very same emotions.

What Can Be Done?

What can be done? First, realize that first impressions lay the foundation for deepening interactions. A musician warmly reminisced on the sensitivity of his pastor: "When we were candidating, Pastor had flowers sent to my wife and me at the hotel. And the following day, he *personally* drove us around the town. Just after we accepted the position, I came to a staff meeting one day and shared my wife's distress over the fleas infesting our new home. Pastor suggested I leave immediately. An hour later he was at our door: 'What can I do?' I can't tell you how much his caring attitude impressed us."

One musician suggested a simple but often overlooked exercise: "Spend lunch together telling each other how you came to know the Lord. Walk through your spiritual odyssey. This is not a trite exercise! I've found that after exercises like that, the issue of authority isn't as much an issue. One's perception of position is different."

Another music director echoed a similar emphasis: "Team teach a Sunday school class. Claim a verse together. The way my pastor prayed for my family really touched me. It drew us together. He told me, 'I want our relationship to be strong. If our relationship fragments, the entire church will know it.'"

This emphasis on intercessory prayer and pastoral care definitely needs underscoring. "Minister to, not just through, musicians."[23] Worship leaders need pastoral care and attention! People involved in true ministry feel the weight of the ministry. They carry the burdens of those under their care in addition to their own family cares. As pastors and musicians sensitively listen to one another and pray over these "weights," they can be refreshed.

Pastor Melvin Amundson eloquently shares his position on feedback: "My door is always open, and your suggestions are always welcome. I only ask that you use your ideas like seeds, not bullets. Plant them so they will grow, not wound."[24]

> *Do nothing out of selfish ambition or vain conceit, but in humility consider others better than yourselves. Each of you should look not only to your own interests, but also to the interests of others.*
> Philippians 2:3–4

Questions for Reflection and Discussion

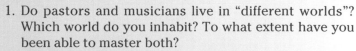

1. Do pastors and musicians live in "different worlds"? Which world do you inhabit? To what extent have you been able to master both?
2. What joint activities could strengthen the pastor/musician relationship?
3. Can you recall a time when you felt exceptionally loved and appreciated by the church community?

IDENTIFYING AND ATTRACTING
WORSHIP MUSICIANS

The days of the church musician as a silent partner in the religious enterprise are over. The tangled web of conflicting musical philosophy . . . makes it absolutely mandatory for the church musician to become an articulate spokesman and teacher.

Calvin M. Johansson, *Music and Ministry*

So far we have learned that an ideal music director is a musician, an administrator, an educator, and a pastor. What about the spiritual gifts and worship leadership? What roles can the musician perform that Scripture indicates are important? How can we identify and attract good music leadership? What are the benefits of musical improvisation? These are some of the questions we'll address.

The Worship Pastor and the Spiritual Gifts

Donald P. Hustad received a letter from a former student, serving as a worship pastor, who asked the following question: "In Ephesians 4:11–12 Paul lists the ministries God has given the church. Where does music fit in?" Here is the passage:

It was he who gave some to be apostles, some to be prophets, some to be evangelists, and some to be pastors and teachers, to prepare God's people for works of service, so that the body of Christ may be built up until we all reach unity in the faith and in the knowledge of

219

the Son of God and become mature, attaining to the whole measure of the fullness of Christ.

Before we get to Hustad's answer, New Testament scholar Gordon Fee makes a helpful comment concerning the various lists of the spiritual gifts (Rom. 12:6–8; 1 Cor. 12:6–11, 28–31; Eph. 4:11–12). He says: "They are ad hoc, and probably representative, not exhaustive or definitive."[1] No two lists are identical. Fee believes they are intended to show the "diverse ways" that the Spirit manifests himself.[2] Now Hustad.

Hustad's answer indicates that, while music doesn't appear on Paul's list in Ephesians 4, the worship pastor's position can relate to each of the five roles below. Hustad speaks of the chief musician as a prophet, evangelist, pastor, teacher, and apostle, respectively. Though not exhaustive, Hustad's exegesis also helps pastors consider what to look for in identifying a chief musician.

1. [As music prophets or "forth-tellers," worship leaders] are as concerned with the words of hymns and anthems as they are with their music. . . . They must choose texts that bring the whole Word to the whole person, and they will equip themselves theologically to do this. . . . They "break the bread of life" in the anthem text, explaining it verbally in the choir rehearsal (sometimes even in the corporate worship service), or in writing in the church bulletin. . . .

2. [As evangelists, worship leaders should] be prepared to address another person with a simple, personal witness to "the old, old story." Furthermore, the solo or the invitation hymn may be the direct tool of the Holy Spirit in achieving . . . a decision that leads to Christian discipleship.

The graded choir program too contributes to evangelism and church growth. Young children are attracted by musical activity, learn to sing the truth of God, and often come rather easily and naturally to personal faith. . . .

3. [As pastors, music leaders] show love and special concern for the members of their musical groups, giving counsel when needed, visiting them in their homes or in the hospital, and standing by them in the occasions of celebration as well as in the times of crisis and sorrow. . . .

4. [As teachers, worship leaders] teach worship and churchmanship. In choosing music with strong scriptural texts, they teach theology and discipleship. They dramatize the Christian challenge to live and to worship creatively, and perhaps most importantly, they teach stewardship of life and of talent. . . .

5. [As apostles, some worship leaders] "follow in the train" of the *apostles,* the first missionaries! . . . They help churches around the world to develop their own indigenous expressions of musical worship.[3]

Kevin E. Lawson's extensive research of associate church staff who are thriving after at least seven years of ministry, clearly indicates that ministers of music who excel in their positions over the long term are pastorally inclined and nurture oriented.[4] They receive their greatest satisfaction in seeing youth and adults grow not only musically but spiritually through the music ministry. Spiritual formation appears to be the primary motivating impulse, not musical performance. That's something to consider when you are interviewing a candidate

A Reading and Improvising Church Musician

While we are talking about ministry, how does music improvisation relate to ministry? What are its key benefits? Can it be learned systematically like music notation, or do some people just "have it"? Does its importance vary from denomination to denomination? Let's address these questions.

In gathering musicians for your ministry, seek those who are good at *both* reading music and improvising. The ability to do both is what I strongly want to emphasize—at least as an ideal. I do not wish to imply, however, that a musician who does not improvise is not valuable or cannot be competent in ministry.

Unfortunately graduates from music conservatories and colleges possess good technique and read well, but few improvise fluently; it is not emphasized in their curriculum. This needs addressing, especially in Christian colleges. On the other hand, self-taught musicians improvise but tend to read poorly. We need balance. Did you know Bach, Beethoven, and Mozart could read *and* improvise expertly?

What about improvisation in the various denominations? We see "two systems"—reading and improvising—operating in a continuum that extends over the whole spectrum of Protestant church culture, from the mainline to the Pentecostal churches. Mainline churches, such as the Episcopal (Anglican), Lutheran, and Presbyterian churches, emphasize the written tradition, whereas the charismatic and Pentecostal-styled churches rely on improvisation.

Mainline churches, for example, use a worship book with weekly Scripture readings laid out in advance for the year, fixed creeds to recite and prayers to read, and short speaking or singing responses. The current mood, however, is to reduce the fixed features "to the bare essentials and to allow considerable mixing of homemade components with official ones. . . . The program has become wide open."[5] The new rites "allow for hymnody [and worship choruses] all over the place. . . ."[6] Because of this new flexibility, mainline churches could benefit greatly by focusing more on improvisation. Improvisation can contribute enormously to the worship ministry (for help see appendix 3).

In charismatic and Pentecostal-oriented churches a different culture prevails. Structure must yield to the Spirit. The order of service may be laid out with no assurance it will be followed. The worship requires musicians who know the tunes by memory and can improvise on the spur of the moment. More often than not, their reading skills are elementary, while their improvisational skills are advanced.

Toward the middle of this continuum fall the various Baptists, Brethren, C&MA, Evangelical Free, Nazarene, and Independent Bible churches, most of which have a free rather than fixed order of service, but they usually follow their order of service.

Practical Benefits of Improvisation

What are the practical benefits of improvisation? They are more extensive than most people realize. I can think of at least four practical benefits of improvisation.

1. *Improvising allows us to be spontaneous and talk in real time.* As an analogy, let's use a foreign language. It's marvelous to be able to read German when you are vacationing in Germany—this gives you access to maps, newspapers, and the meaning of signs along the road. But it's also valuable to be able to *talk* live in real time—that's improvisation. Musical improvisation is the ability to talk spontaneously in musical phrases. Improvisation occurs when you don't know what the next note will be, just as in ordinary conversation we have an idea we want to express but can't predict the exact word that will come out of our mouth in the next sentence.

Let's apply improvisation to pastors. When delivering a sermon, it's essential to be able to cut from one's notes and clarify a point in a personal way when the audience needs that.

Finney thought this way. He strenuously objected to preachers who bury their eyes in their written text and read their sermons without impromptu comments:

The preacher preaches right along just as he has it written and cannot observe whether he is understood or not. . . . [But] if a minister has his eye on the people he is preaching to, he can commonly tell by their looks whether they understand him. And if he sees they do not understand any particular point, let him stop and illustrate it. If they do not understand one illustration, let him give another.[7]

That's the sort of thing a musical improviser can do too.

 2. *Music improvisers are valuable because they can listen and respond to what the Spirit is doing and the people are feeling at any given moment. They also adapt more readily to changes in style.* Improvisers can respond to the emotional and spiritual dynamics happening in a worship service. They can highlight certain words in the text. They can drop the key when the congregational voice is rusty in morning services. They can improvise smooth transitions between numbers and help services flow.

Improvisers can play the "lay-back" rhythms of contemporary churches that are not easily captured in music notation. Whole congregations of young people today are "dropping" these rhythms "right in the pocket." These rhythmic subtleties aren't learned effortlessly. Improvisers are more adept at dealing with these kinds of ongoing cultural adaptations than are more traditionally trained musicians.

3. *Improvisers are able to take full advantage of the potential of synthesizers and the latest music technology.* To take advantage of synthesizers, for example, synth players often have to revise what is on the written page. Some presets cannot perform short note values. If a spacy "pad" has slow-developing attacks, that preset will require fewer notes. If you have a string preset, melodic lines and spacings must be created from the score. Playing block chords isn't effective. If you're playing a guitar or brass preset, you need to innovate the kinds of voicings and lines appropriate for those instruments. Your ear must tell you what sounds right.

In other words, skilled synth players function as orchestrators, bringing out the unique potentials of each sound. This is important, for congregations today expect to hear more than just piano and organ sounds.[8] Plus, guitarists have their pedals, fuzz boxes, and MIDI capabilities, and percussionists have MIDI today too.

The proper perspective is to see acoustic and electronic instruments as complementary, not competitive. Electronic instruments can augment or "pinch hit" for acoustic instruments. If the bass player is sick or out of town on business, the synth can fill in. "Sampled strings" of a very high quality are available today. They can produce the sound of a first-class string section when you don't have the luxury of 30 string players in your church. Yet a couple of live violinists alongside the sampled strings not only improve sonic realism, they add drama and visual presence. The combination can be stunning.

Advice: When purchasing an all-purpose electronic keyboard for church use, buy a "weighted" keyboard, which allows octaves to be played cleanly.

4. *Improvising avoids copyright infringement.* Improvisation is a means of avoiding the moral quagmire of illegal photocopying. Since improvisation is not a "fixed" form, improvisers are free of copyright infringement and can create spontaneously for any vocal or instrumental combination, any hymn, any chorus.

Isn't Improvisation a "Gift"?

Some people may feel as if they have no aptitude for improvisation at all, but I believe this holds true for only a very small percentage of musicians. Almost any musician can learn to supply an accompaniment for a chart with pop symbols (a low form of improvisation). My first questions are these: Are you working at it? Do you know *how* to work at it? The process is quite similar to learning a new language. Improvisation does *not* fall from the sky! It is based on knowledge.

Improvisation takes sustained, patient, and systematic practice, just like the skill of sight reading. If you are a beginner, close the book and start playing your favorite hymn or chorus. You may want to begin with just three chords (C, F, and G, in the key of C). Transpose the song to other keys. Add substitution chords. Seek out a gifted church improviser in your area, and/or study the keyboard books available online. See appendixes 2 and 3 for resources and software.

I do not wish to belittle those who don't improvise. Looking down on these musicians results only in deepening chasms, resentments, and jealousies that separate those who improvise and those who don't, those who champion the traditional music versus modern music, or art music versus folk music. Robin Sheldon expresses the devastation:

> Deep wounds have been inflicted, sufficient indeed to cause total breakdown of communication. . . . Organists have no longer been able to continue where so-called inferior music is used because of their classically oriented entrenched attitudes; conversely, music

groups with their light instrumental accompaniments of guitars, synthesizers, percussion and the relevant electronic gadgetry have been insensitive to those who would naturally wish to use other styles. . . . Humanly speaking, reconciliation is merely a hope because the natural gulf is often so deep.[9]

"Do nothing out of selfish ambition or vain conceit, but in humility consider others better than yourselves" (Phil. 2:3).

Resentments from musicians are sometimes aimed at pastors:

. . . through ignorance or disinterest . . . [pastors] fail to clutch and build on the crucial relationship with their musicians which is so essential a factor. When pastors equate their authority with autocracy, is it surprising that disastrous consequences result?

Disbanding a traditional choir or organist doing a good job is one of the most unforgivable of actions, yet it frequently occurs. It causes untold hurt and can, as evidence shows, permanently alienate people from the Church. To what purpose is this waste, especially when as in many instances there is nothing, or nobody, available as a viable replacement?[10]

Are we hearing the pain in this paragraph? "Unforgivable actions," "untold hurt," "permanently alienated"—the words of "establishment musicians" being replaced! Robert Hayburn observes, "Almost everyone is making music in the church, except trained musicians."[11] That should make us think twice. In the Old Testament, an elaborate training system, the levitical "guild," was established for the very purpose of learning to lead worship.[12] We too need to train and retrain rather than replace so we can grow together rather than sever members from Christ's body.

Though church leaders may need to call for change, sensitivity needs to be demonstrated to musicians in this threatening predicament. To get to their present musical level has already been tremendously arduous and financially draining. The acquisition of new styles comes for most musicians with great difficulty.

A soloist at church once said to me while we were rehearsing, "Forget that Baptist stuff. Can you give it a jazzy feeling?" That comment impelled me to learn how to improvise various Latin rhythms as well as jazz and funk "feels." I know the tremendous effort it takes to internalize them. After being immersed in your own "mother tongue" style for so many years, it's a truly daunting challenge to speak fluently (no less masterfully) in a new musical style. Consider this: "Your favorite style of music is likely to be the one that was most part of your life in your *adolescence*. No matter how many years have passed, that music is your type of music, your music dialect, if you will."[13]

So, *when you hire someone, obtain at the very outset a clear idea of their stylistic comfort zone and church music philosophy*—you may have to live with it! Ask your candidate, "What music did you like most in your adolescence? Describe the music culture of your youth." It usually does not work to ask musicians to adopt new styles.

How Do You Attract Good Musicians?

Premier church consultant Lyle E. Schaller contends:

> The expansion of the ministry of music can be *the most effective single avenue* not only for enriching the peace and joy of the heart, but also for the expansion of the program, for reaching young children and enabling them to express their creativity, for the quick assimilation of new members, for expanding group life, for a ministry with the developmentally disabled, and for creating a distinctive community image.[14]

But seasoned pastors have told me they believe it is harder to find quality music leaders than quality pastors. Pastors frequently ask, "How can I attract good music leadership?" At times we feel the task is overwhelming and the supporters too few. Here are eight suggestions for making the music ministry of your church as effective as possible.

1. *Do what you can, with what you have, where you are.* We all know people with shelves of unread books, unused recipes, and untasted spices—wasted resources. Use the resources you have—your current team of musicians and people willing to lead prayer, read Scripture, fashion banners, and so on—to create the proper environment for worship. Write down your goals; goals unwritten are seldom achieved. Seek to develop the right conditions in your heart and in your congregation.

Have you preached on worship lately? Has your worship committee read and discussed a worship book together? Have you hosted a banquet honoring the volunteers at your church? If so, did you include your musicians?

2. *Be committed to adequately compensating those who are professionally equipped.* Why should church musicians be paid when Sunday school teachers, for example, are not? The question deserves an answer. A musician is like an athlete. Trained musicians must commit time weekly to maintain and extend their skills—a necessity seldom appreciated. They have made an enormous financial investment in their instruments, their private lessons, and college training. Sunday school teachers and other volunteers have not had to make a comparable investment nor must they practice their skills each week.

3. *Indicate your willingness to minister pastoral care to musicians.* Remember that your musicians are part of the church body. The church has nothing to lose and much to gain when it ministers to them.

4. *Personally contact the visible worship leaders in your area.* Take well-known worship musicians in your area out for lunch and let them know of your need. Share your heart and your vision. Indicate that you have preached on worship; tell them the measures you've taken to develop worship. Invite them to lead a special service of worship at your church. Hire one of them to put on a seminar or to work as a worship consultant for a limited period of time. Show them you are serious!

5. *Frequent the "watering-holes" where musicians congregate.* Attend a worship seminar in your area. Get to know some of the participants and attendees. Attend a concert; visit a music store or a Christian record shop; post a notice.

6. *Understand that one good musician attracts another.* If you can attract one good musician to your church, others may follow.

7. *Search large churches for potential musicians.* Often large churches have an abundance of musicians, and some become frustrated when they are used infrequently.

8. *Pray.* One pastor told me he prayed six years for a worship leader before God sent someone to him.

If you do these things now, when the talented person comes along, you can show a *demonstrated* interest in worship. And from reading a book like this you should know the issues, have a few ideas to share, and be able to defend your future worship leadership. That will be highly attractive to a potential worship leader!

Christian worship is the most momentous, the most urgent, the most glorious action that can take place in human life.

Karl Barth

Questions for Reflection and Discussion

1. "Your favorite style of music is likely to be the one that was most part of your life in your *adolescence*." Does this accord with your experience?
2. The benefits of music improvisation extend beyond mere evangelistic playing. Discuss.
3. Did Jesus display an improvisatorial style in his ministry?

SIXTEEN

WHY SEMINARIES SHOULD TEACH WORSHIP

Worship is a gift between lovers who keep on giving to each other.
C. Welton Gaddy, *The Gift of Worship*

Seminaries are failing to exert leadership in worship today. Leadership in worship renewal has come from the grassroots—a multitude of local pastors, musicians, and parachurch ministries. Jack W. Hayford asserts it's authenticity: "I want to underscore the reformation in worship that is in progress. It's already begun, and its fruit has been tested and proven worthy in a sufficient number of situations to show we are not simply dealing with a fad."[1]

The leadership deficiency from seminaries continues to do incalculable harm. It's not a peripheral factor; it's a central impediment to worship in local churches. The lack of theological foundations in contemporary worship is due in part to the lack of leadership at the seminary level. We cannot expect Maranatha workshops to develop the theological foundations of worship. That ought to be the responsibility of our schools of theology. If we are to move ahead effectively, pastors, musicians, parachurch organizations, and seminaries must forge a strong partnership.

The assertion that worship has received scarcely any attention in most North American seminaries or schools of theology for decades is not mere hyperbole. It can be documented. A study of 150 Midwestern pastors indicated that only 3 percent rated their seminary

worship experiences as most significant (1985).[2] Of 103 seminaries sur-
veyed, only *8* offered degree programs in church music (1978).[3] In theological institutions that do offer church music programs, music professor Paul Wohlgemuth reported that a "cloudy picture emerges" of
nonuniform standards, of "courses taught only in interim sessions that
may be cycled every second or third year with no assurance that they
will actually be taught" (1983).[4] Little has changed since these studies
were conducted.

J. W. Schwarz found that seminary students are "aware of their need
for training in church music."[5] Pastors today are also aware of the need.
The impact of the media, the cultural and ethnic diversification of society, the rise of a formidable, separatistic youth culture, and the pressure for small and medium-sized churches to compete with large
churches have combined to make the leadership of worship much
more daunting for the average pastor. Intergenerational worship has
become more difficult to achieve. And there are additional problems.

The Great Divorce

Those who become worship pastors receive a *different* education
in a *different* location than seminarians. Musicians receive their education at conservatories, colleges, or universities, whereas pastors
and church educators receive theirs at seminaries and schools of theology. Musicians experience no contact with seminarians, nor do they
study theology or the pastoral dimension of ministry. The two groups
share no common core courses where they can dialogue with each
other, nor do they have the privilege of rubbing shoulders together in
practicums. In the few seminaries that teach worship, the music and
worship programs are often not combined.

Moreover, since musicians and artists are not present at most seminaries, their practical skills and talents are not available for modeling
worship. Consequently, seminarians tend to experience not only
impoverished expressions of worship in their chapels but also missed
opportunities for spiritual formation. How lamentable! At the very least,
seminaries could consider *utilizing adjunct church musicians drawn
from the community* to assist in their chapel services and to co-lecture
in their classrooms.

On the other side of the ledger, theologically naive musicians exhibit
a woeful lack of theological grounding. Bruce Leafblad has observed
that musicians have "a limited understanding of, and appreciation for,

the true nature and work of the church."[6] No wonder then, when musicians and preachers are thrown together in a pastorate, a lack of understanding and trust arises!

The problem has become more acute because the new worship confers an enlarged role to music expression. Only time will tell if the enlarged role accorded worship leaders will ultimately benefit the church. In many churches today, worship leaders are the primary theologians of local assemblies—the songs they choose are remembered and ultimately shape the theology of the average church attender. Worship leaders function, at the least, as prominent elders. More training ought to be available to them.

Robert Webber attests to the state of affairs in seminaries:

> I speak from experience. I graduated from three theological seminaries without taking a course in worship. Even though I was planning to become a minister, no one ever sat down and said, "Look, worship is one of the most central aspects of your future ministry. Now is the time not only to learn all you can about the subject but also to become a worshiping person so you can offer mature leadership to your congregation." The simple fact is that my seminary professors knew little about the subject. . . .
>
> What is needed . . . is the recognition of worship as a legitimate discipline among the other disciplines . . . it is a field in its own right. Indeed it is an interdisciplinary study demanding expertise in biblical, historical, and systematic theology as well as the arts, practical expertise, and personal formation.[7]

What can be done? An endowed chair of worship at a seminary could have very positive results. Concerted pressure from pastors acting as concerned alumni to bring about corrective change is also needed. Seminary leaders will listen to pastors. If the current state troubles your spirit, *write your letters and make your phone calls!* In the past this is how pastoral care, counseling, and Christian education emphases found a place in seminaries. Cracks of real concern in seminaries are beginning to appear. They are most welcome!

The present state of affairs, as observed by Martin E. Marty and Paul Westermeyer, engenders disharmony and strife:

> The pastor has had little or no training in worship. The musician has had little or no theological training. . . . The pastor may see all of worship related to preaching, pastoral care, [or evangelism]. The musi-

cians may see all of worship related to art, as the world views art, or to teaching higher standards of taste, or to performance. The schizoid condition of much American worship is the inevitable result. . . .[8]

What musicians find most disturbing is that although pastors lack preparation and training in worship, they make the key decisions. This condition has led a growing number of musicians to undertake additional training to become pastors themselves!

Ten Reasons Seminaries Should Teach Worship and Music

1. Worship is central to every pastor's ministry.
2. Music is central to evangelical worship, and the new worship has intensified this centrality: Music now makes up 50 percent of the service.
3. A peer relationship between pastors and musicians is demanded in contemporary worship.
4. Worship requires interdisciplinary study. Seminaries, as an institution, are most able to offer the variety of resources needed to provide a platform for teaching worship.
5. Worship nurtures spiritual formation.
6. Pastors need a theology of worship and music and a better understanding of the arts.
7. Musicians need theological grounding and a better understanding of ministry and the nature of the church.
8. Pastors and musicians should share classes, practicums, and become comfortable with each other prior to their partnership in ministry.
9. Pastors should experience numerous, varied, quality worship experiences in seminaries and have opportunities to design and execute them.
10. Some pastors and musicians have gifts in both preaching and music. Why should only one be developed?

Worship deserves formal recognition in the seminary curriculum. Seminaries need to assume a more significant role in the training of leaders for worship. At the very minimum, call for a worship course and chapels that model good worship leadership and a wide range of service styles and experiences. Furthermore, Web-based certificate programs ought to be developed for worship leaders, lay and professional, who cannot attend theological schools as full- or part-time students.

Properly understood, worship relates to all of life. Donald P. Hustad insists, "To experience full and authentic worship, 'in spirit and in truth,' is the greatest need of the church today."

> *I am of the opinion that we should not be concerned about working for God until we have learned the meaning and the delight of worshiping Him. A worshiper can work with eternal quality in his work.*
> A. W. Tozer, *Whatever Happened to Worship?*

THE ARGUMENT BEHIND CHAPTER 2

Chapter 2 takes the position that the instrumental view best describes the meaning of Colossians 3:16 and Ephesians 5:18–21. Let's address Colossians 3:16 first. You will recall that the opening clause of Colossians 3:16—*let the word of Christ richly dwell within you*—has the central verb ("let dwell").[1] The balanced symmetry of the remainder of the verse is directly dependent on this verb, as shown in this literal rendering:

Let the word of Christ richly dwell within you,
   in all wisdom
      teaching and admonishing one another
         [with] psalms and hymns [and] spiritual songs,
   in the grace
      singing to God
         in your hearts.

Note that there are two qualifying prepositional phrases: "in all wisdom" and "in the grace."

And there are three participles: "teaching," "admonishing," and "singing."

Keep these observations in the back of your mind. You will see their crucial role as we go on.

Spirit-Inspired Songs That Teach and Admonish

Translations differ in how they relate the participles and clauses in this verse. Should they be coordinated, subordinate clauses, or should they be uncoordinated, equivalent, imperative statements, separated by semicolons or periods? For example, the New Revised Standard Version (NRSV) renders Colossians 3:16 as three separate, imperative statements separated by semicolons:

> Let the word of Christ dwell in you richly; teach and admonish one another in all wisdom; and with gratitude in your hearts sing psalms, hymns, and spiritual songs to God.

On the other hand, the New American Standard Bible (NASB) subordinates the two phrases ("with all wisdom teaching and admonishing" and "singing with thankfulness") to the opening, primary statement ("let the word of Christ dwell"), and connects the participles, "teaching and admonishing," to the "psalms and hymns and spiritual songs":

> Let the word of Christ richly dwell within you, with all wisdom teaching and admonishing one another with psalms and hymns and spiritual songs, singing with thankfulness in your hearts to God.

Which is better? Significantly different meanings result from each translation. In the NRSV, "teaching and admonishing" is not connected to the singing of psalms, hymns, and spiritual songs, whereas in the NASB it is.

Why do these translations vary so much? Part of the answer is that participles present a formidable challenge to translators. Translators like to think of Greek as a precise, unambiguous language, but when participles are involved, plausible alternative renderings are possible. Why? The relation of the participle to the rest of the sentence "is not expressed by the participle itself . . . but is to be deduced by the context."[2] A certain amount of subjectivity on the part of the translator is involved. For example, depending on the translator's view of the context, the three participles—"teaching," "admonishing," "singing"—can be rendered as (1) an imperative, (2) an attendant circumstance, (3) a result, or (4) an instrumental (modal) force.

Four Views

Let's examine each of four possibilities in detail. During this process, a rationale will be presented for why the instrumental interpretation is judged best.

A. *Imperative Emphasis*

A large number of translations render Colossians 3:16 with three separate imperative statements. For example, in the three translations below, "teaching and admonishing" are separate commands, unconnected to the opening statement, "Let the word of Christ dwell." In all cases, the semicolons and periods convey the sense that the statements are separate ideas:

> Let the word of Christ, in all its richness, find a home with you. Teach each other, and advise each other, in all wisdom. With gratitude in your hearts sing psalms and hymns and inspired songs to God (NJB)

> Let the word of Christ dwell in you richly; teach and admonish one another with all wisdom; and with gratitude in your hearts sing psalms, hymns, and spiritual songs to God (NRSV).

> Let the message of Christ dwell among you in all its richness. Instruct and admonish each other with the utmost wisdom. Sing thankfully in your hearts to God, with psalms and hymns and spiritual songs (NEB).

A number of factors, however, point away from the validity of the imperative view. First, a participle (in itself) is never imperative, and to view it so "is the work of the interpreter to a large extent rather than of the grammarian."[3] Second, translators rarely choose to translate participles as imperative in the New Testament. Third, when they do so, the participles are independent of a main verb—which is *not* the case here in Colossians 3:16.[4] Greek scholar A. T. Robertson states, "No participle should be explained in this way [as imperative] that can properly be connected with a finite verb."[5] Fourth, scholars note an exception: Imperative participles can occur before the main verb—*but not after.* D. A. Carson says a participle "is not normally imperatival when it follows the imperative."[6] Yet this is precisely what happens in Colossians 3:16—all three participles *follow* the main verb "let dwell." Detwiler concludes, therefore, that neither the "grammar nor the context provide us with any particularly compelling reason to see the participles of Colossians 3:16 as primarily imperatival."[7]

Imperative View

Let the word of Christ dwell richly
teach and admonish one another
sing with gratitude

B. Attendant Emphasis

Attendant translations use the word "as" or "while" to indicate the participle has a *loose,* dependent relationship on the primary statement ("Let the word of Christ dwell"). The popular New International Version and the Contemporary English Version convey the sense that the "teaching and admonishing" are to occur *along with* or *alongside* the indwelling word of Christ:

> Let the word of Christ dwell in you richly **as** you teach and admonish one another with all wisdom, **and as** you sing psalms, hymns and spiritual songs with gratitude in your hearts to God (NIV).

> Let the message about Christ completely fill your lives, **while** you use all your wisdom to teach and instruct each other. With thankful hearts, sing psalms, hymns, and spiritual songs to God (CEV).

Daniel Wallace indicates, however, that the participles here do not fit the normal pattern for attendant participles in the Greek. He reports that 90 percent of the attendant participles occur in narrative literature, are aorist in tense, and precede the main verb—aspects lacking in Colossians 3:16.[8] Furthermore, he states that if a participle makes good sense as an instrumental (adverbial) participle—and that is what is advocated—we should not treat it as attendant.[9] Consequently, there do not appear to be strong reasons for translating the participle with attendant force.

Attendant View

238

C. Resultative Emphasis

In a resultative translation, "teaching and admonishing with psalms, hymns, and spiritual songs" would be the result of the word of Christ dwelling in us, which seems somewhat unnatural here. Wallace notes that result participles follow the main verb (which is the case here).[10] No Bible translations employing this category were found, however; although commentator Peter O'Brien, from his comments, appears to hold to it:

> As the word of Christ richly indwells the Colossians, so by means of its operation they **will** "teach and admonish one another in all wisdom by means of psalms, hymns, and spiritual songs. . . . the teaching and admonishing in all wisdom **arise** from the indwelling of the word. . . . (emphasis added)[11]

David Detwiler concurs that the resultative emphasis is a better choice, grammatically and contextually, than the imperative and attendant emphases, but he favors the instrumental view.

D. Instrumental Emphasis

The instrumental emphasis implies that the word of Christ dwells *by* or *by means of* "teaching and admonishing one another," and *by* or *by means of* "singing . . . to God." This view makes contextual sense, for in this case the word or message of Christ becomes integrated into hearts by means of texts that teach about Christ. It's also a very natural rendering. Having commanded them to let the word of Christ dwell richly, it is logical to expect Paul to talk about the means by which this could be accomplished. Concurring with this rendering, New Testament scholar David Peterson states: "*with all wisdom, teaching and admonishing one another,* gives a definition of the way in which they are to let the word of Christ dwell richly in their midst."[12] This view is also supported by other reputable scholars including Gordon Fee, Murray Harris, Petr Pokorny, and H. A. W. Meyer.[13]

Lingering Questions

Questions may be lingering in your mind. You may be asking, If the Word of Christ is to dwell by means of teaching psalms, hymns, and

Instrumental View

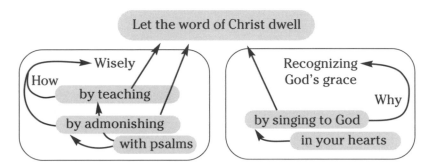

spiritual songs, why did translators miss seeing this? Fee offers two thoughts here.

1. Many earlier translators, he says, saw the context of Colossians 3:16 as dealing "not with worship but with Christian life in general"— i.e., that Paul's words were addressed not to the gathered church but to the individual believer as a general *personal* admonition to each of us—an emphasis he contends the context does not support.[14] Fee points out that the *public* nature of Colossians 3:16 is also supported by the parallel passage in Ephesians 5:19, 21, which shows individuals involved relationally, because worshipers are both speaking to one another and submitting to one another: "speaking to one another in psalms and hymns and spiritual songs . . . submitting to one another in the fear of God" (NKJV).

2. Others, Fee says, entered into the task of translation and commentary with their own presuppositions, doubting that songs could actually teach and admonish. Fee quotes Ridderbos as typical of those who had a prior mind-set to disconnect songs from teaching: "The idea that this mutual teaching and admonishing must be carried out by means of songs seems rather unnatural to us."[15] This kind of thinking, says Fee, "lurks" below the surface of discussions by several commentators.

You may also be asking, Given the variety of interpretations, how *certain* can we be that the instrumental interpretation is the right one? I asked New Testament scholar Clint Arnold,[16] an authority on Colossians and Ephesians and David Detwiler's teacher and thesis advisor, this question: "On a scale of 1 to 10, how certain are you of the instrumental view?" He replied, "I would give it a 7 or 8 out of 10. The instrumental/means use of the participle is actually a very common way of interpreting the participle—far more common than result."[17]

Arnold shared with me that instrumental participles occur elsewhere in Colossians. In Colossians 1:28 NASB, the main verb ("we proclaim him") is followed by two present participles that should be interpreted as instrumental/means (by "admonishing" and by "teaching"). This verse is significant because it uses the same participles as Colossians 3:16.

Similarly, in Colossians 3:12–13, the main imperative verb ("clothe yourselves") is followed by two present participles, indicating the means (by forebearing . . . and by forgiving). And again, in Colossians 4:5 NKJV, the main imperative verb ("walk in wisdom toward those who are outside") is followed by a present participle indicating the means ("by redeeming the time").

Be Continually Filled with the Spirit

Ephesians 5:19–21 has a similar structure to Colossians 3:16—both passages begin with a command. Now, however, there are four balanced dependent clauses (not two) and five participles (not three)—"speaking," "singing," "psalming," "giving thanks," and "submitting."

> Do not be drunk with wine, which is excess,
> but be continually filled with/by the Spirit
> **speaking** to one another
> with psalms and hymns and spiritual songs
> **singing** and **psalming**
> in your heart
> to the Lord
> **giving thanks**
> always for all things
> in the name of our Lord
> to our God and the Father
> **submitting** to one another
> in the fear of God.

Which of the four interpretations (imperative, attendant, result, or instrumental) provides the best translation?

As in the case of Colossians 3:16, the imperative and attendant emphases appear frequently in translations, but they are not the best choice for the same reasons discussed previously. The resultative and instrumental emphases seem more appropriate.

Favoring the resultative emphasis, a number of commentators believe the participles express the *consequences* of being filled with the Spirit.[18] The New Living Translation, for example, employs the word *then* to express a resultant emphasis:

> Don't be drunk with wine, because that will ruin your life. Instead, let the Holy Spirit fill and control you. **Then** you will sing psalms and hymns and spiritual songs among yourselves, making music to the Lord in your hearts.
>
> Ephesians 5:18–19

Popular pastor and writer John MacArthur Jr. adopts the same view, stating the "consequence" of a Spirit-filled life is "a heart that sings. When the believer walks in the Spirit, he has an inside joy that manifests itself in music."[19] And again, "The Spirit-filled life produces music."[20] Detwiler takes issue with the MacArthur quotes: "Notice that MacArthur emphasizes *not* the community but the individual believer. In Colossians, however, Paul is speaking in community terms to the gathered church, not to individuals. He is focusing on the presence of the Holy Spirit in the community. He talks of the community speaking to one another with psalms and submitting to one another."[21]

Detwiler argues (once more) that the instrumental view is preferable. The instrumental emphasis occurs in the World Publishing translation, which employs the preposition *by* for the first clause:

> Don't get drunk on wine, which leads to wild living. Instead, be filled with the Spirit **by** reciting psalms, hymns, and spiritual songs for your own good. Sing and make music to the Lord with your hearts. Always thank God the Father for everything in the name of our Lord Jesus Christ. Place yourselves under each other's authority out of respect for Christ.

Unfortunately the translation continues on with four imperatives: "sing," "make music," "always thank," and "place yourselves." In this respect, the New King James Version better captures the four dependent clauses and the five participles of the instrumental emphasis:

> And do not be drunk with wine, in which is dissipation; but be filled with the Spirit, **speaking** to one another in psalms and hymns and spiritual songs, **singing** and **making melody** in your heart to the Lord, **giving thanks** always for all things to God the Father in the name of our Lord Jesus Christ, **submitting** to one another in the fear of God.

A number of commentators, however, reject the instrumental view. For instance, Wallace accepts the instrumental view as a grammatical possibility, but writes, "It is almost inconceivable to see this text suggesting that the way in which one is to be Spirit-filled is by a five-step, partially mechanical formula."[22] Detwiler, though, would not view the passage as being so "rigid and absolute." He counters that Wallace's criticism could apply equally to a result emphasis: "It would be equally inconceivable to view the text as suggesting that being filled with the Spirit results exclusively in the four specifically mentioned activities."[23] Nor does Clint Arnold view the passage rigidly: "I think it is really important to stress that Paul is not thinking in some formulaic way, but rather is stressing the connection between corporate worship and the filling of the Spirit. This is something that many people may know intuitively and by experience. Thus there is some appropriateness to the expression: 'I can't wait to go to church this Sunday: I really need to get my battery charged up again!'"[24]

In summary, the instrumental version appears to offer the best alternative. Speaking personally, it was shocking to learn that the meanings of widely recognized (and widely read!) Bible translations could differ so greatly and have the power to influence one's worship philosophy so radically. Some translations appear to be of no help at all—even misleading. That was an eye opener! Given the challenges and difficulties of translation, painstaking scholarship has garnered in my mind an increased respect.

RESOURCES AT
WWW.WORSHIPINFO.COM

Worshipinfo.com exists to equip, educate, and provide original resources for worship leaders, pastors, performing musicians, and technical staff. Materials supplementing *The New Worship* are currently available there for your use. In addition, other books, articles, keyboard tutorials, worship guides, arrangements, and CDs are at the site.

Web Materials Enhancing *The New Worship*

The New Worship Supplement: Material that didn't get into the book for lack of space is presented here for your use (illustrations, discussions, etc.). Other authors and experts will be invited to share their views. There will be updates.

The New Worship Musician Software: Making Praise Flow by Barry Liesch. A free, downloadable tutorial with 160 musical examples to help musicians learn how to modulate and improvise. Freeware for Windows and Macintosh. See appendix 3 for more details.

The New Worship PowerPoint Presentations by Barry Liesch and David Russell: 16 free, downloadable PowerPoint slide shows, one for each chapter of *The New Worship,* are available. Designed for worship leaders, teachers, and seminar presenters, users have permission to rewrite, add, or delete any of the slides. They are intended to provide a foundation on which you can build your own presentations.

Other supplemental materials for The New Worship: additional materials will be made available.

Worship Book

People in the Presence of God: Models and Directions for Worship (Zondervan) by Barry Liesch is available at www.amazon.com and is described in detail at worshipinfo.com. The book offers a panoramic look at the biblical foundations of worship, interspersing many practical applications derived from five biblical models of worship: (1) the patriarchs; (2) the tabernacle/temple; (3) the synagogue; (4) Pauline worship; and (5) worship in the Book of Revelation.

Keyboard Tutorials

A series of keyboard tutorials by Dr. Barry Liesch for improving worship improvisation skills. Each book includes MIDI files and uses many hymns and choruses for demonstration purposes.

The New Worship Keyboardist: Part 1, Added Seconds
The New Worship Keyboardist: Part 2, Quartals
The Jazz Worship Keyboardist: Part 1, Raised 11ths
The Jazz Worship Keyboardist: Part 2, Raised 9ths

More keyboard books and other materials are forthcoming.

THE NEW WORSHIP MUSICIAN
SOFTWARE

Have you ever wanted to sit down at the piano and lead a group of people in a time of free flowing praise? That's what this free, downloadable, supplemental software for Mac and Windows helps you do.

The responsibility to segue from chorus to chorus and hymn to hymn falls to a knowledgeable musician—usually the keyboardist or a guitarist. Yet many struggle, finding the performance of modulations baffling because little is taught or written about it.

This supplemental software teaches you how *to create modulations yourself* and *develop a sense of flow*. Pastors or music directors may want to give this software to their musicians. College music departments will also find it useful. This printable resource offers:

- A mini-course on modulation and improvisation
- 125 pages and 160 examples
- coverage of classical and contemporary styles

An intermediate background in piano or organ will be beneficial. This software is primarily intended for musicians who have little or no experience in improvising, but even seasoned improvisers may find information that will clarify their thinking. *Whenever you see this computer disk logo in the margin of* The New Worship, *it's your signal that follow-up material is available in this software.*

Ten chapters are divided into two sections. The first section focuses on various modulations. The V7 I and ii7 V7 I progressions are employed initially, and then the Vsus9 is introduced to smooth chord connections and add color. A summary chapter puts a flowing praise service together and shows how to make modulations flow.

The second section focuses on improvisation. Added seconds and quartal chords are presented.

Contents

Modulation

1. Basic Stuff
2. Modulations Up a Half Step
3. Modulations Up a Whole Step
4. Modulations with Color and Resonance
5. Modulations in Free-Flowing Praise: A Demonstration

Improvisation

6. Ten Thoughts on Developing a Ministry
7. Fourteen Principles on Intelligent Improvisation
8. Reshape V7: Use "Four over Five"
9. Reshape Triads: Use Added 2/Quartal Chords
10. Shop Talk: Insights from Tom Keene

The software is available free of charge in Macintosh and Windows versions. The self-extracting, printable archive takes 2.2 Mb and is available at www.worshipinfo.com.

NOTES

Chapter 1 Culture, Choruses, and Hymns

1. John Witvliet makes some telling comments in his review of four worship books in "At Play in the House of the Lord: Why Worship Matters" in *Books and Culture* (November/December 1998): "Worshipers in nearly every Christian tradition experience some of what happens in worship as divine encounter. Differences in Christian worship arise not so much from whether or not God is understood to be present, but rather in what sense. Those who mock supposedly simplistic theories of sacramental realism at the Lord's Supper wind up preserving sacramental language for preaching or for music. Speaking only somewhat simplistically: the Roman Catholics reserve their sacramental language for the Eucharist, Presbyterians reserve theirs for preaching, and the charismatics save theirs for music. In a recent pastor's conference, one evangelical pastor solicited applications for a music director/worship leader position by calling for someone who could 'make God present through music. . . .' No medieval sacramental theologian could have said it more strongly. Dare we call this 'musical transubstantiation'?"

2. From Kenneth A. Myers, *All God's Children and Blue Suede Shoes: Christians and Popular Culture* (Westchester, Ill.: Crossway, 1989). Quoted by reviewer Douglas Groothuis in *Christian Scholar's Review* (June 1992), 422. See also Milburn Price, "The Impact of Popular Culture on Congregational Song," *Hymn* (January 1993), 11–19; and Paul Westermeyer, "Beyond 'Alternative' and 'Traditional' Worship," *The Christian Century* (March 18–25, 1992), 300–302.

3. Some of these deficiencies were culled from Jeremy Begbie's lecture at Regent College, Vancouver, B.C., June 1994, "Where Is Church Music Going?" (tape RAV 24 9407).

4. Gordon D. Fee, *God's Empowering Presence: The Holy Spirit in the Letters of Paul* (Peabody, Mass.: Hendrickson, 1994), 878.

5. Of the 63 students submitting a written response to my question in class, "How many hymns are you familiar with, or how many could you recognize?" The data was as follows: 10 percent know 5 or fewer hymns; 25 percent know 10 or fewer hymns; 50 percent know 20 or fewer hymns; 75 percent know 40 or fewer hymns; 6 percent know 100 or more hymns. I played and sang several hymns as examples before asking for a response, and made sure they understood I was asking how many hymns they were merely acquainted with. My sense is that this data is fairly representative.

James L. Melton, director of choral activities and associate professor of music at Vanguard University of Southern California (another Christian college), believes their students, on the average, are acquainted with fewer than 10 hymns (personal communication, 19 June 2000).

6. See Begbie, "Where Is Church Music Going?" Also see Harold Best, *Music through the Eyes of Faith* (HarperSanFrancisco, 1993), 71–73, 190, for ideas relating

to one's musical center. I find that some of my students, however, cannot identify a musical center for themselves. Interesting! See the section The Main Problem later in this chapter.

7. The chart is adapted from Harry Eskew and Hugh T. McElrath, *Sing with Understanding: An Introduction to Christian Hymnody* (Nashville: Broadman, 1980), 47.

8. Roland H. Bainton, *A Life of Martin Luther: Here I Stand* (Toronto: New American Library of Canada, 1963), 267.

9. For an insightful Christian perspective on the media, see Quentin J. Schultze et al., *Dancing in the Dark* (Grand Rapids: Eerdmans, 1991).

10. This story is adapted from Kenneth W. Osbeck, *101 Hymn Stories* (Grand Rapids: Kregel, 1982), 126, 172.

11. Before launching into such a project, read the insightful book by Charles Arn, *How to Start a New Service* (Grand Rapids: Baker, 1997). Understand that Arn, a church growth leader affiliated with Fuller Seminary, is a passionate advocate of evangelism and multiple-style services. His book is the result of a five-year (at least), hands-on study.

12. Bill Gibson, worship leader, personal communication, 2 June 2000.

13. James Melton, personal communication, 19 June 2000.

14. Dianne Bowker (ThM, MCM), personal communication, 2 June 2000.

15. James Melton (personal communication, 19 June 2000) believes hymns are theologically and doctrinally better because bad hymns "have been weeded out over the years by new hymnal editions and committees. Also, theologians have written the hymn texts, [whereas] primarily musicians (and not very good ones) are writing the majority of the new choruses."

16. Best, *Music through the Eyes of Faith,* 67. For a secular example of "living pentecostally," listen to Pat Metheny's gorgeous CD, *Secret Story* (Geffen GEFD 24468).

17. Listen to Bob James's CD *Fourplay* (Warner Bros. 9 26656—2), cut one, 2:29–2:57.

18. For a high level of musicality and serious intent (with accessibility), the vocal and piano CD by Tony Bennett and Bill Evans, *Together Again* (Rhino R2 75837) is hard to beat. For an instrumental CD involving keyboards (acoustic/electronic), guitar, bass, and percussion, listen to James, *Fourplay* (Warner Bros. 9 26656—2). For examples of CDs with excellent Christian performers, listen to *Count Me In* (Integrity 08942), featuring saxist Justo Almario and friends; *The Gospel According to Jazz* (Warner Gospel 47113–2), Kirt Whalum and friends; and *Jars of Clay*, (Silvertone Records 01241–41580–2).

19. Martin Luther, *Luther's Works,* gen. ed. Helmut T. Lehmann, vol. 49 (Philadelphia: Fortress, 1972), 68–69.

20. The worship leader's edition of *The Worshiping Church: A Hymnal* (Carol Stream, Ill.: Hope, 1991) contains a copyright index indicating which hymns are public domain. The telephone numbers of publishers are given.

21. See below a "blues" or "black" rendering of "Blessed Assurance."

Notice the right hand voicings (above) make much use of the pentatonic scale (C, D, E, G, A, C) for the basic chords in the key of C (C, F, G). Look at the D's and A's in the right hand; they tend to give the passage its black sound. To further clarify the style, below are two chord progressions (A1, B1). A1 is what you would expect to encounter in an ordinary hymnbook harmonization (I–IV–I or C–F–C), whereas B1 is its black counterpart (I–ii–I or C–Dm–C). Notice, again the C–D–C movement in B1.

A2 and B2 (below) extend this idea a little further, giving a feeling of musical context, with (again) A2 representing a conventional hymnbook sound and B2 a black sound.

Below, find an exercise to assist you in improvising in black style. It's in C major, but practice it in other keys. Measure one centers on the C chord (I), measure two F (IV), and measure three G (V), the three chord areas you are most likely to encounter.

251

22. See *Maranatha! Music Praise Hymns and Choruses,* expanded 4th edition by Maranatha! Music (1997), 1. Also, look at the bridges created in *Acoustic Hymns* (Get Down Records, a ministry of Christian Assembly, 2424 Colorado Blvd., Los Angeles, CA 90041). Bridges like these could be useful in a congregational setting too. James Melton (personal communication, 19 June 2000) adds that the Maranatha! arrangement of "I Am Thine, O Lord" (Crosby) with "Jesus, Draw Me Close" (Founds) also works well.

23. See Bob James's *Playin' Hooky* (Warner Bros. 9 46737—2, cut 1) for a clever updating of Chopin's *Etude in E Major;* Eddie Daniel's *Beautiful Love* (Shanachie 5029, cut 1) for a jazz version of Bach; David Grusin's *Collections* (GRD—9579, cut 9), which combines Baroque and bossa nova styles.

24. The word *prostitutes* is shocking, but the Wesleys were proclaiming the gospel to all segments of their society. The word *harlots* was also used.

Chapter 2   Teaching, the Spirit, and Our Congregational Songs

1. David Franklin Detwiler, "The Role of Music in Worship according to Paul: An Exegetical Inquiry" (Master's Thesis, Talbot School of Theology at Biola University, 1997).

2. Ibid., 65.

3. Fee, *God's Empowering Presence,* 649.

4. The concept of "dwelling" occurs repeatedly in Paul's writings: See in NASB Rom. 8:9, 11; 1 Cor. 3:16; 2 Cor. 6:16; Eph. 2:22; 3:17; 2 Tim. 1:14.

5. David Peterson, "Worship in the New Testament" in *Worship: Adoration and Action,* ed. D. A. Carson (Grand Rapids: Baker, 1993), 78.

6. David Peterson, *Engaging with God: A Biblical Theology of Worship* (Grand Rapids: Eerdmans, 1992), 213.

7. Detwiler, "The Role of Music," 85. See also Markus Barth and Helmut Blanke, *Colossians* (New York: Doubleday, 1994), 427.

8. The Septuagint translators also do not differentiate between *psalms, hymns,* and *spiritual songs* when translating the Hebrew Old Testament into the Greek language. They use all three words extensively for psalm titles, for example. Moreover, Philo and Josephus do not use the word *psalm* for a song of praise. They use the word *hymn* when quoting from David's psalms.

9. Fee, *God's Empowering Presence,* 653.

10. Donald P. Hustad, *Jubilate II: Church Music in Worship and Renewal* (Carol Stream, Ill.: Hope, 1993), 148.

11. Fee, *God's Empowering Presence,* 654n.71. A stronger argument for singing in tongues could be made from 1 Corinthians 14:13–16. Some adopt a trinitarian view of psalms, hymns, and spiritual songs: psalms to God, hymns to Christ, spiritual songs to the Holy Spirit.

12. Ibid., 653–54.

13. Ibid., 650.

14. Clinton E. Arnold, *The Colossians Syncretism: The Interface between Christianity and Folk Belief at Colossae* (Tübingen, Germany: J. C. B. Mohr, 1995), 310.

15. Clinton Arnold is professor of New Testament at Talbot School of Theology and author of *Ephesians: Power and Magic* (New York: Cambridge University Press, 1989), as well as *The Colossians Syncretism* cited above (personal communication, 27 May 1994).

16. Dianne Bowker, personal communication, 3 April 2000. See the chapter "Hymnody as Theology" in her master's of theology thesis, "Theology through the Arts: Tree Imagery in Christian Hymnody as an Exposition of the Person and Work of Jesus Christ" (Regent College, 1999).

17. Robert D. Dale, *To Dream Again: How to Help Your Church Come Alive* (Nashville: Broadman, 1981), 54.

18. Clint Arnold, personal communication, 8 May 2000.

19. Hampton's piece, though popularly called a chorus, has characteristics of a hymn, for it has two stanzas (and a refrain).

20. John M. Frame, *Contemporary Worship Music: A Biblical Defense* (Phillipsberg, N.J.: P & R Publishing, 1997), 100.

21. Ibid., 99.

22. This quotation by Thomas H. Troeger appears in his review of a book on the poetry of the psalms in *The Hymn: A Journal of Congregational Song* 44, no. 3 (July 1993): 55.

23. Commenting on Ephesians 5:18–21, Markus Barth concurs: "By quoting, transforming, and composing hymns, in the writing of Ephesians, the author of the epistle has given his readers an example of the feasibility, usefulness, and beauty of the directive given here." *Ephesians 4–6* (Garden City, N.Y.: Doubleday, 1974), 582.

24. Fee, *God's Empowering Presence*, 656.

25. Best, *Music Through the Eyes of Faith*, 192. David Peterson concurs, "One part of the meeting cannot be 'the worship time' (e.g., prayer and praise) and another part 'the edification time' (e.g., preaching), since Paul's teaching encourages us to view edification and worship occurring together." "Worship in the New Testament," 83.

26. Fee, *God's Empowering Presence*, 655.

27. Ibid., 655.

28. Kenneth S. Wuest, *The New Testament: An Expanded Translation* (Grand Rapids: Eerdmans, 1961), 474

29. Fee, *God's Empowering Presence*, 655, 580–81. Philip hears the eunuch reading aloud (Acts 8:30). Daniel, Jesus, the Pharisee, and the tax collector all pray aloud (Dan. 6:10–12; John 17; Luke 18:9–14).

30. Ibid., 722.

31. Detwiler, "The Role of Music," 106.

32. Ibid., 111.

33. Ibid., 114.

Chapter 3 Free-Flowing Praise

1. For a more scholarly analysis of the variety of Protestant worship traditions, see James F. White, *Protestant Worship: Traditions in Transition* (Louisville, Ky.: Westminster, 1989), 23ff. He lists nine groups: Lutheran, Reformed, Anabaptist, Anglican, Separatist/Puritan, Quaker, Methodist, Frontier, and Pentecostal.

2. John Wimber was the senior and founding pastor of the Vineyard at Anaheim Hills, California, before his death. This parent church has planted about three hundred Vineyard churches throughout the United States and Canada in about fifteen years. Their music and worship style have been central to their success.

3. Paul Anderson, "Balancing Form and Freedom," *Leadership* (spring 1986), 26.

4. For License Kit and licensing and copyright information, contact Christian Copyright Licensing, Inc., 6130 N.E. 78 Court, Suite C–11, Portland, OR 97218.

5. Charismatics like Judson Cornwall and Bob Sorge make a distinction between "praise" and "worship." This distinction is confusing because praise is a part of worship. What they are attempting to say, I believe, is that in the dynamics of leading worship, praise and exaltation normally precede adoration and intimacy. Expressing it in this way clarifies the concept and helps avoid confusion.

6. MIDI is an acronym for "Musical Instrument Digital Interface," which makes it possible for electronic instruments from different manufacturing companies to talk (relate) to each other. Thus the organ keys can trigger a synthesizer, "fire" several synthesizers at one time, and even connect with a drum machine.

7. Try modulating up a P4 when repeating, "Let there be glory and honor and praises" (D to G-major).

8. *Hymns II* (InterVarsity Press, 1976) has pop chord symbols and uses the keys guitarists perfer.

9. Also available are a book and two audiotapes on worship drumming: *Drums in Worship* by Mike Kinard, Mike Kinard Productions, P.O. Box 476627, Garland, TX 75047; (214) 771-0205.

10. For an automated music accompaniment software program for use with IBM, Atari, or Macintosh computers, contact PG Music, Inc., Suite 111, 266 Elmwood Ave., Buffalo, NY 14222.

11. Harold Best, "Authentic Worship and Faithful Music Making," at www.worship info.com.

12. Ibid.

Chapter 4 Journey into the Holy of Holies

1. See Graham Kendrick, *Learning to Worship as a Way of Life* (Minneapolis: Bethany House, 1984), 141–51; and Judson Cornwall, *Let Us Worship* (South Plainfield, N.J.: Bridge Publishing, 1983), 153–58. This chapter borrows from them.

2. Adapted from Hayyim Schauss, *The Jewish Festivals: History and Observance,* trans. Samuel Jaffe (New York: Schocken Books, 1962), 170–84.

3. Cornwall, *Let Us Worship,* 156, emphasis added.

4. Ibid., 109–10.

5. Ibid., 157.

6. Ibid., 157–58.

7. Ibid., 158.

8. James F. White claims that the desire to begin the service with confession actually stems from the medieval emphasis on penance (*Protestant Worship,* 66, 74).

9. I feel tentative in talking about the combination of worship and evangelism within a single morning service, for I have not recently had the privilege of serving for an extended time at a church where that was achieved continuously and effectively. I have *attended* churches, however, where the two purposes were powerfully comingled on Sunday mornings.

10. My appreciation to Daniel Bauman, pastor and former dean of Bethel Seminary, for these thoughts (3 March 1994).

Chapter 5 Designing the Service

1. Hustad, *Jubilate II,* 117.

2. Ibid., 234–37, 346, 391.

3. Some would add the weekly or frequent observance of the Lord's Supper to this list.

4. Robert E. Webber, *Worship Is a Verb* (Waco, Tex.: Word, 1985), 50.

5. Hustad, *Jubilate II,* 320; appears here in an adapted form.

6. Ibid., 333. See source for an example of an extended prayer in contemporary language.

7. Ibid., 322.

8. Donald P. Hustad, *Jubilate! Church Music in the Evangelical Tradition* (Carol Stream, Ill.: Hope, 1981), 178.

9. Ibid., 320.

10. I'm assuming most readers are most accustomed to thematic services. For these readers, I hope the exposition of liturgical and open worship services may suggest new possibilities for use within the thematic framework. This kind of cross-fertilization seems to be precisely where interesting things are happening today.

11. Ronald Allen and Gordon Borror, *Worship: Rediscovering the Missing Jewel* (Portland, Oreg.: Multnomah, 1987), 74.

12. Ibid., 71.

13. Kendrick, *Learning to Worship,* 141.

14. Ibid., 153.
15. Ibid., 157.
16. Ibid., 161.
17. Ibid., 164.
18. Ibid., 199–200.
19. Ibid., 169.
20. Ibid., 170–71.
21. Ibid., 165.
22. Ibid., 166.
23. I understand many evangelicals believe the day of prophecies and tongues "has ceased." I am not trying to make a theological point. I think it does us good, however, to let Scripture "fall out" just as written and try to understand, feel, and experience what the early church experienced.

Chapter 6 Drama, Scripture, Technology

1. I have borrowed from my book *People in the Presence of God* (Grand Rapids. Zondervan, 1988) rather freely in this section. This book (available at www. amazon.com) offers a much more complete treatment of worship in the Book of Revelation with five chapters devoted to the subject.
2. Liesch, *People in the Presence of God,* 280.
3. Steve Pederson, *Drama Ministry* (Grand Rapids: Zondervan, 1999). Also see, *Christians in Theatre Arts* (www.cita.org; 864-271-2116); *Drama Ministry,* a creative resource publication (www.dramaministry.com; 800-992-2144); Michael Slaughter, *Out on the Edge: A Wake-up Call for Church Leaders on the Edge of the Media Reformation* (Nashville: Abingdon Press, 1998).
4. See Liesch, *People in the Presence of God,* for two ready-for-performance examples in the appendix with permission to reproduce.
5. *Worship Leader,* call 800-286-8099 for subscription; *Church Production Magazine,* call 877-241-7461 for subscription.
6. *Worship Builder* is produced by DONline Solutions: www.worshipbuilder.com (210-215-1703).
7. Nine software programs are: *ChurchView* at www.churchview.net (800-989-7287); HymnShow at www.tempomusic.com (800-733-5066); *Presentation Manager* at www.creativelifestyles.com (248-685-8179); *Prologue* at www.prologue.cc (877 274-7277); *SongBase/VideoPresenter* at www.songbase.com (800-717-7833); Song-Screen at www.songscreen.com (719-550-1719); *SongShow Plus* at www.song show plus.com (208-898-0756); *Worship Software* at www.worshipsoftware.com (800-239-7000); *Worship Song Programmer* at www.omegaconsultantsinc.com (360-754-1805). This information was gathered from an article by Tim Eason, "PowerPoint and Beyond, Part III: Worship Software Overview," in *Church Production Magazine* (March/April 2000), 38–73.
8. Personal communication, 14 June 2000. David Russell is the director of instructional resources at Biola University.
9. See Marva Dawn, *Reaching Out Without Dumbing Down* (Grand Rapids: Eerdmans, 1995); Neil Postman, *Amusing Ourselves to Death: Public Discourse in the Age of Show Business* (New York: Penguin Books, 1985).

Chapter 7 Inspiring the People's Song

1. A 56-minute video, *Sing and Rejoice: Help for Hymn Singing with Alice Parker,* is available from Worship Works, a National Worship Resource Network, 10619 Alameda Drive, Knoxville, TN 39932; 615-966-0103; the cost is $39.95.
2. Composed by Dr. Jack Schwarz, head of the Music Department at Biola University, La Mirada, California (ca. 1987).
3. Kenneth W. Osbeck, *101 Hymn Stories* (Grand Rapids: Kregel, 1982); *The Worshiping Church: A Hymnal,* worship leader's edition (Carol Stream, Ill.: Hope, 1990).

4. Personal communication, 13 June 2000.

5. Ibid.

6. John Wesley, *The Works of John Wesley* (1872; reprint, Grand Rapids: Baker, 1978), 346.

7. Tom Kraeuter, *Developing an Effective Worship Ministry* (P.O. Box 635, Lynwood, WA 98046: Emerald Books, 1993), 92.

8. The tunes in this paragraph can be found in the *Maranatha! Praise Chorus Book* (distributed by Word, 1983).

9. The text is from Isaiah 6:3; tune by Nolene Prince; choreography by Dorie Mattson, October 1985.

Holy Holy Holy Is the Lord of Hosts

Isaiah 6:3

Words/Music by
Nolene Prince
arr by Barry Liesch

whole earth is full of your glo - ry   Ho-ly is the Lord.

10. A few of these points were culled from Jay Martin, "That Congregational Singing," *Journal of Church Music* 25, no. 5 (May 1983).

11. See Harold P. Geerdes, *Music Facilities: Building, Equipment, and Renovating* (Reston, Va.: Music Educators National Conference, 1987); Harold P. Geerdes, *Worship Space Acoustics: A Guide to Better Sound in Your Parish* (Washington, D.C.: The Pastoral Press, 1989).

Chapter 8 Is Worship a Performance? The Concept

1. Personal communication, 4 January 1992. Tom Keene has produced, performed, and arranged for more than three hundred Christian albums.

2. Daniel Bauman comments: "Bruce Leafblad talks of 'evangelistic music' for the outsider. Are we using outsider music for the insider?" (3 March 1994).

3. Personal communication, 23 May 1986 with John Cochran, a Christian drama instructor.

4. Søren Kierkegaard, *Purity of Heart Is to Will One Thing* (New York: Harper, 1938), 160–66.

5. Adapted from Edwin Lindquist, "The Dusty Demands of Worship Prompting," *Leadership* (spring 1986), 37.

6. *Webster's New Collegiate Dictionary* (1960), 625. "Perform is the general word, often applied to ordinary activity as a more formal expression than DO, but usually implying regular, methodical, and prolonged application or work." *Random House Dictionary of the English Language: The Unabridged Edition* (1967), 1070. "Perform, often a mere formal equivalent for do, is usually used for a more or less involved process rather than a single act." *Webster's New World Dictionary: Third College Edition* (1994), 1003. "Perform implies action that follows established patterns or procedures or fulfills agreed-upon requirements and often connotes special skill." *Merriam Webster's Collegiate Dictionary,* 10th ed. "When you perform or play a piece of music or dance, etc., you do something to entertain an audience." *Collins Cobuild English Language Dictionary* (London, 1988). The word "rendition" has become as popular as performance in the sense of providing musical, dramatic,

or other forms of entertainment. Both words mean the accomplishment or execution of acts, feats, or ceremonies." Harvey Show, *Dictionary of Problem Words and Expressions* (N.Y.: Washington SquarePress, 1975).

7. For further references on *ministering,* see the NASB 1 Kings 8:11; 1 Chron. 6:32; 2 Chron. 8:14; 23:6; Neh. 10:39; for *serving,* see Num. 8:11, 19, 22, 24; 1 Chron. 6:48; 25:1; Luke 1:8.

8. A number of translations use the phrase "to do" (e.g., KJV) in place of the word *perform.* This is the basic meaning of the Hebrew and Greek words. The word *perform* seems less general and more focused. The NASB uses this word in the context of signs and wonders in the Old Testament more than ten times. In the New Testament the NASB translates the New Testament Greek words *poieo, ergazamai, ginomai, ioomai* as "perform," "performs," "performing," "performed" more frequently than the NIV. Moreover, in about thirty instances in the NASB, the Greek words refer to healing, signs, and miracles "performed," whereas, for example, only ten instances of the same occurs in the NIV. The ten occurrences in the NIV refer exclusively to signs and wonders. Obviously the translators of both versions have been reserving the English word *performance* almost exclusively to the overtly spectacular in the New Testament. The NASB uses *perform* in relation to worship in Luke 1:8 and 1 Cor. 9:13.

9. Again, I am not suggesting that you must or should use the word *performance* in the pulpit. I am suggesting ways to mute its negative connotations and keep everyone properly focused.

10. Tasks that appear on the surface to be simple and short yet are absorbing emotionally and intellectually also qualify.

11. In relation to length, though, pastors and the people perceive things differently. Many pastors feel it is more difficult to preach a short sermon than a long one. For the people, however, it is more difficult to hear a long one than a short one, unless the pastor is unusually gifted. When a sermon or a song service is not going well, there is a tendency to extend it inordinately in order to "turn the corner." My experience is that this is seldom effective. We simply may be reaping the fruit of preparation that was inadequate or lacking in insight.

12. Ben Patterson, "Can Worship Leaders Worship?" *Leadership* (spring 1986), 36. Pastor Eugene Peterson says that his Sabbath (practically speaking) is Monday. Sunday he leads others in their Sabbath. Sunday is his "workday."

13. May I share with you something that offends me? Worship leaders are sometimes particularly insensitive immediately after the passing of the cup in the communion service. The people are at a point of repose, reflecting on the Lord, when suddenly the service veers off in another direction as if shot out of a cannon. It is as if the deep reverence felt in drinking from the cup has absolutely no continuing significance. Why can't we linger for a time in that reverence?

Chapter 9   Is Worship a Performance? The Implications

1. See 1 Sam. 16:18; 1 Chron. 15:22; 2 Chron. 34:12; Ps. 33:3; 47:7; Isa. 23:16.

2. I picked up the ideas of "response-able" and the definition of *discipline* from being around Richard Foster and Dallas Willard.

3. C. S. Lewis, *Christian Reflections* (Grand Rapids: Eerdmans, 1967), 10.

4. Ibid., 1.

5. I don't mean to imply that human personality should be expunged or suppressed.

6. The scriptural reminder and thought is from Stelian Parvu, Christian recording artist (14 January 1994).

7. Lyle E. Schaller, *The Senior Minister* (Nashville: Abingdon Press, 1988), 131.

8. Lyle E. Schaller, *The Middle-Sized Church: Problems and Prescriptions* (Nashville: Abingdon Press, 1985), 88.

9. I am not referring to the kind of divine compulsion Paul speaks of in 1 Corinthians 9:16. Rather, I have in mind a more human, ordinary desire to perform.

10. A pastor comments: "When art goes public, the public can say what they want. No one feels compelled to take a course in art before they criticize a painting, nor a course in homiletics before they critique a sermon" (3 March 1994).

11. Richard J. Foster, *Celebration of Discipline* (San Francisco: Harper and Row, 1988), 130.

12. Dallas Willard, *The Spirit of the Disciplines: Understanding How God Changes Lives* (San Francisco: Harper and Row, 1988), 174.

13. The chart is adapted in part from Foster's *Celebration of Discipline,* 128–40.

Chapter 10 Worship: Christ's Action and Our Response

1. Throughout the first half of the chapter I will be borrowing a number of ideas from James B. Torrance, *Worship, Community and the Triune God of Grace* (Downers Grove, Ill.: InterVarsity Press, 1966).

2. Ibid., 17.

3. Ibid., 18.

4. William L. Lane, "Hebrews 1–8" *Word Bible Commentary* 47 (Dallas, Tex.: Word, 1991), 59. The verse does not explicitly refer to the heavenly sanctuary, but the content supports this conclusion.

Victor Rhee (professor of New Testament at Talbot School of Theology) writes, "The Greek word for 'congregation' in both 2:12 and 12:23 is *ekklesia.* It appears to refer to the assembly in heaven, for the author of Hebrews in 2:10–18 is referring to Jesus who was crowned after suffering as the representative of all mankind" (personal communication, 12 May 2000).

Tom Finley, professor of Old Testament at Talbot School of Theology, says: "In Hebrews 2:12 the worship sense is *secondary,* whereas the primary point appears to be our identification with Christ as brothers. In the Psalms reference (Ps. 22:22), however, worship is *primary,* a response to God's deliverance. A similar twist occurs in Hebrews 2:13, where in the original reference (Isa. 8:18), Isaiah himself is the 'I' of the quote. There appears to be an analogy. As Isaiah could speak of himself along with his children as 'signs' pointing to the Lord, so Hebrews applies it to Christ. It is the *identification* with 'his brothers' that enabled Christ to be 'a merciful and faithful high priest' (Heb. 2:17–18)" (personal communication, 15 May 2000).

5. John Calvin, "The Epistle of Paul the Apostle to the Hebrews," *Calvin Commentaries* 12, trans. William B. Johnston (Grand Rapids: Eerdmans, 1963), 27.

6. The references in this paragraph are Hebrews 2:11, 17 (NRSV); 4:5, 10, 15, 5:2; and 9:14.

7. Torrance, *Worship,* 24.

8. Ibid., 30.

9. William L. Lane, "Hebrews 9–13," *Word Bible Commentary* 48 (Dallas, Tex.: Word, 1991), 410.

10. George Westley Buchanan, "To the Hebrews," *Anchor Bible* 36 (Garden City: Doubleday, 1972), 208.

11. Lane, "Hebrews 9–13," 411.

12. Ibid., 397.

13. Tom Finley (personal communication, 15 May 2000). Dianne Bowker (personal communication, 1 June 2000) adds: "I agree with the above and would extend that to specifically include *all* the senses. In our worship, how can we incorporate the sense of smell, for example, or touch, along with our hearing/speaking/singing and seeing? Even the sense of sight is greatly underutilized in evangelical worship, when we consider the sterility of much of our architecture, and our lack of banners, stained-glass windows (in some sanctuaries, windows of any sort), sculpture, and other visual arts. The biblical principle that supports the use of our bodies in

worship is based on Romans 12:1—to 'present our bodies [the physical] as holy and living sacrifices is our spiritual work/service of worship'! There is no body/spirit dichotomy here. As Wendell Berry has said, God's dust and God's breath come together to make a living soul."

14. Jack R. Taylor, *The Hallelujah Factor* (Nashville: Broadman, 1983), preface, 16.

15. Andrew E. Hill, *Enter His Courts with Praise: Old Testament Worship for the New Testament Church* (Grand Rapids: Baker, 1996), xxx.

16. Ibid.

17 J. D. Davies, *Liturgical Dance: A Historical, Theological and Practical Handbook* (London: SCM, 1984), 86.

18. Ralph P. Martin, *The Worship of God: Some Theological, Pastoral, and Practical Reflections* (Grand Rapids: Eerdmans, 1982).

19. Hill, *Enter His Courts,* xviii.

20. Compare Deuteronomy 4:24.

21. For the Old Testament terminology, I have borrowed liberally from Hill, *Enter His Courts.*

22. Johannes Botterweck and Helmer Ringgren, eds., *Theological Dictionary of the Old Testament,* (Grand Rapids: Eerdmans, 1974), 4:249.

23. Martin, *The Worship of God,* 11. Also, the word *bless* means "to kneel."

24. Botterweck and Ringgren, ed., *Theological Dictionary of the Old Testament,* 4:249.

25. David Peterson writes concerning the Greek word *proskynein:* "It is not legitimate to suggest that in religious contexts the terminology expressed intimacy with God or affection toward him. Submission is the fundamental disposition. . . ." ("Worship in the New Testament" in *Worship: Adoration and Action,* 53). Yet I have heard *proskynein* used repeatedly (and incorrectly) as an argument for intimacy in worship. See also Walter Bauer, *A Greek-English Lexicon of the New Testament,* 2d ed. (Chicago: University of Chicago Press, 1958), 716.

26. "To fall down" is also associated with worship in the Old Testament. See Josh. 5:14; 2 Chron. 20:18; Job 1:20.

27. Tom Kraeuter, *Developing an Effective Worship Ministry,* 92.

28. See Colin Brown, gen. ed., *The New International Dictionary of New Testament Theology,* vol. 3 (Grand Rapids: Zondervan, 1978), 550–55.

29. Paul Waitman Hoon, *The Integrity of Worship* (Nashville: Abingdon Press, 1971), 219.

30. Tom Finley responds: "This seems like an Old Testament emphasis also, especially from passages like Deut. 6:4ff. Also *abad* (another form of *abodah*) means 'to serve.'"

31. Peterson, *Engaging with God,* 206.

32. Ibid., 181–82. Also, Tom Finley notes that the same emphasis is found in Deuteronomy 6:13: "Fear the Lord your God, serve *[abad]* him only" (personal communication, 15 May 2000).

33. See Gerald F. Hawthorne, "Philippians," *Word Biblical Commentary* 43 (Waco: Word, 1983), 104–6.

34. Dianne Bowker (personal communication, 1 June 2000) suggests that the tendency to view the worship service as an evangelistic event (a seeker's service) has resulted in a reductionism in several areas: visual symbols of worship have been eliminated, congregational participation has been limited to musical segments, and the music is sometimes more a performance by the worship team than it is the work of the people.

35. Bruce Leafblad, *Music, Worship, and the Ministry of the Church* (Portland, Oreg.: Western Conservative Baptist Seminary, 1978), 21. Leafblad, in using the word *first,* is addressing the issue of priority.

36. Ibid., 21–39.

37. Jack W. Hayford, *Worship His Majesty* (Waco, Tex.: Word, 1987), 56.
38. Jack W. Hayford, *Church on the Way* (Grand Rapids: Chosen Books, 1983), 53.
39. Ibid., 48–49.
40. Ibid., 78–80.
41. Ibid., 51.

Chapter 11   Worship That Models the Purpose of the Church

1. This chapter draws from David B. Pass's book *Music and the Church: A Theology of Church Music* (Nashville: Broadman, 1989), which attempts to provide a comprehensive model for church music. Particular phrases from his book are used without endnoting. He presents a survey of ten theologians, which provides an international consensus for his model (pp. 75–78): Bonhoeffer, Hoekendijk, Dulles, Kelsey, Trimp, Gelineau, Nxumalo, Bosch, Moody, and Deschner.
2. Other Greek words relating to the overall purpose of the church include *didache* and *diakonia*.
3. Fee, *God's Empowering Presence*, 230–31.
4. Dianne Bowker (personal communication, 2 June 2000).
5. Fee, *God's Empowering Presence*, 245–46.
6. William Lock, professor of church music at Biola University (personal communication, 7 June 2000).
7. Pass, *Music and the Church*, 118.
8. A study of the Pauline worship services described in Scripture will show that the sheer number and variety of elements involved is astonishing. See Liesch, *People in the Presence of God*, chapter 5, for a descriptive chart and an extended discussion.
9. Craig Douglas Erickson, *Participating in Worship: History, Theory, and Practice* (Louisville: Westminster/John Knox, 1989), 36–37.
10. Chuck Smith Jr., "Leading People to an Encounter with God," *Worship Leader* (August–September 1992), 50.
11. Elmer Towns, *An Inside Look at Ten of Today's Most Innovative Churches* (Ventura, Calif.: Regal, 1990), 56–67.
12. Ibid.
13. Quoted in Sally Morgenthaler, *Worship Evangelism* (Grand Rapids: Zondervan, 1995), 66.
14. Ibid. Morgenthaler cites the following verses as biblical support of the worship evangelism concept: Num. 15:14; Deut. 26:10–11; 2 Sam. 22:50; Ps. 18:49; 40:3; 57:9–10; 67:5–7; 96:3, 10; Isa. 66:19; Acts 10:34–35; Rom. 15.9–11; and Rev. 15:4. See also the argument for believer services in Ron Owens, *Return to Worship: A God-Centered Approach* (Nashville: Broadman and Holman, 1999), 83–89.
15. This hymn can be found in *The Worshiping Church*, #436.
16. Personal communication, July 1978.
17. Fifteen instances of *leitourgia* (in its various grammatical forms) occur in the New Testament. The NIV translation uses a wide array of words to express its wide range of meaning: minister, ministry, ministering, ceremonies, service, serves, servants, help, care, and share.
18. Theodore Jennings, *Life as Worship* (Grand Rapids: Eerdmans, 1982), 11.
19. Peterson, "Worship in the New Testament," 71.
20. Ibid., 67.
21. Symbols are created when something interior and spiritual finds expression in something exterior and material. Some examples are the bread and wine, cross, candelabrum, Lord's Table, altar, open Bible, world missions map or globe, cornucopia, banners, *icthus* fish, dove, robes, vestments, incense, processionals, recessionals, laying on of hands, church building architecture, placement of choir(s), pulpit(s), baptistry, artwork, and liturgical action.

22. Joseph Gelineau, "Music and Singing in the Liturgy," in *The Study of Liturgy,* eds. C. Jones Wainwright and E. Yarnold (London: S.P.C.K., 1978), 443.

23. Pass, *Music and the Church,* 100.

24. Ibid., 128.

Chapter 12 Resolving Tensions over Musical Style: Peter

1. See Elmer Towns, *Ten of Today's Most Innovative Churches,* 15. This source was found in Russell Chandler's *Racing toward 2001* (Grand Rapids: Zondervan, 1992).

2. Bill Gaither is reported to have said the same thing at a seminar of the 1986 Gospel Music Convention (Nashville) in David B. Pass, *Music and the Church,* 18 n. 3.

3. Some may object to the assumption that fifteen geographical locations implies fifteen languages, but both the NIV and NASB seem to support this position, for they use the expressions "own language" or "native language." In fact an alternative reading for "language" in the NASB is rendered "dialect" (2:6, 8). Moreover, if only Greek, Latin, and Aramaic were spoken, why were the expressions of amazement so intense? Also see Best's discussion on the musical implications of Acts 2 in *Music Through the Eyes of Faith,* 66–69.

4. Music innovation, though, is not exclusively tied to language. For a comparison of language and music, see Doris Stockmann, "Interdisciplinary Approaches to the Study of Musical Communication Structures," in *Comparative Musicology and Anthropology of Music,* eds. Bruno Nettle and Philip V. Bohlman (Chicago: University of Chicago Press, 1991), 328–35. It can primarily involve rhythm, dance, and interlocking music textures (Christopher A. Waterman, "Uneven Development of Africanist Ethnomusicology," in *Comparative Musicology and Anthropology of Music,* 178). Innovation involves a response to human personality, nature sounds, any sounds, the kinds of materials available (bamboo or metal or electronic), and other media. It involves a selective response to one's total culture (Stockmann, "Interdisciplinary Approaches to the Study of Musical Communication Structures," 75).

Reporting on tribal music in India, enthnomusicologist Carol Babiracki remarks that a number of ethnomusicologists have noted the following: "The music . . . of a tribe that has maintained a unique linguistic and cultural identity also tends to be unique, different from that of both its tribal and nontribal neighbors. Even linguistically related tribes living within the same geographical region appear to differ from each other more musically than they do linguistically" (Bhattacharya 1990: 66, 68; Parmar 1977a: 47; Nag 1981: 323). *Comparative Musicology and Anthropology of Music,* 75.

5. Others interpret "afar off" to indicate a later time period.

6. The phrase comes from F. H. Chase, *The Credibility of the Acts of the Apostles* (London: Macmillan, 1902), 79.

7. He has at this point ministered to the half-Jewish Samaritans, just as Jesus did.

8. Harold Dollar, "The Conversion of the Messenger," *Missiology* 21, no. 1 (January 1993), 17.

9. Paul agrees with the assessment that the Cretans are "liars, evil brutes, lazy gluttons" (Titus 1:12), but he does not tell his workers not to associate with them.

10. I'm not saying they, in fact, would have reacted this way, but that is how I felt.

11. Best, *Music through the Eyes of Faith,* 81–82.

12. Daniel Bauman: "I have argued that God has no particular favorite style—he looks at the heart" (3 March 1994).

Chapter 13 Resolving Tensions over Musical Style: Paul

1. Harold Best takes the same position in *Music through the Eyes of Faith,* 42, 54–60.

2. Osbeck, *101 Hymn Stories,* 127. The generic fallacy in logic states that a statement can't be faulted simply because the source is not credible. If Hitler stated the earth was round, the killing of six millions Jews wouldn't necessarily make the statement invalid (Garrett Brown, personal communication, 13 August 1994).

3. For a fuller treatment, see Liesch, *People in the Presence of God,* 174–79. Daniel Bauman says: "This must be taught. It doesn't happen by osmosis" (2 March 1994).

4. Fee, *God's Empowering Presence,* 619.

5. Ibid.

6. This is not to undervalue the larger issues that ensue from an apparently simple act.

7. See Paul Hindemith, *A Composer's World* (Cambridge, Mass.: Harvard University Press, 1952), 12–15, for a contrasting view—that of Greek philosopher Boethius. His idea is that music has power over behavior. It has moral power.

8. Calvin M. Johansson, *Discipling Music Ministry. Twenty-first Century Directions* (Peabody, Mass.: Hendrickson, 1992), 46.

9. Ibid., 47.

10. Ibid., 109.

11. Ibid., 23.

12. Ibid., 20.

13. Ibid., 52, 55.

14. Ibid., 55.

15. Ibid., 26.

16. Ibid., 25.

17. Pass, *Music and the Church,* 44.

18. Ibid., 102.

19. Ibid., 45.

20. Johansson, *Discipling Music Ministry,* 25.

21. Ibid., 108.

22. Ibid., 72.

23. Ibid., 71.

24. These comparisons were culled from Best's *Music through the Eyes of Faith* and Johansson's *Music and Ministry: A Biblical Counterpoint* (Peabody, Mass.: Hendrickson, 1984); and *Discipling Music Ministry*

25. Best, *Music through the Eyes of Faith,* 52–53.

26. Graham Cray, "Justice, Rock, and the Renewal of Worship," in *In Spirit and in Truth: Exploring Directions in Music in Worship Today,* ed. Robin Sheldon (London: Hodder and Stoughton, 1989), 22.

27. A survey by Hannelore Wass, "Adolescent Interest in and Views of Destructive Themes in Rock Music," *Omega: Journal of Death and Dying* (1988–89), 177–86, indicates that adolescents themselves "expressed concern about destructive lyrics in rock music." Moreover, another study by Isadore Newman, "Drugs, Suicide, and Rock and Roll" (paper presented to the annual meeting of the Ohio Academy of Science, Dayton, Ohio, April 1990), reported that for those youths involved in clinical treatment, patient preference for heavy metal music "was related to suicide ideology and drug involvement." Adolescents not involved in clinical treatment were not as much affected.

28. Gerhard von Rad, *Old Testament Theology,* vol. 1 (New York: Harper, 1962), 24.

29. Sigmund Mowinckel, *The Psalms in Israel's Worship,* vol. 3 (Oxford: Basil Blackwell, 1962), 81.

30. Eric Werner, "The Conflict between Hellenism and Judaism in the Music of the Early Church," *Hebrew Union College Annual* 20 (Cincinnati: Hebrew Union College, 1947).

31. Hustad, *Jubilate II,* 56.

32. Ibid., 48–49.

33. See Liesch, *People in the Presence of God,* and the subheadings entitled "Percussion Instruments," "Harps Were Like Guitars," and "Discrimination in Reverse," 194–96.

34. This subsection adapted from Hustad, *Jubilate II,* 67.

35. For sources with a different viewpoint, see Johansson, *Music and Ministry,* especially chapter 5; "Aesthetics" and "Boethius" in *The New Grove Dictionary of Music and Musicians* (1980), vol. 1: 22 and vol. 2: 844, respectively; and the "Doctrine of Affections," in *The New Harvard Dictionary of Music* (Cambridge, Mass.: Harvard University Press, 1986), 16.

Chapter 14   Volunteer and Staff Relations

1. Garth Bolinder, "Closer Harmony with Church Musicians," *Leadership* (spring 1986), 95.

2. See Brooks Faulkner, "Ethics and Staff Relations," in *Review and Expositor* (1989), 547–59. The whole issue is devoted to ethics.

3. Johansson, *Music and Ministry,* 1.

4. Schaller, *The Senior Minister,* 66.

5. Doran C. McCarty, *Working with People* (Nashville: Broadman Press, 1986), 75.

6. Ibid., 62.

7. Ibid., 61.

8. Schaller, *The Senior Minister,* 114.

9. Paul Westermeyer, *The Church Musician* (San Francisco: Harper, 1988), 101.

10. My thanks to Laurey Berteig for bringing this emphasis to my attention (24 May 1994).

11. Bolinder, "Closer Harmony with Church Musicians," 99.

12. Schaller, *The Senior Minister,* 117–18.

13. See the excellent article by Kent Hughes, "Going to Your Left," in *Leadership* (summer 1993), 110, on learning to work on our weaknesses.

14. McCarty, *Working with People,* 101.

15. Schaller, *The Senior Minister,* 173.

16. Ibid., 174.

17. Ibid., 107.

18. Hustad, *Jubilate!,* 49–50.

19. Schaller, *The Senior Minister,* 99.

20. Bolinder, "Closer Harmony with Church Musicians," 97.

21. The racehorse, music grinder, and trifler images come from Westermeyer, *The Church Musician,* 6, 90, 92.

22. H. W. Beecher, *Lectures on Preaching,* 2d series (1873; reprint, New York: n.p., 1973), 115.

23. Bolinder, "Closer Harmony with Church Musicians," 96.

24. Melvin Amundson, "Building Positive Staff Relationships," *Journal of Church Music* (March 1986), 13–14.

Chapter 15   Identifying and Attracting Worship Musicians

1. Fee, *God's Empowering Presence,* 707.

2. Ibid., 886.

3. Adapted from Hustad, *Jubilate!,* 50–51.

4. Kevin Lawson, *How to Thrive in Associate Staff Ministry* (Bethesda, Md.: Alban Institute, 2000). Lawson, professor of Christian Education at Biola University, studied 500-plus associate staff members in 16 denominations. The most important factors (reported) for having longevity and satisfaction in the music ministry were: (1) a spouse who supports me in my ministry; (2) seeing my type of ministry as "real ministry," not just a stepping stone to something else; (3) supervisors who treat me as a partner in ministry, not just an assistant; (4) a clear sense of calling

from God; (5) a strong burden, passion or vision for this kind of ministry; (6) a good awareness of my gifts/abilities, and knowing this ministry is where they fit best; (7) supervisors who let me do my work without "looking over my shoulder" all the time; (8) supervisors who stand by me when I receive criticism; (9) affirmation from the people where I serve.

5. Colin Buchanan, "Music in the Context of Anglican Liturgy," in *In Spirit and in Truth,* 110–11. I would endorse biblical liturgies, however, and would decisively reject inclusive language that tampers with, changes, or repeals the male gender of God.

6. Ibid., 105.

7. Quoted in an article by Nathan O. Hatch, "Evangelicalism as a Democratic Movement," in *Evangelicalism and Modern America,* ed. George Marsden (Grand Rapids: Eerdmans, 1984), 74.

8. Martin Luther encouraged a variety of instruments: "Christian musicians should let their singing and playing . . . sound forth with joy from their organs and whatever beloved music instruments there are (recently invented and given by God) of which neither David nor Solomon, neither Persia, Greece, nor Rome, knew anything." *What Luther Says: An Anthology,* vol. 2, comp. World M. Plass (Saint Louis: Concordia, 1959), 982.

9. Sheldon, ed., *In Spirit and in Truth,* viii.

10. Lionel Dakers, "The Establishment and the Need for Change," in *In Spirit and in Truth,* 86.

11. Robert Hayburn, *Papal Legislation on Sacred Music* (Collegeville, Minn.: The Liturgical Press, 1979), 408.

12. See Liesch, *People in the Presence of God,* 183–85, 188–91, 192–95, 227–28.

13. Pass, *Music and the Church,* 92. True, one's college education can also influence one's musical tastes.

14. Schaller, *The Senior Minister,* 131.

Chapter 16   Why Seminaries Should Teach Worship

1. Hayford, *Worship His Majesty,* 21.

2. Norman W. Regier, "Self-Evaluation of Pastor's Church Music Education and the Resultant Philosophy of Music in the Worship Service" (Ph.D. diss., University of Missouri-Kansas, 1985), 26.

3. Robin A. Leaver and James H. Litton, eds., *Duty and Delight: Routley Remembered* (Carol Stream, Ill.: Hope, 1985), 93.

4. Ibid., 91–92.

5. J. W. Schwarz, "The State of Church Music Education for Ministerial Students in Protestant Seminaries in the United States," *Dissertations Abstracts International* 36, 1600 AD (University Microfilms no. 75–19043), 65.

6. Leafblad, "What Sound Church Music?" *Christianity Today* (19 May 1978), 20.

7. Robert E. Webber, "An Evangelical and Catholic Methodology," in Robert K. Johnson, ed., *The Use of the Bible in Theology: Evangelical Options* (Atlanta: John Knox Press, 1985), 139–40.

8. Westermeyer, *The Church Musician,* 82, xi.

Appendix 1   The Argument behind Chapter 2

1. The concept of "dwelling" occurs repeatedly in Paul's writings: See NASB Rom. 8:9, 11; 1 Cor. 3:16; 2 Cor. 6:16; Eph. 2:22; 3:17; 2 Tim. 1:14.

2. Fredrick and Alfred Debrunner, *A Greek Grammar of the New Testament and Other Early Christian Literature,* trans. and rev. Robert W. Funk (Chicago: The University of Chicago Press, 1961), 215. Daniel B. Wallace remarks, "The context has more influence on participles than on any other area of Greek grammar" (*Greek Grammar beyond the Basics* [Grand Rapids: Zondervan, 1966], 613).

3. A. T. Robertson, *A Grammar of the Greek New Testament in the Light of Historical Research* (Nashville: Broadman, 1934), 1133.

4. Cleon Rogers, "The Great Commission," *Bibliotheca Sacra* 130 (July–September 1973), 259.

5. Robertson, *A Grammar of the Greek New Testament,* 1133–34.

6. D. A. Carson, "Matthew," *The Expositor's Bible Commentary* 8 (Grand Rapids: Zondervan, 1984), 595.

7. Detwiler, "The Role of Music," 78.

8. Wallace, *Greek Grammar beyond the Basics,* 641–42.

9. Ibid., 640.

10. Ibid., 639.

11. Peter T. O'Brien, "Colossians, Philemon," *Word Biblical Commentary,* 44 (Waco, Tex.: Word, 1982), 207.

12. Peterson, *Engaging with God,* 222 n. 7. See also Peterson, "Worship in the New Testament," 80, where he says psalms, hymns, and spiritual songs are "the means of teaching and admonishing one another."

13. Fee, *God's Empowering Presence,* 651; Murray J. Harris, *Colossians and Philemon: An Exegetical Guide to the Greek New Testament* (Grand Rapids: Eerdmans, 1991), 168; Petr Pokorny, *Colossians: A Commentary* (Peabody, Mass.: Hendrickson, 1990), 174; H. A. W. Meyer, *Critical and Exegetical Handbook to the Epistles to the Philippians and Colossians,* trans. W. P. Dickson (New York: Funk and Wagnalls, 1875), 448.

14. Fee, *God's Empowering Presence,* 649.

15. Ibid., 652.

16. Books relevant to the topic by Clinton E. Arnold include *Ephesians: Power and Magic, The Colossian Syncretism,* and *Powers of Darkness: Principalities and Powers in Paul's Letters* (Downers Grove, Ill.: InterVarsity Press, 1992).

17. Clint Arnold (personal communication, 25 April 2000).

18. The formidable list includes Fee, *God's Empowering Presence,* 650, James D. G. Dunn, *The Epistle to the Colossians and Philemon* (Grand Rapids: Eerdmans, 1966), 239, Andrew T. Lincoln, *Ephesians,* World Biblical Commentary 42 (Dallas: Word, 1990), 345, as well as John Eadie, Francis Foulkes, Arthur G. Patzia, John Stott, Richard A. Young, Craig S. Keener, and Wayne Grudem. See Detwiler, "The Role of Music," for the complete references.

19. John MacArthur Jr., *The MacArthur New Testament Commentary: Ephesians* (Chicago: Moody, 1986), 256.

20. Ibid.

21. David Detwiler (personal communication, 26 April 2000).

22. Wallace, *Greek Grammar beyond the Basics,* 639.

23. Detwiler, "The Role of Music," 111.

24. Personal communication, 25 April 2000.

INDEX

Barry Liesch (Ph.D., University of California at San Diego) is a professor of music at Biola University. He has served as music/worship director for a number of churches as well as the worship leader for Richard Foster's Renovaré. He is active as a worship leader, pianist, and MIDI arranger/orchestrator. Dr. Liesch has written *People in the Presence of God*, numerous journal articles, five keyboard improvisation books, and has partnered a web site rich in worship materials (www.worship info.com).

If you have questions regarding this book, you may contact the author in the following ways:

Biola University
Music Department
13800 Biola Avenue
La Mirada, CA 90639

Fax: 310-903-4748

e-mail: barry_liesch@peter.biola.edu